# WOMEN of ACTION in TUDOR ENGLAND

Nine Biographical Sketches

# WOMEN of ACTION in TUDOR ENGLAND

## Nine Biographical Sketches

*Pearl Hogrefe*

Iowa State University Press
AMES, IOWA

PEARL HOGREFE is Professor of English, Iowa State University, and author of several books in her fields of creative writing and Renaissance literature. Among them are: *The Process of Creative Writing; The Sir Thomas More Circle; The Life and Times of Sir Thomas Elyot, Englishman;* and *Renewal,* a book of poems. She holds the Ph.D. degree from the University of Chicago. She has published also in the journals of her fields and, in her appointment at Iowa State, has been cited by the faculty for her creative writing activities and her outstanding and inspiring service on the staff. A major portion of her research for this book and others has been carried on at the Folger Shakespeare Library in Washington, D.C., since much information about women is in print but has not been analyzed and assembled. She did research on the background in England and also secured photostats of many important documents through friends or through correspondence with the proper officials in England.

She has had grants to aid her research: two from the Folger Shakespeare Library (1951, 1961), a fellowship from the American Association of University Women (1952-1953), two grants in recent years from the funds of the Alumni Achievement Awards, Iowa State University, and one from Delta Kappa Gamma.

Two permanent endowment fellowships bear her name: the Pearl Hogrefe Endowment Fellowship from her former students and friends and from others who wish to support creative writing or research in literature at ISU, and the Wood-Hogrefe AAUW National Fellowship, open to competent women in any area of scholarship.

© 1977 The Iowa State University Press
Ames, Iowa 50010. All rights reserved

Composed and printed by
The Iowa State University Press

First edition, 1977

**Library of Congress Cataloging in Publication Data**

Hogrefe, Pearl.
    Women of action in Tudor England.

    Includes bibliographies.
    1.  Women—England—Biography.  I.  Title.
HQ1595.A3H63        920.72'0942        76-28496
ISBN 0-8138-0910-X

# Contents

# Illustrations

# *Preface*

The aim of this book is to present the lives and activities of women who had both the desire and the drive to accomplish something individual outside the domestic circle—something they considered a contribution to the public welfare. The aim is not to present women of rank who led self-centered lives nor to comment on women in drama or in other literature of the period. Some of these women were apparently good wives and mothers, but they are not included for that alone. Queen Elizabeth was the only one who refused to become a wife; Bess of Hardwick was the only one who became an unsatisfactory wife, in her fourth marriage, at least in the eyes of her husband, the Earl of Shrewsbury. With the exception of Bess of Hardwick again, each woman wished to do something for the public good. Thus these Tudor women were unlike the equally vigorous women of the fourteenth and fifteenth centuries, who tended to use their energies in managing or defending the material possessions of the family.

The nine women chosen for this book do not include all who made a contribution in the Tudor Age. Others deserve biographical sketches. At the end of the seventeenth century William Wotton, in *Reflections on Ancient and Modern Learning,* made an interesting statement about the number of outstanding women, although his main purpose was to emphasize modern learning:

> It [learning] was so very modish that the fair sex seemed to believe that Greek and Latin added to their charms, and Plato and Aristotle untranslated were frequent ornaments of their closets. One would think by the effects that it was a proper way of educating them, since there are no accounts in history of so many great women in any one age as are to be found between the years 1500 and 1600.

The selection of nine women from many possibilities is partly subjective, partly based on a desire to emphasize active women who have been mentioned only in biographies of their husbands, and partly guided by the aim of presenting the areas influenced by women. Each of these women made a contribution in one area at least. Some, like Margaret Beaufort, Catherine of Aragon, and Catherine Parr, supported many enterprises — educational, religious, philanthropic, political, literary — all concerned with the public welfare. Mildred, Lady Burghley, made a large contribution by understanding and supporting her husband's political life; she furthered the Puritan religion whenever she could; she practiced a philanthropy growing from a desire to help others help themselves or from her great compassion. Anne Cooke Bacon and Catherine, Duchess of Suffolk, tried to further religion, each in her own powerful way. Bess of Hardwick was a maverick but one who cannot be ignored; she amassed a fortune, founded dynasties, and built great houses. Mary Sidney Herbert, Countess of Pembroke, exerted a many-sided literary influence. She persuaded her brother Sir Philip Sidney to write; after his early death she edited and published his works; she encouraged, trained, and gave a good home to other writers; she made and published translations; she used her poetic talent in lyrical versions of the Psalms. Queen Elizabeth used her powers in governing an England that she loved. Though all these women were individualists, she was certainly the most unusual. For each of the others, life, character, and contribution to the period are emphasized; but stating facts about the life of Elizabeth would be like carrying coals to Newcastle. In the chapter about her, the emphasis is on the qualities that made her a successful queen.

Of the nine women, nearly all came from families able and willing to give their daughters a thorough classical education. Again the exception was Bess of Hardwick. Apparently she made her way by early physical charm plus native shrewdness. Four of the nine belonged to royal families either by birth or by marriage; two owed their influence partly to an unusual education and partly to marriages to men who became prominent in the government; three achieved positions in the peerage by their marriages. The practical need of a classical education for men, the resulting emphasis upon a thorough classical education for women, the plan of employing tutors for the family, and the class system in general did not favor the education of middle-class women. But middle-class fathers who were wealthy merchants or fathers with more modest means, like those of the nobility and gentry, were beginning to ask tutors they employed to give the same education to both sons and daughters. The influence of the court and the enormous influence of Sir Thomas More on the education of women touched mainly the upper class by force of circumstances, not by any desire of More himself. Hence the educated and the outstanding women of the sixteenth century tended to be from the upper class.

When this research began, there was no thought of two books. But gradually the material developed what might be called a split personality, resisting organization into one unit. Gradually also a plan for two books evolved: *Tudor Women: Commoners and Queens,* organized by topics and using middle-class as well as upper-class women to illustrate ideas; and this book of biographical sketches. Since the research was one process for many months, it seems necessary to repeat from the earlier book some details about form.

Since this book is intended not only for general readers interested in the history of women but also for serious students of the Renaissance, every effort has been made to secure simplicity and clarity without sacrifice of sound scholarship. Important sources are usually named in the discussion. For each chapter a list of Notes and Sources is available at the back of the book, sometimes with only a general comment and sometimes with chapter or page numbers. Since early printed books often have uncertain or inaccurate paging and since they are sometimes mentioned here for prefaces or for large themes involving the entire book, detailed references are avoided if they seem mere pedantry. But when page references are accurate and promise to be useful, they are given. When a book listed in the *Short-Title Catalogue* is mentioned in the discussion, a modern spelling, if there is a standard one, usually appears for title and author, with the early spelling in the Notes and Sources. In quotations from early authors standard contractions have been expanded and sixteenth-century spelling has been modernized, with conjectures or explanations in brackets. The *STC* numbers of books are also given in the Notes since some are difficult to find. A reader who is not a serious student of the period will find it easy to ignore these Notes if he wishes.

It seems necessary also to repeat most acknowledgments, both to organizations and institutions and to individuals. A grant from the American Council of Learned Societies years ago was useful for exploratory work at the British Museum; though it did not lead to immediate publication, it helped to create a thirst that lingered. Two grants from the Folger Shakespeare Library, in 1951 and 1961 by Director Emeritus Louis B. Wright, were of inestimable value. When the American Association of University Women awarded me the Founders Fellowship for 1952-1953, they made possible a year of freedom from academic responsibilities. As a result *The Sir Thomas More Circle* was eventually completed and published. My gratitude easily extends over the years to their act of pure faith. Without these grants other work and this book would never have been planned. Two grants in recent years from the Alumni Achievement Fund, Iowa State University, were a definite help to the study of sixteenth-century women. In addition, a research grant given by Eta Chapter, Delta Kappa Gamma, Ames, Iowa, for work in the summer of 1973 enabled me to complete other details and to assemble illustrative material for this book.

Individuals have contributed, of course. Dozens of fellow readers at the Folger Shakespeare Library, where much of my research has been done, have been helpful with their stimulating comments and questions at lunch or tea, though details have vanished in the haze of the past. My gratitude is happily extended to a few administrators and to many men who were my colleagues and who encouraged me by granting me a tacit or a spoken equality before it became popular to welcome women into academic life. Colleagues and friends, including Professor Albert L. Walker, read earlier and later chapters to my profit. Representing the general readers to whom the book may appeal, Mrs. Albert L. Walker and Mrs. Emerson W. Shideler (Mary McDermott Shideler) either listened to or read early material and gave valuable suggestions. Both have had experience in editing, in writing, and in research (though not about the sixteenth century) and both are interested in the topic. The persistent faith of Thomas Dunne, Senior Editor of St. Martin's Press, in both my material and my writing, has been a genuine asset.

Three other people have the real gratitude of the author: two at Iowa State University are Donald S. Pady, Reference Librarian, for tireless efficiency about other material and interlibrary loans; and Mrs. Gerald A. Dorfman (a graduate student in art working with Professor Mary L. Meixner) for her help on illustrations, especially line drawings. The third person is the Earl of Ancaster, Grimsthorpe Castle, Bourne, Lincolnshire, England, who answered himself the questions addressed to his agent and generously granted all permissions.

Staff members of the Folger Shakespeare Library have been helpful. In addition to Director Emeritus Louis B. Wright (the friend of all earnest scholars, great or humble) they include Director O. B. Hardison with his friendly encouragement; Laetitia Yeandle, Curator of Manuscripts, who aided me in my search for illustrative material; and Dorothy M. Mason, Research Librarian from the early days of the library to 1973, who listened to my ideas and produced material far beyond the call of duty or of friendship.

Several historians have raised pertinent questions or suggested valuable material: Eric McDermott, S. J., Georgetown University;

Glenn C. Nichols, once at Iowa State University now at the University of Maryland; Marjorie Gesner, Michigan State University, who also secured material for me in England; and Kenneth G. Madison, Iowa State University. Richard Ormond, Assistant Keeper, National Portrait Gallery, London, has been most helpful in answering definite questions about portraits. On legal details I was able to consult the late Lewis M. Simes, Professor Emeritus, University of Michigan, and more recently at Hastings College of Law, San Francisco. These professionals have saved me from errors of fact and of wording, but they are absolved from responsibility for any errors that may remain.

To these groups and individuals and to others whose help I have never consciously recognized or have forgotten, my sincere thanks.

# INTRODUCTION

# *Pre-Tudor and Tudor Women*

Before the Tudor Age, English women were not usually the fragile, protected beings that some imagine them. This comment applies to women in royal families, other aristocrats, wives of the landed gentry, and prosperous or less prosperous middle-class families. In the thirteenth, fourteenth, and fifteenth centuries women were often intrepid or even ruthless, possessing a high degree of executive ability. With some exceptions their education was narrow, emphasizing only the skills they would need in daily life. Their activities were narrow also, centered in the domestic life of the family. As Tudor women retained some of these qualities, continued to pursue some of these activities, but broadened greatly their education and their activities, it seems advisable to summarize first the facts about the earlier women and then to compare them with women of the sixteenth century.

In pre-Tudor centuries queens of England did not rule in their own right (with the doubtful exception of Matilda), but they were vigorous and fearless, with an enormous capacity for action. Women like Eleanor of Aquitaine, Eleanor of Provence, Margaret of Anjou, and Cicely Neville had a finger or even a whole hand in the political pie. But they were not much concerned with ideas about the effective government of all England; instead, they were supporting one member of a family or one royal house against opponents. Some of these queens were skillful in both political and military action, and some were ruthless; one at least was so ruthless that she defeated herself.

In these same earlier centuries women who were not royalty but inherited a great estate and a title when the male line failed might find that they had also inherited the office of sheriff of a shire, in a few counties where the king had not yet acquired the power of appointment. Instead of naming deputies as the law permitted them to do, a number of women served as sheriffs themselves. At one time the sheriff had been almost the ruler of his shire; and though the duties were gradually decreasing, in the sixteenth century they still included arranging for Quarter Sessions and serving through them, making public any proclamations of a ruler, and reporting the results of shire elections. The position required vigorous initiative and other qualities usually considered masculine but not the exclusive property of men.

In the same early centuries the wives of the manor lords or of other men with great landed estates were apparently vigorous, intrepid, and able as executives. They acted as lord and as lady when their husbands were absent. And husbands were often absent on personal business in London or at the court, in a period when the court followed the ruler. Husbands went to war. They traveled to the Continent on diplomatic missions. They held offices in the king's household. Forming a poorly paid but efficient system of government, they traveled an area of England on commissions of the assize, of jail delivery, of the peace. Of course the wives had servants as well as bailiffs or stewards, but the wives often made all the major decisions for great farming operations and for complex households that were almost self-sustaining. But these women were not working for the general welfare; they were concerned with the family.

In the first half of the fifteenth century, Isabel Berkeley was such a woman. She traveled to London to act as her husband's solicitor, or she took over legal and business affairs at home while he went to court. While she was representing him in a property dispute, she was seized by one of his enemies and imprisoned in a strong castle. After the king had finally been persuaded to sign the order for her release, she died in prison. Her biographer believed, with some reason, that she was murdered.

Later in the fifteenth century, Margaret Paston was another woman of action. Her husband John Paston had property willed to him by Sir John Fastolf, and thus he had acquired enemies who envied him and wished to take the property from him. Margaret was at Gresham with only a dozen of her people when a thousand armed men of Lord Molyneux came to recover it for him. She refused to come outside or to surrender, even when men began undermining the room where she sat. Finally they carried her outside and took possession. She also struggled for weeks against the men of the Duke of Suffolk for possession of the manor of Drayton, with each side trying to assert ownership by collecting the rents and holding the manor court. As the men of the Paston household were going in fear of their lives, only the chaplain and one other man went with her to hold the manor court; sixty of the duke's men reached the place first and prevented her from doing so. But next morning she arrived first to meet the justices of the peace. Telling her full story in the presence of the duke's men, she won a decision for the Pastons. Margaret Paston, like Isabel Berkeley, was competent in practical action, but both were concerned mainly with the property of the family.

During these same early centuries husbands frequently appointed their wives to execute last wills and testaments, even for the greatest estates in England; and widows often held the wardship and marriage of the son who would inherit. Men on all levels of society, of different occupations, and in all parts of England followed the tendency to name the wife as "whole and sole executrix" or as one of several executors. A woman so named must have been familiar already with all the details of her husband's affairs and had proved her ability to manage and to accept responsibility.

During the pre-Tudor centuries middle-class women from both upper and lower economic levels were active as women of business. Wives or widows of wealthy London merchants often managed large enterprises. Margery Russell of Coventry was one of them. About 1413 she applied for letters of marque and reprisal, according to the custom then, declaring that men of Santander, Spain, had robbed her of merchandise worth £ 800. Signed by the kings of England and Spain, these letters gave her the right to cover her losses by seizing property from other Spaniards. But Margery's agent, it seems, took too much. A Spaniard who lost his small ship and his wines brought suit to recover and received an order on the Exchequer for a refund. Perhaps he had encountered Margery before, for he was sure that he would never get the money due him. But whatever the accounts leave unexplained, it seems clear that Margery carried on a large business and that she knew how to use freedom of action for her own benefit.

In the earlier centuries also, many middle-class women who carried on small businesses proved that women had the right to such activity and that large numbers of them had the energy to exercise the right. Numbers of women were carrying on various trades and crafts (including those conventionally considered masculine) in Oxford, Norwich, York, through the West Riding of Yorkshire, at places in Berkshire, and doubtless in other localities. Most of these women with small businesses were members of gilds; usually they needed to belong to a local gild to secure the freedom of the city and to buy and sell legally. Most medieval gilds admitted women freely (maids, wives, and widows); some gilds stated in their rules that women members must help make new rules; and some named specifically the rights of women to become apprentices, to establish a business at the close of a successful apprenticeship, to take apprentices, and even to employ journeymen.

Women were admitted to membership also in a number of the great trading companies of London, with evidence of their membership often dating from about 1348, though they may have belonged before they were mentioned in the records. They were also members of the Barber-Surgeons Company of London. Their place in the printing business of the sixteenth and seventeenth centuries, usually as widows, is well documented by the records of the Stationers Register; but these records, resulting from the strict control over religious and political ideas, sometimes lead students to the erroneous conclusion that a woman could not establish her own business but was limited to the right of continuing her husband's business after his death.

Business ventures seem to have been open freely to any single woman or widow who had the necessary energy and the capital. Chances were furthered for a married woman (known as a feme covert, a protected woman under the guardianship of her husband) by the provision that she could establish her own business (if her husband gave his consent) and operate, for her business only, as if she were a feme sole (a single woman or widow). In London and in a number of other municipalities a married woman had this right. Though the rules varied from place to place, usually her husband was not responsible for her business debts; if someone brought suit against her in connection with her business, she had to answer the plaintiff herself and to satisfy him if the judgment went against her. If she brought suit, she was required to name both her husband and herself as plaintiffs, with his name appearing first.

During the sixteenth century some of these activities continued to be possible or actual. No woman seems to have inherited the office of sheriff of a shire during that century (male heirs may have been more plentiful), but the right remained. In the seventeenth century the Lady Anne Clifford became sheriff of Westmorland and performed some of the duties herself. Wives of men who held landed estates, great or small, continued to make decisions for both lord and lady when their husbands were away from home; or as widows, they held the wardship and marriage of sons who were heirs to great titles and estates. In all classes of society except perhaps the lowest, where records and property scarcely existed, wives continued to be named as executors of their husbands' wills. The practice continued even up to the middle of the seventeenth century.

Great changes were developing about 1500. Many-sided evidence suggests that fewer women were engaged in business enterprises, either large or small. This sharp decrease in numbers was apparently not caused by any sudden weakness in women themselves; and in spite of some local restrictions placed on them from time to time, it did not result from oppressive statutes directed against women. Such statutes do not appear in the records. Many causes may have been operating; but the known or possible causes were changes in English life, mostly economic and large enough to be outside the control of the individual. Important changes included these developments: the invention of machinery such as looms with twelve to twenty-four shuttles worked by the hand of one man; a shift from the exporting of raw wool to the exporting of wool cloth; an enormous growth in the demand for wool cloth both in England and on the Continent; the resulting development of large-scale capitalism, especially in the woolen industry, with the family unit or the domestic unit giving place to the factory plan; the decline of the gilds, with statutes forbidding them to do the things for which they were organized—these statutes being directed not against *women* but against *persons;* the growing wealth of the merchants and their tendency to become landed gentlemen, with new outlets for wives who might otherwise have gone into large-scale business; great changes in population, with sharp declines in the fourteenth century followed by rapid growth in the sixteenth; and a change in philosophy from the idea that property was a trust to be used for the common good to the idea that it might justly be used entirely for the owner's personal satisfaction.

Another great change, beginning about 1500 or a little later and continuing almost to the end of the century, was the tendency of women to achieve a sound classical education. With this education a new breed of women developed—women with broader aims and ideas but with the practical intelligence and fearless vigor of women in earlier centuries. Perhaps they owed much to the generations of free-wheeling women who had preceded them, even though the earlier women pursued mainly financial interests for the family. These new women were shaped by the Renaissance, by the theories of the early English humanists, and especially by the concern of Sir Thomas More about the education of women. They enlarged their interests from the physical property of the family to the welfare of all England and of other countries. Through the classics mainly, they became interested in abstract ideas—theories of politics and government, religious differences, the bases of a sound philanthropy, ideas about philosophy, literature, and other intellectual affairs. Speaking Latin well, and also French or Italian, they had an equality in communication with their husbands' guests and friends from the Continent. They used their education in other ways; their learning was not a mere decoration. They were the outstanding women of the Tudor Age.

Another important change in the sixteenth century concerned the position of women as queens. With a new climate of tolerance developed in many countries through the Renaissance and with their own sound training in ideas and in enlarged communication skills, they no longer used their abilities only as the wives of kings. They ruled as queens in their own right.

To keep the evidence from being one-sided and thus inaccurate, it seems well to mention that a woman, both earlier and later than the Tudors, was limited in other ways. She had almost no rights under public law. "In the camp, at the council board, on the bench, at the jury box," according to Pollock and Maitland, there was almost no place for her. She could not vote for a candidate seeking office, be a candidate for an elective office herself, help make or repeal laws, and except in a few kinds of cases she could not give evidence in a court of law. In the thirteenth century, probably no woman could have inherited the throne of England. Many of these restrictions continued into the twentieth century.

But under private law a single woman or a widow had almost the same rights as a man (at least in theory): she could inherit property, make a contract, sue or be sued, give or sell her property, and make a last will and testament. But her right to inherit property might be circumvented by a principle developed as part of the common law—that male heirs were preferred before female heirs. Thus a daughter who expected to inherit because her father had no sons sometimes found that her father's brother, his nephew, or even his half-brother claimed her inheritance, fought for it in the courts, and kept it from her during years of litigation. Also her father had freedom of testation in the sixteenth century, with no significant restrictions; that is, he could will property as he pleased. A father who wished to leave his estate undivided and to perpetuate the family name, but who had no son, might ignore daughters and leave his lands to his brother or to his brother's son. Enough examples exist to indicate that such actions were not empty threats. One daughter who almost lost her property was Catherine Willoughby, her father's only direct heir. When her father died about 1526, his brother tried to claim the estate as next male heir. But Charles Brandon, Duke of Suffolk, bought Catherine's wardship from the king; and his influence apparently saved for her most of her property. A woman with a similar problem was Lady Mary Cholmondeley; when her father died in 1581, his half-brother claimed all the family estates. After she had brought suits for forty years, friends persuaded the opponents to accept equal shares. Thus they secured a final settlement. A father who acted to disinherit his daughter Anne was George Clifford, Earl of Cumberland. Dying in 1606, he willed his estates to his brother, and after him to his nephew. They were not to return to Anne unless the male line failed. These estates, it is said, had been entailed to pass to a father's direct heir, whether that heir was a son or a daughter. Though Anne's mother, Anne herself, and at times Anne and her husband, kept bringing suits, she did not secure the properties until 1643 when the male line failed. These two methods of keeping a woman from her inheritance illustrate a larger truth: law is not rigid but flexible, as it is handled by individual lawyers and judges or swayed by powerful men.

A young girl approaching her first marriage while she was still under parental control had small chance of choosing her husband, and most parents did everything in their power to have their daughters married before they came of age. Girls of royal or aristocratic families were sometimes married at fourteen; daughters of other families with substantial property were usually married at sixteen or seventeen. Marriage involved a business contract. The bride's father gave a portion or a dowry, an amount that varied from ten to fifteen dollars (in U.S. money) to isolated instances of ten to fifteen thousand dollars, to her new husband. The bridegroom's father had to arrange a marriage settlement or a jointure to bring the bride an income if she became a widow and also to provide living expenses for the couple. Neither a daughter nor a son and heir could hope to make a desirable marriage without such arrangements. Parents who did not wish to force an early marriage or who might wish to change their minds later drew up a contract for the future. It was easier to break a contract or an unconsummated marriage; and popular medical treatises were available warning that early sexual activity or the early birth of a child might be dangerous. In theory, at least, a daughter (or a son) could repudiate at twelve a contract made earlier by the parents. But financial arrangements were still formidable barriers.

When a father made his will, he often provided a maintenance allowance to be paid a single daughter until she married, and also a portion for her marriage. He often added that a daughter who refused to marry the man chosen for her by either parent, by a guardian, or by an executor or executors of the will would forfeit these amounts and any other property assigned to her in the will. So the portion, especially, which held great interest for any prospective husband, might compel obedience. Though attitudes were changing in the latter part of the sixteenth century, people in northern England remained conservative longer. In 1599 William Shaftoe in Northumberland willed his daughter as if she had been a cow or a sheep herself: "To my daughter Marjerie, LX sheep, and I bestow her in marriage upon Edward, son of Reynold Shaftoe."

Tudor parents, with some outstanding exceptions, were not soft-hearted enough to yield to a daughter's entreaties or tears about her choice of a husband. The practice of placing a child with a wet nurse at birth and leaving it there for two years or more, with occasional visits from the mother, did nothing to foster affection in the family. An occasional mother, when her daughter resisted a marriage, beat her into submission. For example, when the parents of Lady Jane Grey ordered her to marry Guildford Dudley as a part of the plot to make her queen of England, she refused at first, it has been reported; but her father cursed her and her mother beat her until she surrendered. Judging from the character of her parents and the way they punished her in other situations for mere trifles, one is inclined to believe the report.

When a woman married, for all practical purposes she also lost any control over her property while the marriage lasted. She became a feme covert, sheltered under the guardianship of her husband. Her chattels, including her wearing apparel and jewels, belonged to her husband; he could alienate them (transfer the ownership to another person) if he wished. Her chattels real, "such as a term of years, a wardship, a statute merchant or staple," became his, so that he could alienate them; but if he did not do so while he lived, they belonged to her at his death. He could not will them to others, and they did not pass to his nearest kin as his own chattels did. During the marriage the husband had complete control over his wife's freehold interest in land, with no check of any kind over him. If no child was born alive of the marriage and if the wife died first, her lands went to her heirs; the widower had no claim on them. But if a child had been born alive—the test being that it uttered a cry even if it died immediately after it cried—the widower was "entitled to an estate in the whole of his wife's lands for his life." He did not lose the right when he married again. This right was known as "tenancy by the curtesy" or "tenancy by the law of England." The origin of his claim may have been the reasonable assumption that he should become the guardian of his child; but if so, a gradual but irrational change had developed in favor of the man.

Dower for a widow, however, was a carefully defined and a well-protected right. According to Pollock and Maitland, "A widow is entitled to enjoy for life under the name of dower one-third of any land of which the husband was seised in fee during the marriage." As the wording implies, it did not include his equitable estate. She might claim half instead of a mere third, by local custom, but to do so she had to prove the custom. The husband could not deprive her by conveying property to another person without her consent; and if she seemed to consent, she was examined without her husband present, so that officials might discover if her consent was voluntary or forced. Support from her husband's estate was to be "incontinent" (immediate); and if necessary, she was temporarily assigned part of a large property until a complex estate could be settled. Dower was supported by the church, sometimes confirmed by local custom, accepted by men trained in the common law, established by a statute of Parliament, and regulated from time to time by additional statutes. No right of a woman was better protected, it seems, than her right to dower.

Though the dower rights seem fair and even generous, the rights of Tudor women under public law were nonexistent; and when they married, all their property came under the control of their husbands. But it would be unfair to summarize the restrictions on women without adding that sons also were treated unjustly. Tudor society was patriarchal, not merely antifeminine. The principle of primogeniture, which had developed because it protected an overlord, was unfair because it gave the estate to the first-born son. Other sons were sometimes made stewards of family property or granted small annuities; but for them desirable marriages, by the standards of their own families, were seldom possible. And they could not consider seeking employment outside the family. Even the son and heir who married while his father was still living had to depend upon his father to provide living expenses for himself and his wife and a jointure for her if she became a widow. So the father sometimes decided when his heir should marry and also selected the bride. But it is still true that Tudor women who contributed to the public welfare did so in spite of restrictions.

# WOMEN of ACTION in TUDOR ENGLAND

Nine Biographical Sketches

*Above: Portrait of Mildred Cooke Cecil painted about 1565, probably by a follower of Hans Eworth.*

*Left: Detail of Theobalds, the last and most magnificent of the places built by Lord Burghley. The great house, under construction from 1563-1585, has been called ". . . the most important architectural adventure of . . . Elizabeth's reign."*

# CHAPTER ONE

# *Mildred Cooke Cecil, Lady Burghley*

## 1526-1589

Perhaps no portrait ever did a greater injustice to its subject than the well-known one of Lady Burghley. Attributed to Hans Ewarth and now at Hatfield House, it was used by Conyers Read in *Mr. Secretary Cecil and Queen Elizabeth*. It may be an excellent physical likeness. It presents a richly dressed woman in the fashion of the later sixteenth century—but one whose long, intellectual face with its firm lips and chin is unsmiling, without any suggestion of feminine charm. Her appearance might lead some to say, "What a formidable woman!" But the real person back of the portrait was human, compassionate, and on the word of her husband, a "matchless mother." She was wise, with the educational, religious, and political understanding that made her a genuine helper of her husband, Sir William Cecil, Lord Burghley.

Some men who knew her saw only the physical exterior. The Count de Feria, lingering at the court after the accession of Elizabeth, was one of them. He reported to his king that the wife of Secretary Cecil was a tiresome pedant. Guzman de Silva, Spanish ambassador from 1564 to 1568, was one of many more perceptive observers, both native and foreign. Describing her in one of his letters as a furious heretic, he also reported that she discussed important problems with her husband. She had told the ambassador that the queen would never marry Leicester

*Among Mildred Cecil's many bene- factions was sponsorship of a weaving project among the women of Cheshunt. She provided materials, paid for the spinning and weaving, and gave the cloth to the poor.*

3

and probably no one else unless it might be the archduke, whom Cecil himself favored. If anyone knew, he added, it was Cecil's wife, for she was clever and had great influence with her husband.

Mildred Cooke was the oldest of five known daughters of Sir Anthony Cooke and his wife, Anne Fitzwilliam, who lived at Gidea Hall near Romford, Essex. Three other daughters who lived into maturity were Anne, Elizabeth, and Catherine; another daughter Margaret, who married Ralph Rowlett in 1558, died only a few weeks after her marriage. If Mildred was born in 1526, as we assume, she was six years younger than her husband William Cecil. Whether they were married December 21, 1545 (the date Conyers Read accepts from one record by Cecil), or in 1546 the date Cecil gave in another list of family events) does not seem important. Historians admit that Cecil was inconsistent about the dates he gave for events in his own life. In either case, Mildred was nineteen or twenty, a little beyond the usual age in that period for a first marriage. The earlier date may be correct; for a property transaction dated November, 1545, tells us that Richard Cecil, father of William, conveyed to William and Mildred "the manor of Essington in Rutland and Lincolnshire and all his other lands in Essington, Carelby, and Ryall in Rutland and Lincolnshire. . . ." These lands would surely provide for the living expenses of the couple and for a jointure when and if the bride became a widow—the usual obligations of the bridgroom's father. An item recently published by J. George in *Notes and Queries* indicates that 1545 was the date of the marriage. He states that on November 21, 1545, William Cecil and Mildred Cooke applied for and were granted a dispensation for the marriage without banns and within the prohibited time, that is, within Advent, usually a period including four Sundays before Christmas. The dispensation was granted by the Archbishop of Canterbury's Faculty Office. Whether Sir Anthony Cooke provided a portion for Mildred and for his other daughters we do not know.

For William Cecil it was the second marriage. While he was at St. John's College, Cambridge, with John Cheke as his tutor, he had been attracted to Cheke's sister Mary. The father of the Cheke family had died; and the mother, perhaps with Mary's help, was keeping a wine shop to support the family. Records in William Cecil's own handwriting tell us that he left St. John's College and came to Gray's Inn on May 6, 1541, to study law; that on August 8 of the same year he was married to Mary Cheke; that May 5, 1542, their son Thomas was born; and that

Mary Cecil died at Cambridge on February 22, 1543, and was buried in St. Mary's Church. It is doubtful whether Cecil ever brought Mary to London. If these dates are correct, William Cecil lacked several weeks of being twenty-one at his marriage to Mary Cheke; thus he needed his father's consent.

It is easy to fall into the trap of thinking that Mildred Cooke married a great statesman. But at the time of their marriage William Cecil was an unknown young man of twenty-six; he held no position at the court of Henry VIII (who died in 1547), though he was in the Parliament of 1543. He held minor offices under Edward Seymour, the Protector, and was one of two secretaries for the Duke of North-umberland (after that ambitious climber had made himself a *de facto* ruler while Edward VI was still a king in name); he was also a member of the Privy Council. But his career really began in 1558 when Elizabeth named him her principal secretary on the first day of official business. She said to him, "This judgment I have of you that you will not be corrupted by any manner of gift and that you will be faithful to the state; and that without respect of my private will you will give me the counsel that you think best. . . ." At that time the Cecils had been married twelve or thirteen years.

Those who write about the Cecils are not in complete agreement about the happiness of that marriage. A contemporary, Roger Ascham, considered that Mildred was extremely fortunate. Writing to his friend Johann Sturm in 1550 and describing Mildred Cecil as one who spoke Greek almost as easily as she spoke English, Ascham could not decide "whether she was to be envied more for her knowledge, for having Anthony Cooke as her father and teacher (the associate of John Cheke in instructing our young king), or for having married William Cecil. . . ." Since Ascham was writing to a personal friend on the Continent, he may not have had ulterior motives for praise; and his contacts with the court gave him a chance to know the facts.

Modern doubters apparently evaluate a marriage on the basis of passionate emotions. Tudor men and women were more likely to judge it by rank and property, with depth of affection developing later by chance if at all. Others, who feel that the union was fortunate, estimate it by shared interests and principles and by the events of the years that followed. William and Mildred Cecil had in common a sound training in the classics. Though the tradition that he read Greek lectures at Cambridge without pay when he was nineteen lacks firm evidence, it may be true. And Sir Henry Peacham the Younger reported in *The Complete Gentleman* that Cecil, to the day of his death, carried with him a copy of Cicero's *De officiis* because he considered it "sufficient . . . to make both a scholar and an honest man." Cecil is also credited by some with being the great classical influence on the sixteenth century, but Sir Thomas More had laid the foundation, especially for the thorough classical education of women, before Cecil was born. And Cecil's wife Mildred, who could speak Greek easily, was his equal in scholarship.

Mildred and William Cecil also shared religious attitudes and ethical principles, a fact that became apparent when he realized that he was being drawn inevitably into the plot of John Dudley, Duke of Northumberland, to alter the succession. Earlier, Northumberland had contrived the execution of Edward Seymour, the Protector. His plan was to get an illegal declaration from the dying King Edward, naming Lady Jane Grey as his successor, and later to summon a Parliament to change the statute that named Mary, the older daughter of Henry VIII, as the next heir to the throne. With the help of Lady Jane's parents, he brought about a marriage between Jane and his oldest unmarried son, Guildford Dudley. When the plan unfolded, Cecil suffered from conflicts in loyalties. As a subject he owed obedience to his ruler; as a man trained in law he supported statutes; by religious convictions he favored Lady Jane Grey; but he had supported the Tudor dynasty—and Mary, with the best claim as a Tudor, was a Catholic. Though he had more religion than some historians suppose, his love of England surmounted religious dogma, which in his life so far had behaved like a chameleon. Cecil decided that he had three choices: escape from England (an act contrary to his conscience), imprisonment, or death. He took extreme measures. He removed money, plate, and papers from the Cannon Row house, placing part with a servant named Sere and part with a Mr. Nelson in Essex. He arranged two hideouts, one in his mother's home at Stamford Baron and one at Nelson's place in Essex near the Thames. He conveyed movable property and leases to others and put his lands in the name of his son Thomas.

Meantime Cecil did all that he could to keep from supporting Northumberland; but as he and Sir William Petre were the two principal secretaries of the duke, and Cecil was also a member of the Council, he had his difficulties. Whenever he could manage to do so, he excused himself from drafting documents; as long as he could, he postponed signing as a supporter of Northumberland, trying to appear last as if he were a mere witness, not a participant. After Lady Jane had been proclaimed, Cecil used his influence in Northamptonshire and

Lincolnshire to keep aid from Northumberland and to prevent the
hundred men he might have raised at Wimbledon from joining the
duke. Cecil also tried to turn other important men against the plot. He
kept horses ready for joining Mary when it seemed desirable, but he
had no need to join her secretly. After she was proclaimed, the Council,
now eager to support her, sent Cecil to her on official business. The
Earl of Arundel and Sir William Paget had already spoken in his favor;
and for some reason Anne Cooke (as Conyers Read reported from information given by a servant of the Cecils) was with Queen Mary. Why
Anne was there must remain conjecture; it does not seem that a woman
with her strong prejudice against "papists" would have been there of
her own volition merely to welcome Mary as queen. But one who has
tried to understand the whole life of Mildred Cecil with her political
astuteness in other situations might venture to suggest that Anne was
there because her sister had sent her to do what she could for William
Cecil. A further conjecture might be added—that Mildred had been
watching and hearing reports on events, with a keen understanding of
the issues involved. At least when Cecil arrived, Queen Mary listened
to a detailed account of what he had done, decided that he was a "very
honest man," and permitted him to be the first member of the Council
to kiss her hand. Later she issued a pardon for him.

If these conjectures have a basis in fact, the letter William Cecil
wrote his wife at the height of his crisis would come to her as no
complete surprise. He trusted Sir Nicholas Bacon with its delivery; he
did little explaining of facts; but apparently he thought that his wife
would appreciate his ethical and religious attitudes. He asked her to
look after the education of his son Thomas (at that time they had no
living child), to devote herself to the study of scripture, and not to
mourn for him because he meant to die in the faith. He asked her to tell
his friends, "my renouncing of all the world's fortune is to save my
conscience clear which hath in public service suffered many torments,
and to be a free man before the sight of God I am content to be a
bondsman to the world." He concluded the letter: "These things, my
good wife, do I utter, being well strengthened in mind after long
consultation betwixt God and my conscience, and seeing great peril
threatened upon us by the likeness of the time, I do make the choice to
avoid the peril of God's displeasure."

In another account of his crisis Cecil said that he did not try to
escape from England because Sir John Cheke reminded him of the
dialogue in which Socrates refused to avoid death by escaping, because
a good citizen must obey the law. Thus the Christian conscience of Cecil
and his knowledge of classical ideas united in a profound effect upon his

own future and the future of England. No doubt his wife, with her classical scholarship and her depth of religious feeling, understood his ideas. And his letter, written after years of marriage and while he was under threat of death, may be better evidence of a satisfactory relationship than evanescent passion without mutual principles.

Mildred Cecil was not always as fortunate as Roger Ascham assumed, when he was writing Sturm in 1550, but for other reasons than the emotions or the ideas she shared with her husband. She had family problems, and most of them were beyond her control. Her stepson Thomas (the son of Mary Cheke) was one of them, though he may have been her husband's problem more than hers. That relations between her and the boy were not intimate is implied by the request Cecil made to his son about 1561 when he was on the Continent, "Write at every time somewhat to my wife." Difficulties may have risen from the fact that Thomas had only average ability and did not feel easy in the presence of either his father or his stepmother. If Mildred gave the boy his early education (and she is said to have taught the sons of her husband), his feeling of inferiority may have grown in spite of her efforts and her good teaching.

But Thomas improved after his return from an educational tour of the Continent. When he married about 1564, and Stamford Baron was still in the hands of his grandmother as her dower, Cecil turned Wimbledon over to him. Family relations also improved. At one time when the Cecils were planning a trip that would take them near Wimbledon and were uncertain about stopping, Thomas learned of the hesitation and wrote them a cordial request to do him and his wife the honor of visiting them. Eventually Thomas inherited the Cecil home at Stamford Baron (which his father rebuilt for him as Burghley House) and also the title Lord Burghley. But Robert, the son of Mildred, inherited what was best adapted to him, his father's office as secretary to the queen, the magnificent Theobalds which was nearer London, and some other property. And Mildred Cecil was certainly not the person to resent the fact that Thomas, instead of her son Robert, inherited as the older son.

The Cecils had misfortunes about their children, mostly misfortunes beyond their control. They had been married more than eight years before the birth of a child was mentioned. Whether there had been miscarriages or stillbirths is uncertain, for even in the late sixteenth century children born dead or those who died shortly after birth were usually not mentioned in family records. Among the aristocracy where more complete records exist, 100 out of 1,000 died between the twenty-ninth week after conception and the first seven days after birth, according to Sigismund Peller; and of those born alive, 193 out of 1,000 were likely to die during the first year.

The first child mentioned for the Cecils, a daughter Francisca, was born in 1554 but "did not long survive." The next child, their daughter Anne, was born in 1556; she lived to make an unfortunate marriage to Edward de Vere the Earl of Oxford. In 1559 they had a son William, but again he "did not long survive." Two years later another son was born and was also named William, but he soon died. On June 1, 1563, a third son came; this time they named him Robert. He survived to become Earl of Salisbury and a statesman under Elizabeth and James I. The last child recorded, Elizabeth, was born in Westminster, in July 1564. Queen Elizabeth was godmother to the son Robert and also to her namesake Elizabeth. This last daughter lived to marry William Wentworth in 1582; and though not a brilliant match, it brought the whole family happiness for a time. But the husband died before a year had passed, probably of the plague, and Elizabeth herself died a short time later. Anne, Countess of Oxford, lived till June 1588, when she was about thirty-two. Of six known children, only Robert remained when their mother died.

The marriage of Anne to Edward de Vere, seventeenth Earl of Oxford, in 1571 when she was about sixteen, proved to be tragic for the entire Cecil family. At one time it was assumed that she would marry Philip Sidney, and that union, it seems, would have prevented much unhappiness. Cecil may have wished for his favorite child a status the Sidneys could not give her, or Anne may have been headstrong. The marriage is more difficult to understand because Oxford had been a ward in the household, unless his character did not reveal itself fully until he was out of Cecil's control.

Oxford disowned Anne's first child (a daughter), accused her of unfaithfulness, and for a time refused to live with her; but in 1582 they were reconciled; she bore him a son who died and two other daughters who survived. Anne's three daughters joined the Cecil household because their father did not care to hamper himself with them. At one time Oxford accused Anne's mother of alienating her daughter's affection from him; and he treated her distinguished father with callous contempt. The death of Anne, which her mother faced after more than forty years of marriage, and the loss of four other children, may have seemed even less tragic than Anne's life as Countess of Oxford. But, medical knowledge then being limited, Anne's unhappiness was the only grief that might have been avoided—if her father had had the gift of foreknowledge. Probably the grandeur of Anne's funeral in the grey old Westminster Abbey in June 1588 gave Cecil and his wife little consolation.

But Robert, now about twenty-five, was giving them some satisfaction by this time. He had survived adolescence (a period that ended many a young man of good family in the sixteenth century); had followed his father to St. John's, Cambridge, and to Gray's Inn; had devoted himself to intellectual pursuits in a period on the Continent; had begun a first term in the House of Commons before he was twenty; and was taking on duties that might lead him to work with his father.

Earlier, his physical condition probably caused his mother anxiety. He was small, perhaps two or three inches over five feet; and, especially by his enemies, he was called a hunchback. Less hostile people suggested that he had a large head with some curvature of the spine and that his slight deformities were exaggerated by the ruff and other details of fashionable dress. A tradition reported that his physical abnormality had been caused by a nurse who dropped him when he was a baby, but the larger family record suggests heredity.

Two other Cooke sisters, Anne and Elizabeth, bore children who were not completely normal in health or physique. Anne Bacon had only two sons, Anthony and Francis; Anthony was a semi-invalid all his life, with many ailments and at one time the threat of blindness. Elizabeth Cooke Hoby's son, Thomas Posthumous Hoby, was so small that he was ridiculed and considered no matrimonial prize. Enemies referred to him as ''a scurvy urchin'' and ''a spindle-shanked ape''; and James Howell, writing to the Countess of Sunderland in 1629, described him as ''the little knight that useth to draw up his breeches with a shooing-horn, I mean Sir Posthumous Hoby. . . .''

Further evidence for heredity rises from the fact that a daughter of Robert Cecil began life with a deformity. Robert had a son William and two daughters, Catherine and Frances. Though biographers have disagreed about which girl was deformed, letters in the Cecil papers make clear that it was Frances—a conclusion that F. M. Handover had correctly drawn in *The Second Cecil*. Letters between Robert Cecil and Lady Sturton, his wife's sister, emphasize the father's fear that if his daughter came to court she would be the victim of cruel laughter; they state that he had sent a man to examine her, that the man promised ''great amendment,'' and that Lady Sturton would soon bring her back to London, where this man could work with her.

A letter from Hugh Baylye to Robert Cecil removes any possible doubt:

> The charge which I have taken in hand for the cure of Mistress
> Frances Cecil that she should go well and perfect of herself;
> now, thanks be to God, she is well and out of her instruments.
> My bargain was, when I took her in hand, to receive for the
> curing of her, £100. I desire you, therefore, that I may be
> satisfied.

The letter was endorsed, "1599, Oct. For £100 for curing the Lady Fr.
Cecil." Later Frances was mentioned as a suitable match for men of
title, and in July 1610 she was married, with a magnificent celebration,
to Lord Clifford, the oldest son of the Earl of Cumberland. Her cure
must have been permanent.

Mildred Cecil died April 5, 1589, less than a year after the funeral
of her daughter Anne. The marriage of her son Robert had been
arranged at that time but not celebrated. Thus she never knew that his
marriage to Elizabeth Brooke was unusually happy, that he had a
deformed child, and that the child was cured.

Mildred Cecil gave outstanding service to her husband and to
England as the hostess of great houses. Though Wimbledon, in
Wimbledon Park about eight miles from the present Waterloo Station in
London, was one of their earlier homes, it was not one of the great
houses, and neither was the Cannon Row house, Westminster. The
great ones were Cecil House in London, near the Strand, south of
Covent Garden, and Theobalds in Hertfordshire. She seems never to
have lived at Stamford Baron (later called Burghley House), the
paternal home of the Cecils across the river Welland from Stamford in
Northamptonshire. But she visited her husband's mother there, making
a five-day trip from Wimbledon for the purpose. When William Cecil's
father died in 1553, Stamford Baron was assigned to the widow as
dower for her life. As Cecil said in 1585, she was the owner while she
lived "and I but a parmour." He never presumed to entertain the
queen there during his mother's life, though the queen came to the
town in August 1566, while he was there. But his daughter Anne had
smallpox at the time; thus he had a reason for lodging his guests in a
house at the Grey Friary in Stamford. Cecil's mother lived until March
1588, about a year before the death of his wife.

About 1550 to 1553, however, Cecil began acquiring land near
Stamford and making other plans to enlarge the paternal home, which
was only a mile and a quarter from the town, preparing it for his older
son, Thomas. It seems doubtful whether William Cecil ever made it his

residence after his mother died because of his precarious health and the distance of the place from London, and no available records indicate that he ever entertained the queen there. But it was associated with his name, for along with Theobalds and perhaps Cecil House it became one of his architectural triumphs.

Wimbledon was the chief home of the Cecils for about ten years, and many details of their life there are available. When Cecil leased it in 1550, it was known as the Old Rectory. Though the house burned down later, a survey of it, made about 1650, gives an approximate view of the whole as it appeared when it was the home of the Cecils. On the first floor were a hall, a parlor, two smaller rooms, the kitchen, the pantry, the larder, the buttery, and two dairy rooms. Upstairs, ten bedrooms were built around a gallery. Like those of the usual manor house, the buildings nearby included a brewhouse, a bakehouse, a stable for fourteen horses, two coach houses, a coal house, and a cage for hawks used in hunting. Where William and Mildred Cecil lived from the time of their marriage, about 1545, until they moved to Wimbledon seems uncertain. They may have been at the manor of Essington, since it was a part of Richard Cecil's provision for his son when he was married to Mildred Cooke; but that may have seemed too far from London by 1550, the year Cecil became a manager of real estate for the Princess Elizabeth and also one of two personal secretaries for Northumberland.

At Wimbledon the family included Cecil, his wife, his son Thomas, his sister Margaret, his wife's sister Elizabeth, a ward named Arthur Hall, a John Stanhope who may have been a relative of his wife, and an unnamed gentleman. The twenty-five servants included a steward, chaplain, schoolmaster, clerk, chamber-keeper, tailor, joiner, cook, under-cook, butler, scullion, three maids for general work, two grooms of the stable, a gardener, and two farmhands. Cecil's payroll for them was about £50 a year, and the cost of feeding the household about £200 a year. As a matter of thrift and principle, Cecil grew his own grain and raised his own animals for beef; hence two farmhands were a necessity. He gave liveries with his badge embroidered on them to his servants. Menus were provided for seven days a week, one for the chamber table where the family ate, one for the parlor table where members of the staff ate, and another for the hall where the servants ate. Boiled beef was a part of every meal at every level along with much other meat and poultry, except on Friday and Saturday, which were fast days with no meat and much fish. Wine, beer, and bread were not formally listed on the menus, though the cellar lists included a good supply of wine. As usual in the period, fruits and salads were seldom mentioned. Compared with later years, the household at Wimbledon was modest; but order and thrift without undue stinting prevailed there and continued later.

After William Cecil inherited property from his father in 1553, he was considered a man of some wealth; but in 1557 when Anne of Cleves died, both he and his wife attended the sale of her effects and spent about £100 on clothing. The most expensive single item they bought was "a rich kirtle with pearls and wire," for £23. Apparently the Cecils remained thrifty enough to look for a bargain when an opportunity offered itself.

One may guess, without any claim to being a mind reader, that Mildred Cecil remembered Wimbledon with some nostalgia. Her whole life suggests that she was modest, not yearning for grandeur, though later she sometimes had it thrust upon her. Her husband apparently had more time for family life about 1553 to 1558, for though he held offices under Edward Seymour and under Northumberland and had some assignments under Mary, he was not an Atlas-laden official until the accession of Elizabeth. At Wimbledon four of the six children were born and three of them died. At Wimbledon the Cecils experienced many intimate joys and sorrows of their marriage.

As the years passed, the Cecil household grew larger with the building of Cecil House and Theobalds, but even in the earlier years Cecil had given a home to one or two wards. Since Cecil also carried more and more of the burdens of government, in 1571 he was rewarded with the title Lord Burghley; and his wife had the right to be called Mildred, Lady Burghley. In 1561 Cecil had been appointed master of the Court of Wards; later he became guardian of all the royal wards. Eight of them belonged to the noblest families of England. They included the Earl of Rutland (Edward Manners), the Earl of Oxford (Edward de Vere), Philip Howard (son of the Duke of Norfolk), the Earl of Essex (Robert Devereux), and the Earl of Southampton (Henry Wriothesley). Philip Sidney also spent time with the Cecils, though he was not a ward and was not in Cecil's service. Not all of the young noblemen named above were wards at the same time, and some of them did not live with the Cecils. Essex, for example, who inherited the title in 1576 when he was ten, was sent to the household of the Earl of Huntingdon with his brother and his two sisters; but as his father had asked to have him under Lord Burghley's supervision, he spent some time with the Cecils. The Earl of Oxford came in 1562 when he was about twelve. The Earl of Rutland became Cecil's ward in 1563 at fourteen. Philip Howard probably joined the household at fifteen in 1572, the year his father was executed. Southampton (Shakespeare's patron later) inherited the title in 1581 when he was eight. He lived in the Burghley household until 1585, when he entered St. John's College, but returned for vacations. A woman of compassion like Mildred Cecil would probably give special attention to an eight-year-old who joined her big family or to older boys if they needed her care. Of course young noblemen had tutors and servants, swelling the number of residents beyond the scope of modern imagination.

The anonymous biographer of Burghley, who had spent about twenty-five years in his service, said of the household, presumably in the later years, "I have numbered in his house, attending on his service, twenty gentlemen of his retainers, of £1,000, some 3, 5, 10, yes £20,000, daily attending his lordship's service." The same biographer said that most of the principal gentlemen of England tried to place their sons in his service, sometimes for their education while the fathers were still living, sometimes for their care as the fathers confronted death. The Duke of Norfolk, on the night before his execution, asked that Burghley, his political enemy, might bring up his sons. Walter Devereux, first Earl of Essex, asked at his death that his son and heir might be under Burghley's supervision. Widows with troublesome sons wished to place them in his charge. Lady Elizabeth Russell, his sister-in-law, once wrote asking him to take over an insolent Posthumous Hoby, her son by her first marriage. In 1571 the Countess of Lennox asked him to take her son Charles, who was a source to her of "anxiety and vexations." No evidence indicates that he assumed the burden of these two widows. But as Catherine, Duchess of Suffolk, had been his firm friend for years, he is reported to have taken into his household for a time Peregrine Bertie, her son by her second marriage.

But the Cecil household, wherever they lived and whoever the young men were who joined it as wards and retainers, with their servants, remained an orderly place. They had prayers every day at eleven, "where his lordship and all his servants were present"; they seldom went to dinner without prayers; and they had "prayers again at six o'clock before supper." When Burghley was absent, his steward followed the same routine. At meals all was in good order. In later years several different tables were provided: a standing table for gentlemen and two other long tables "many times twice set out," one of them for yeomen and the other for the "clerk of the kitchen." In the Wimbledon days there had been a small family table in a separate room. Such an orderly household could hardly have been maintained without the full involvement of Mildred, Lady Burghley.

Study plans for any young man living in the household also tended to be definite, according to a document cited by Conyers Read under the heading, "Orders for the Earl of Oxford's Exercises." From seven to seven-thirty in the morning the young nobleman practiced dancing, for the next half hour he was at breakfast, from eight to nine he studied French; then he gave a half hour to writing and drawing. Common prayers and dinner followed. At one o'clock he gave an hour to cosmography, an hour to Latin and a second hour to French, followed by a half-hour for exercises with his pen. After four-thirty he might spend the rest of the day "in shooting, dancing, walking, and other commendable exercises." On holidays he was to read the Epistle and the Gospel in his own tongue and also "in the other tongue," probably Latin. His tutor must have been responsible for the study schedule, though it had to be adjusted to the prayers and meals of the entire household.

Such facts as we have about the wards and the young men in service connected with the household suggest that Lady Burghley had one of the most difficult and demanding positions in England, except for the queen, as the lady of a great household. When the group reached the maximum number of wards with all their servants and tutors, probably at Cecil House or Theobalds, the household must have resembled a great resort hotel. Perhaps the only real privacy Lord and Lady Burghley had for discussing problems came after they had retired to their sleeping quarters for the night.

The Cannon Row house was an earlier, simpler home of the Cecils, but they continued to use it after they had more spacious residences because it was near Parliament and near the queen when she came to Whitehall. In a Parliament about 1555 (the anonymous biographer reported) a matter that Queen Mary wished to have adopted was being debated: the question of confiscating the property of the Protestants who had gone into exile. Opposing the queen's view were Sir Anthony Kingston, Sir William Courtney, Sir John Pollard, and "many others of value, especially western men." Since they approved the work of their spokesman Sir William Cecil, they came to him when the House rose and offered to dine with him that day. They would be welcome, he said, if they did not speak of any Parliament affairs during the meal; he may have wished to follow his usual custom of acting as the affable host and creating friendly laughter. They probably went to the Cannon Row house, Conyers Read suggested in telling the incident. How many guests there were and how much warning Lady Cecil and her steward had were not reported.

In 1559 another important guest, the Earl of Arran, James Hamilton (son of the Duke of Châtelherault and heir presumptive to the throne of Scotland), was received at the Cannon Row house and kept there in concealment. He had just escaped from France because of hostility to the development of his Protestant views. After a private interview with the queen he went on to Scotland.

Cecil House, a magnificent place in London that Cecil felt it necessary to acquire, was near the Strand, with Covent Garden (really a garden then) on the north. Built between 1560 and 1563 with spacious grounds, unlike a modern city dwelling, it was developed from a large house begun by Sir Thomas Palmer. Before the place was finished in July 1561, the queen came to supper with the Cecils. Having been at the Charterhouse, she came across the fields to Cecil House, and her Council met with her there till midnight. Where the members of the Council had supper is uncertain. Perhaps Mildred Cecil had to direct her servants to furnish food for all.

Later, many private guests at Cecil House were listed; and the accounts of a careful steward, who was a member of the household from 1575 to 1577, mentioned a dinner to the Privy Council. According to the *Acts of the Privy Council,* the group met at Cecil House in May 1579, twice in June 1579, and three times in November 1587. All these meetings were in the lifetime of Lady Burghley. While there is no definite statement that food was served each time, it seems probable in those days of slow travel and lavish hospitality that a feast would be furnished for a great group, including the attendants of the queen and the members of the Council. In the minutes of many Council meetings the place is not mentioned; it is omitted for some two hundred fifty meetings between 1578 and 1587. Hence many other meetings, while Lady Burghley was living, may have been at Cecil House.

Family celebrations were sometimes held there. But though it is probable that Robert was born there, and though his father recorded the birth as June 1, 1563, he said nothing about a celebration of the event. Having lost two sons earlier (each named William) he may have been wary. But he did report that his daughter Elizabeth was born there and was christened July 6, 1564, with Lady Lennox and the queen as her sponsors. He added, "The same night the queen supped at my house." Cecil had "fourscore persons in family, exclusive of those who attended him at court," said his anonymous biographer; and his expenses were £30 a week when he was absent and £40 to £50 a week when he was in residence. His yearly expenses at Cecil House and Theobalds together were about £2,704. His stables cost him a thousand marks a year. Cecil House was used for another elaborate family affair:

the marriage of Anne to the Earl of Oxford in Westminster Abbey on December 19, 1571, was followed by entertainment at the house. The queen was present with all the great men of England and some foreigners, including the French ambassador, La Mothe Fénélon.

Great public affairs as well as family celebrations were planned for Cecil House. About 1581 Lord Burghley gave a dinner there for the French commissioners who came to treat about the queen's marriage to Alençon. Members of the Privy Council, six important peers, and twenty-one other Englishmen were guests — and probably the wives of the Englishmen also, since they were usually invited to state dinners. The number of French guests, probably large, was not reported. Among the interpreters were Thomas Cecil, Francis Bacon, and Henry Killigrew. The kitchen bill for the occasion was more than £204, and the total cost exceeded £362. The expense included carrying charges from Stamford for rushes, flowers, pewter, carpets, and the queen's picture. Sums were paid to carpenters, plasterers, and glaziers; but according to Conyers Read, it is uncertain whether these sums covered alterations before or repairs after the dinner. Perhaps only a few modern women would envy Lady Burghley her duty to plan and serve as hostess for such a dinner, even though she had many servants.

The last and the most magnificent of the places Lord Burghley built was Theobalds. He bought the manor by that name in 1562 or 1563 (until 1570 he was buying other properties nearby to enlarge the estate), he began actual building about 1563, and did not complete all details until 1585 or about that time. Of course the Cecils were using it years before it was completed, the queen having made her first visit there in 1564. The anonymous biographer recorded that Burghley had "meant it for a little pile, as I have heard him say, but after he came to entertain the queen so often there, he was forced to enlarge it, rather for the queen and her great train . . . than for pomp and glory." Lord Burghley gave similar details about 1585, in a letter to a friend on the comments of his enemies:

> If my buildings mislike them, I confess my folly in the expenses. . . . I mean my house at Theobalds, which was begun by me with a mean measure but increased by occasion of her majesty's often coming, whom to please I would never omit to stir myself to more charges than building it. And yet not without some special direction of her majesty. Upon fault found with the small measure of her chamber, which was in good measure for

me, I was forced to enlarge a room for a larger chamber, which
need not be envied of any for the riches in it, more than the
show of old oaks with painted leaves and fruits.

Thus Theobalds grew—as a modern architect, Sir John Summerson, says—from the domestic necessities of a great statesman and
from a royal command. Like other great houses of the sixteenth century, it was not the work of a single professional architect, but of skilled
craftsmen guided by an intelligent, cultured mind. Perhaps it was the
product of two such minds, for Mildred Cecil with her knowledge of
great houses and the classics must surely have made her contribution.
Sir John Summerson commented that Theobalds was, "with the
possible exception of Longleat and Wollaton, the most important architectural adventure of the whole of Elizabeth's reign. Certainly it was
the most influential of all."

The location was carefully planned. According to Summerson, the
site was 500 yards west of the road to London and 90 yards south of the
branch road to St. Albans; it was 20 miles from Cecil House in London
and near the highway that led from London up to Stamford. Being near
three royal houses, it was convenient for the queen. It was about twelve
miles from Gidea Hall, Essex, the home of Sir Anthony Cooke and his
wife, and about fifteen miles from Gorhambury, where the Bacons were
building a country home.

The magnificence of Theobalds can best be appreciated by
beginning to observe it at the archway of the entrance gate. From there
one could see "a most stately walk on a raised causeway, shaded by
alternate elm and ash trees," leading to towers, pinnacles, and courts,
giving an impression of great size. The house stood in a park so large
that one could go two miles without coming to an end of the walks. The
plan of the house, as reconstructed by Summerson, included five
courts, three of them (the outer or base, the middle, and the fountain
courts) extending in a direct line from front to back. One could see
through the archways as far as the fountain court. At the right of the
base court and beside it was the buttery court; at the left and beside it
was the dove-house court. The gardens, like those at Cecil House, were
in charge of the eminent herbalist, John Gerard.

Inside, the magnificence of Theobalds is illuminated by passages
from the account of Rathgeb, secretary to the Duke of Wirtemberg. He
was there in 1602 when it was still used by Robert Cecil. He saw a great
hall that had no pillars and was about thirty by sixty feet. Besides
noting other embellishments, he said:

there is a very high rock of all colors, made of real stones, out of
which gushes a splendid fountain that falls into a large cir-
cular . . . basin, supported by two savages. . . .

The ceiling . . . is very artistically constructed; it contains
the twelve signs of the zodiac, so that at night you can see
distinctly the stars proper to each; on the same stage the sun
performs its course . . . by some concealed ingenious
mechanism. On each side of the hall are six trees, having the
natural bark so artfully joined, with birds' nests and leaves as
well as fruit upon them, all managed in such a manner that you
could not distinguish between the natural and these artificial
trees . . . for when the steward of the house opened the windows, which looked upon the beautiful pleasure gardens, birds
flew into the hall, perched themselves upon the trees, and
began to sing.

What Mildred Cecil thought of the magnificence at Theobalds is
not a matter of record; but from what we do know of her whole life and
character, it seems probable that she preferred the simplicity of life at
Wimbledon with emphasis upon the activities of her own family.

The queen found Theobalds both convenient and pleasant to visit.
In his *Progresses* John Nichols reported that she was there at times
during ten or more different years from 1564 to 1589, and she may have
stopped twice in 1577 and also in 1578. Burghley's biographer, who had
been a member of his household, recorded that he entertained her
"twelve several times" at Theobalds and that each visit cost him
£2,000 or £3,000. She was there at his charge "sometimes three
weeks, a month, yes, six weeks together." But Burghley thought that
all he did was too little. Ambassadors and other strangers came to her
at Theobalds where she was "in as great royalty and as well and
magnificently served as at any time or place," to her great pleasure and
that of her retinue. All this was done "at his lordship's charge, with
rich shows, pleasant devices, and all manner of sports. . . ." During
one visit of the queen he gave her a basin decorated with mother-of-
pearl, gold, and silver. The outside was adorned with verses of
scripture and devices from cosmography, and the "layere," (perhaps
meaning the cover) had a fierce lion with a scepter. This gift was in a
case of black velvet garnished with silver, and the handle was made of
white silver.

Sometimes the queen stopped with little or no notice in advance. In
1578, for example, a vague item seems to mean that she had been there
only a short time before, but needed a stopping place in a day of travel.
Hence Burghley asked Thomas Randolph and the queen to dine at

Theobalds. Of course the queen would be attended by a hungry retinue. For emergencies like this, Lady Burghley needed huge supplies of food (without modern refrigeration), a reliable steward, and disciplined servants.

The long residences of the queen at Theobalds are supported by evidence from *Acts of the Privy Council.* In 1575, according to the minutes, the Council met there May 25, 27, 28, 30, and 31 and also June 1, 2, and 6. In 1587 the group met at the same place July 9, 10, 14, 16, 21, 26, 28, 29, and 30 (perhaps twice on the last-named date) and on August 5, 8, 9, and 13 (perhaps twice on August 13). Each group of meetings probably resulted from the fact that the queen was making a visit longer than usual; and since many minutes do not name the place, perhaps others were also at Theobalds.

During the years when Mildred Cecil was being hostess to the queen at Theobalds, it seems uncertain whether the family considered it or Cecil House the chief residence. A great amount of travel, usually by horseback and often with a number of servants, went on between the two places. From a list of items with exact dates of comings and goings, Conyers Read concluded: ''Burghley, when he was approaching sixty years, did not hesitate to take a twenty-mile ride to London one day and back again the next. And Lady Burghley did the same.'' When they brought with them a number of servants from Cecil House to Theobalds, they may have needed extra ones for other special guests or for a visit from the queen. At times Mildred Cecil might well have had the impression that Theobalds was really a home of the queen, not of herself and her own family. She and her husband were both fond of having their children and grandchildren with them, but probably they had to subordinate this desire to the wishes of the queen.

When Rathgeb was listing details about Theobalds for the Duke of Wirtemberg, he summed up by saying that no king need be ashamed to dwell there. James I apparently agreed. In 1607 Robert Cecil, who inherited the place from his father, received a royal request that may have been a command; he moved into Hatfield House and the king took over Theobalds. However, if William Camden was correct when he reported in an edition of *Britannia* that Robert Cecil talked of destroying the place, Cecil may have found ownership a burden and was glad to give possession to the king. Because it became a royal palace. Theobalds met destruction in the struggle between the Puritans and the Cavaliers. Today scarcely a stone remains of that magnificence.

Besides her hostess duties for the family and for public affairs, Mildred Cecil may have made life a little easier for her husband by maintaining good relations with the queen. When Elizabeth succeeded to the throne, the Cecils had been married about thirteen years; and as Conyers Read said, Mildred "participated actively in her husband's intellectual and political life." It has been suggested that the queen was not really fond of her because she lacked feminine charm, but another view was expressed by Thomas Baker in *A History of the College of St. John the Evangelist.* When the queen paid a visit to the college in 1564, Baker said that William Cecil, then chancellor of the university, came a day early, "accompanied by his lady, a person noted for her learning and therefore more acceptable to the queen and the university." There may be reason for Baker's opinion. About 1564 Mildred Cecil dared to petition the queen to let her husband stay at home instead of sending him on a mission to the emperor with Sir Nicholas Throckmorton. She pleaded his delicate health, but Guzman de Silva's report also carried the information that Cecil's enemies wished to get him out of the country and put someone else in his place. Probably Mildred Cecil was fully informed on the political implications of the situation. In 1567, after the murder of Lord Darnley, the queen chose Mildred Cecil as one of two women to visit Lady Lennox in the Tower and talk with her about the death of her son.

An incident of 1573 indicates that Lady Burghley did not approve of the flirtations and the frivolity that the queen sometimes carried on or permitted, as if she wished to enliven daily life. Gilbert Talbot (writing to his father, the Earl of Shrewsbury) reported that the queen was spending much time with Leicester and was showing her usual affection for him and that she was much taken also with the appearance, dancing, and apparent courage of the young Earl of Oxford. Two sisters, Lady Sheffield and Frances Howard, were "far in love" with Leicester; the queen did not like their striving with each other and had placed spies to follow Leicester. Lady Burghley made a critical comment about these goings-on, according to Gilbert Talbot; and if she did so, her comment may have been colored by an unfavorable attitude to Oxford, who had been her son-in-law for some two years. Her remark traveled to the ears of the queen. At first the queen was offended, but soon she and Lady Burghley were reconciled again. One who accepts at all this report by a male gossip must accept its conclusion—that coolness between them was brief and did not affect their relationship for years to come.

But a fundamental difference in the religious views of the queen and Mildred, Lady Burghley, was important. The queen imposed a centralized control of the church by her bishops, she liked a measure of form and ceremony, and she probably suspected that any tendency of local groups to control themselves or to discuss their own in-

terpretations of scripture was subversive. Mildred, like her sister Anne
Bacon, was a Nonconformist, a confirmed Puritan. Her religious
sentiments were stronger than those of her husband, she exerted influence on him, and other Puritans frequently asked her to intercede for
them. In the first ten years of Elizabeth's reign (according to Conyers
Read) Mildred was an active worker for the Puritan cause. Later she
was less active, probably because she realized through her husband
that urging the queen too much stirred her to opposition. Conyers Read
also stated that we hear little about her in the last twenty years of her
life (1569-1589) but that she continued to be at court. Her greatest
influence may have been exerted through private talks with her
husband and with other officials, an influence that would never appear
in any documents. Thus one might hazard a guess that her efforts did
not cease in the later years but were exercised with quiet discretion.

But even if she became more tactful in her approach to the queen,
Mildred Cecil, the three other Cooke sisters, and many influential
women did what they could to aid the Puritan cause. Lawrence Stone
(with his ability to draw large, convincing conclusions) says in *The
Crisis of the Aristocracy* that Puritanism in the first thirty years of
Elizabeth's reign owed much of its success to a few peers, to a number
of peers and knights who were members of the Council, to the
"irrepressible Duchess of Suffolk," and to many other influential
women who were actively religious. Among others he named two of the
Cooke sisters—Anne Bacon, who sheltered Puritan preachers at
Gorhambury, and Elizabeth Russell. Though he did not name Catherine
Cooke, other sources make clear that both she and her husband Henry
Killigrew were aiding the fiery Edward Dering to continue the public
lectures the queen disliked. When the Council failed to stop him, the
queen finally gave the order herself. Mildred Cecil was giving another
kind of quiet support that seems to have continued to the end of her life,
according to a letter that a Doctor Richard Webster wrote to Robert
Cecil about his efforts to get a prebend at Windsor. He had scarcely a
friend to help him, he said, "since it hath pleased God to deprive us of
my good lady and mistress, your most virtuous mother of happy
memory, the staff of poor chaplains in her life time. . . ."

Mildred Cecil apparently worked hand in glove with her husband
while he was securing an accord with Scotland and was working toward
the treaty of Edinburgh, signed in 1560. Her contribution is emphasized

by the letters she was receiving from the leaders in Scotland. But before we can understand her influence, even in part, it seems necessary to summarize the situation in Scotland.

The child who became Mary Queen of Scots was born in 1542. She was the granddaughter of James IV, King of Scotland, and his queen Margaret Tudor, the older daughter of Henry VII of England. Hence Mary had a claim on the throne of England. She was the daughter of James V and his French queen, Mary of Guise. When her father died a few days after her birth, she was his only legitimate heir. Henry VIII tried to secure a contract of marriage between her and his son Edward, who was born in 1537; but he tried threats instead of persuasion and failed. So Mary of Guise arranged the betrothal of her daughter to the dauphin, sent her to France when she was about six years old to be educated there with the royal children, and brought about the actual marriage in 1558. When Henry II died from an accidental head wound he received in a tournament the next year, the dauphin succeeded his father as Francis II. As a result, Mary of Scotland was queen of France from July 1559 to December 1560 when her husband died. Francis II was young, sickly, and lacking in force of character; he listened to his charming wife and allowed members of the Guise family to govern France. When his brief life ended and his eleven-year-old brother succeeded him as Charles IX, their mother Catherine de Medici became the power in France. Members of the Guise family lost their influence, Catherine was hostile to Mary, and Mary's situation in France was becoming intolerable to her.

Meantime much had been happening in Scotland. In 1554 Mary of Guise had become regent for her daughter. Supporters of the reformed or Protestant religion, who called themselves the lords of the congregation, were increasing in numbers and in power. About 1559 the Catholic regent began treating them harshly, and serious civil disorders broke out. The regent called upon the French to help; they fortified Leith for her use and brought in French soldiers. In 1559 also William Maitland of Lethington (one of the most competent of the Scottish leaders), who supported the reformed religion but had continued to work with the regent, decided that she was "full of craft and deceit." He left her service and became a leader in the lords of the congregation. In the same year John Knox returned to his native Scotland to do his best for religious reform. His best was usually effective and sometimes devastating. In 1558 he had published at Geneva *The First Blast of the Trumpet against the Monstrous Regiment of Women*. Resenting his attack on the rule of any woman, Elizabeth refused to let him enter England; and later whenever she developed a brief reluctance to support the Protestants in Scotland, she may have been partly motivated by resentment against Knox.

As early as January 1559 James Hamilton, Duke of Châtelherault and heir presumptive to the throne of Scotland, talked with Sir Henry Percy about the possibility of an understanding with England. A few days later Percy wrote Cecil that Maitland wished to talk especially with him but also with the Council. Within a month William Kirkaldy of Scotland was seeking a conference with Percy; he reported that Maitland wished to confer with the Council and with Queen Elizabeth. In March of 1559 Maitland came to France and to England, had his first meeting with Cecil, and made a friend of Mildred Cecil. These details were given by Conyers Read, who added that Maitland seems to have been in London, again about November 1559 to February 1560; and it is likely that he was a guest in the Cecil home.

At one time Cecil wrote to James Croft that the plan was to give the Scots promises, then money and, when and if it became necessary, to furnish them arms. At the end of 1559 it looked as if the Scots alone would never be able to dislodge the French forces already in Scotland. Cecil had the problem of convincing the Council that help to Scotland was important enough to risk war with France. He convinced the Council, but the queen refused to confirm his plan. But she did send money; and when the agents of the regent became suspicious, she solemnly denied sending any, saying that the regent was hearing only malicious rumors. Even when the lords of the congregation "began paying their troops in English and Flemish coin, and when a thousand pounds was intercepted on its way to them," she continued her denials; but she smiled, as if the whole affair were a great joke.

The queen also sent William Winter with a fleet to Berwick, with instructions to lodge his ships in the Firth of Forth, pretending that he had been driven there by a storm. No matter what happened, he was never to admit that he was there by the command of the queen. His orders were to keep supplies from the regent and to damage French ships all he could, whether they were in the Firth of Forth or at sea. About this time the French were having serious troubles at home; and in Scotland Mary of Guise was mortally ill. She died before the end of 1560. Since Mary Queen of Scots was the direct, legal heir to the crown of Scotland, the lords invited her to return from France and become their queen. She accepted, but months passed before she arrived.

At the end of 1559 or early in 1560 Queen Elizabeth insisted on negotiations instead of wasting lives and money in war. She and the Council finally persuaded Cecil to go to Edinburgh. He went as a doubter, but once there he used all his skill. William Cecil of England and William Maitland of Scotland were chiefly responsible for the negotiations leading to the Treaty of Edinburgh. Scotland agreed to recognize the right of Elizabeth to rule England; Francis II and Mary were to quit using her arms and her title; most of the French troops were to be withdrawn from Scotland at once, and the fortress of Leith was to be destroyed; the government of Scotland was to be carried on by a council of Scottish nobles, that is, by the lords of the congregation. Though Francis II and Mary had given their royal word to ratify the treaty, they found pretext after pretext for refusing to do so. Their refusal did not matter much compared with the fact that French soldiers had been removed and the fortress of Leith promptly destroyed. The Treaty of Edinburgh was signed July 6, 1560. On August 25, 1560, without waiting for the return of Mary Queen of Scots or for her consent, the parliament of Scotland voted to suppress the Catholic faith and to establish Protestantism as the religion of Scotland. Mary Queen of Scots returned to her native land August 19, 1561.

On her return Mary chose two excellent men as her chief counselors. They were William Maitland of Lethington and James Stuart, her illegitimate half-brother, later Earl of Moray. She agreed to the Protestant creed for the country but asked that she be allowed to celebrate Mass for herself. With the firm support of James Stuart and the stubborn opposition of John Knox, her request was granted. At first angry crowds gathered to stop the Mass; but James Stuart, it is said, stood in the door of the building and held them back. After a few weeks people gradually calmed down, won over by the charm of Mary and her willingness to compromise.

The situation in Scotland had been a matter of great concern in England. The problem was both religious and political. As the country turned from the Catholic faith to the reformed religion, or Protestantism, William Cecil recognized a chance that might not come again while he lived: a chance to unite the two countries in the same religion, perhaps to unite them under one ruler, and to get the French out of Scotland lest they use it as a back door for attacking England. No loyal Englishman enjoyed the thought of France taking over Scotland and then moving against the English. Most English Protestants with any depth of religious feeling believed that in the hour of need England should help another Protestant nation; even Queen Elizabeth accepted the idea as a political necessity, though she might struggle against the cost of such help. Mildred Cecil had grasped political ideas easily in other situations and she had now been following her husband's career for some years. She had a greater depth of religious feeling than her husband, it seems; hence her concern with the problem of Scotland would be at least as great as his. It would also be an informed concern, both political and religious.

While Cecil and Maitland were working to bring about an accord between the two countries, Mildred Cecil and Maitland were also working in a common cause, as we learn both from his letters to her and those of other Scotch leaders. Just what these leaders expected her to do is not specific, but it is clear that they considered her work important. Details from their letters will be followed by some conjectures about the influence they expected her to exert.

Maitland wrote Mildred Cecil some time after he had been in London from November 1559 to February 1560 (when it is likely that he had been a guest in the Cecil home). He wrote again on April 18, 1560, from a camp before Leith. He had delayed writing, he said, for fear of increasing her care. But at this time, though they were doubtful about the queen's attitude, he saw nothing to mislike, and the Lord St. John would soon be sent to the queen. When he wrote on April 28, again from a camp before Leith, he begged her to overlook his slowness in writing: the practices of the enemy had kept him in fear of having nothing to bring comfort. But at this time, "praise God," the matter was coming out better. When St. John arrived, she would know more. About two weeks after the treaty of Edinburgh was signed, he wrote her again, this time from Berwick. Now that they had come to the end of their troubles, he said, they would have most need of her help in the affair that she knew he was earnestly pressing. She would hear from others the course of events. He sent her the compliments of the Lord James Stuart, with mention of a present his lordship had sent her, and the compliments of Mr. Melville; he recommended to her the bearer, the Laird of Craigmillar.

About this time Mildred Cecil was corresponding with Sir Henry Percy also about affairs in Scotland, but his letters to her are not available. He had been working on the treaty of Berwick; it was signed February 27, 1560. In this agreement Elizabeth promised to intervene to save the freedom of Scotland; and if the French attacked England, the Scots were to send help.

In September 1560 Robert Melville, another leader of the Scots, wrote Mildred Cecil from Edinburgh. He was working with the Protestant forces, and later he came as an ambassador to England. Melville gave her the names of three men who were coming on a commission to the queen; he also told her that the estates in the parliament had agreed "indifferently" well, and at this time that no sedition or other trouble existed in the country. He was sending her certain presents, and he commended to her the bearer of his letter, his cousin, Walter Melville. He had sent letters to her by Mr. Killigrew (who became her brother-in-law later and was sent to Scotland about this time) but he did not know whether she had received them.

On September 28, 1560, the Earl of Arran, James Hamilton, was writing to Mildred Cecil, saying that if any other than the bearer had been the messenger in "a cause so weighty," he would have been compelled to write her more fully. But he sent only these few lines in addition to what the bearer would tell her. The Hamiltons were heirs presumptive to the throne of Scotland, and the lords of the congregation hoped to bring about the marriage of a Hamilton to Queen Elizabeth.

What did the Scottish leaders expect Mildred Cecil to do for their cause in the months before the signing of the Treaty of Edinburgh and in the period that followed? The number of men who wrote, their importance, the messages and the gifts they sent, their reluctance to make definite statements in their letters, and their reliance on trusted messengers certainly suggest something significant. It seems a reasonable guess that they trusted the enthusiasm of Mildred Cecil for their cause more than they trusted the intentions of Queen Elizabeth or even of William Cecil. When Maitland had suggested that the Scots were doubtful about the attitude of the queen, he apparently meant the English queen. They may have expected Mildred Cecil to persuade a thrifty Queen Elizabeth to send money to support their cause. At least the queen did send them money. And if Mildred Cecil needed at times to persuade the queen that help to Protestant Scotland was more important than resentment against John Knox for his blast against the rule of women, she was probably equal to the occasion.

At least William Cecil did succeed in completing the treaty of Edinburgh while his wife was lending assistance and was receiving gifts and thanks from the most important leaders in Scotland. How much she contributed we can never know. But Conyers Read said of the completed work: "The Peace of Edinburgh was one of Cecil's great achievements and one of the great achievements of Elizabeth's reign." It was in part, it seems safe to conclude, the achievement of Mildred Cecil.

Mildred Cecil maintained friendly relations with leaders of Scotland in other situations. When the younger Earl of Arran developed Protestant views while he was in France, his new views became known and his arrest was ordered. He managed to escape. In his crisis either Cecil sent Throckmorton to bring him to Emden, where he took ship to England, or Killigrew went to the German coast with a fishing boat to bring him in disguise to the Cecil home in Cannon Row. He spent one or two nights there and had a formal audience with the queen before he went on to Scotland. The Cecils were friendly to James Stuart when he was "put to the horn," or outlawed from Scotland because he opposed the marriage of Mary Queen of Scots to Lord Darnley; in this situation he came to London. On October 22, 1565, the queen and Cecil had a long conference with him, according to Guzman de Silva; Conyers Read said he probably stayed in the Cecil home "as he had done more than once in happier days." Later he sent back a letter of thanks to Mildred Cecil for the good treatment she had given a banished man, with his love to Nan (Anne Cecil, then about nine years old).

Apparently Mildred, Lady Burghley accepted the system of gratuities that guided officials of the English government, or at least the system as it was practiced by conscientious officials like her husband. Once at least, in the handling of a wardship, she seems to have accepted a large sum herself. That system (as analyzed by Sir John Neale in *The Elizabethan Political Scene*) was based on the hard fact that officials in the government, even those of high rank, received mere token payments; and some minor officials had no pay at all from the government. People using their services had to compensate them, and thus a system of gratuities or "large-scale tipping" had grown up. When officials were not conscientious, the system easily became bribery.

The queen also had under her direct control a large amount of patronage consisting of hundreds of offices; many suitors were trying to get these offices, the number far outnumbering the positions. Between the queen and the suitors an inner ring of officials and courtiers existed, with admittance to the privy chamber and probable influence with the queen. Suitors usually had to reward one or more of them if they expected to win a suit. The queen may have realized that adequate salaries to officials would have been a wiser plan, but any change required many thousands of pounds that she did not have. She and Burghley tried to manage the system as honestly and wisely as they could and to get competent men into positions. Few men, except Sir Thomas More and Sir Thomas Elyot earlier, refused all fees.

Since wardships were often good business investments, people paid high prices for them. Apparently Lady Burghley accepted a large sum to influence her husband (who was lord treasurer and master of the Court of Wards) about the guardianship of the five-year-old son of Thomas Fermor, Somerton, Oxford. The father had died in August

1580. The accounts of an executor, Bennett Winchcombe, include these items: to Christopher Hatton's son for writing to "my lord treasurer," ten shillings; to Mr. Bradshawe, "who first moved my lady to deal in it," ten pounds; to one of her secretaries, six pounds; to speed her chamberlain, three pounds; for writing two letters to "my Lady Burghley," twelvepence; to "my Lady Burghley for obtaining the wardship," two hundred fifty pounds. Unless part of the money was sticking to the fingers of Mr. Winchcombe, or unless the lady returned part or all of the fee—and no evidence indicates that either of these things happened—Lady Burghley received a larger fee than the queen might have expected for her influence about a wardship. Whether her husband received any fee for the same wardship is a matter for pure speculation. But most competent historians consider that Lord Burghley was moderate and honest by the standards of his time about accepting fees, and he sometimes refused to take any gift for a service.

A letter written from the court by Lady Burghley in October 1573 to her cousin Sir William Fitzwilliam seems worth quoting almost entire as evidence of her political understanding. Sir William was then in his second year as lord deputy of Ireland, and though he was probably one of the most efficient of Elizabeth's officials in that country, he was bitterly attacked by enemies. Her Latin letter was translated by George Ballard in *Memoirs of British Ladies:*

> I am heartily sorry for the great and continual injuries you have, and which I well understood before the receipt of my lady's and your letters. And I wish I were as able to redress them as I have both grieved with you and for you. My lord, I know, both hath and doth continue your defender here (whatsoever he writeth to you there) to the uttermost of his power; and only he alone, I must needs say, is driven to answer in your behalf. I speak not this to crave thanks . . . I know he dealeth faithfully to his prince and country and truly and honestly with all men; and as I would be glad you were delivered from that burdensome service, so do I wish it may be with such credit as I think you have deserved, though I be partial. And therefore I think it best this storm were overblown, and after some service done, a better time may be found to seek your departure. For otherwise, besides further discredit, you shall hardly get recompense for your former service, which would grieve me most of all. For when, upon your misliking, others are sought to be placed, it seemeth that the preferring of another is the disgracing of you. So that though I know not what is, indeed

> I guess that time left [is] to your advantage. . . . It is not you
> that suffer alone, this grief is common to all those that deal in
> princes' affairs. . . . And therefore, good cousin, use your
> discretion in moderating your grief, and bear with the time. . . .

She added a postscript: "Keep close your friends' letters, for craft and
malice never reigned more. Some about you perhaps may be corrupted
to show them, though for my part, I care not — not that I know anything,
before God, but because I know the like practice used with some here."

Besides indicating her concern for a kinsman and friend, the letter
is evidence that she was a realist about evil in her world, that she had
confidence in her husband (not blind faith but an understanding of his
problems), and that she was astute in analyzing political situations. The
letter, like those she received from leaders in Scotland, suggests that
she followed with deep interest the problems her husband faced in
governing England. It seems that Lord Burghley was fortunate in his
marriage; and if the Lady Mildred enjoyed being valued for the
qualities she really possessed and having a chance to use her mental
abilities, the marriage was fortunate for her.


In all areas of life, both personal and public, Mildred, Lady
Burghley was not a status-seeker; she was never guilty of self-
aggrandizement. Unlike her sister Elizabeth, she had no tendency to
quarrel with either inferiors or superiors, no desire to appeal to the Star
Chamber or to the Privy Council, and no tendency to boast that she
knew the law better than legal officials. She made no display of her
learning. She did not prepare Greek and Latin epigrams for the
monuments of her friends or members of her family, as her sister
Elizabeth made a habit of doing. She wrote no books, and she published
no translations from either Greek or Latin. Though she had translated
Saint Chrysostom, when she learned that the same work had already
been done by John Christopherson, she refused to publish her version.
And she was the woman whom Ascham praised for speaking Greek as if
it were English!

No doubt she spoke Latin fluently; every man or woman who was
praised as a classical scholar about the middle of the century or a little
earlier, when she was being educated, seemed to take that skill for
granted. Those who wrote on education — Vives, Elyot, Ascham —
emphasized the teaching of children to use Latin in ordinary talk about
things of everyday life. Since English was not then a language of
diplomacy, one might suppose that she and a Spanish diplomat who

wrote home giving the details of his conversations with her were speaking in Latin and that she often found the skill useful when she was hostess to her husband's diplomatic guests from the Continent.

Richard Mulcaster added his testimony in *Positions,* an important work by an influential teacher at the Merchant Taylors school in London. Any man who was a skeptic about the ability of women trained in the classics to speak the languages (presumably Greek and Latin) should begin a conversation with one of them. He would speedily be changed, Mulcaster suggested, from skeptic to believer.

Writers, especially those who dedicated books to Mildred, Lady Burghley commended her for her knowledge of the classics. In his "praise of Eight Ladies at Queen Elizabeth's Court," Richard Edwards mentioned a "comely" Cooke (apparently Mildred), adding that she compared favorably with Roman women for her learning. In dedications, writers not only stressed her knowledge of Greek and Latin but they avoided the romantic feminine nonsense that appeared in many dedications to women. When Thomas Lodge addressed *A Margarite of America* to Mildred's sister, the self-seeking Lady Elizabeth Russell, he said, "I humbly kiss your most delicate hands, shutting up my English duty under an Italian copy of humanity and courtesy." No writer addressed Mildred Cecil in words like these. When Thomas Drant honored her and her sister in *A Medicinable Moral* in 1566, he merely said, "To the Right Honourable my Lady Bacon and my Lady Cecil, favorers of virtue and learning." A dedication could hardly be more concise or more truthful. In 1582 Christopher Ockland dedicated to Mildred, Lady Burghley, *De pacatissimo Angliae statu.* He described her as "most famous, most learned, most skilled in Greek and Latin literature, and in other literature. . . ." In a Latin poem that followed he said that she was the most illustrious of the four sisters. In 1582 he addressed to her his *Anglorum praelia.* In 1585 John Sharrock issued an English translation of Ockland's *De pacatissimo* with the same dedication and the same poem. All these dedications avoided romantic excess and praised her for qualities she possessed.

The most interesting dedication to her was the one by Ulpian Fulwell in 1579 for *The First Part of the Eighth Liberal Science,* the art of flattery. In a poem of some length he used the name *Mildred Burghley* in an acrostic. In a dialogue with his muse he questioned whether he should dedicate his work to her; his muse advised him to do so, relying on the courtesy of one "Whose noble heart knows all humanity.'' The author answered that he could  not do justice to her learning, virtue, godliness, noble nature, and courtesy. The muse insisted that she would accept his work if he remained modest and did not deal ''with tricks of love or Venus' toys,'' and she would not expect ''a coy conceit of curious eloquence.'' So he dedicated the work ''To the right noble and virtuous lady, the Lady Burghley. . . .'' When he looked at the fountains of flattery, he wished to expose their wicked impudence, but he did not need to turn to Homer for accounts of the sirens:

> And as it is well known that your ladyship have stopped your ears against their magical incantations as a pattern of prudence and discretion for others . . . to imitate. For the abandoning of which filthy art, I refrain to write that which common knowledge and public report do of your ladyship's worthiness daily testify . . . the great courtesy that I have seen and received at your ladyship's hands hath enforced me to express my dutiful gratuity with this . . . unpolished piece of work . . . with my humble and hearty prayer unto almighty God, both for you and my good lord, whom God preserve to the inestimable comfort of the common wealth of this realm.

Fulwell's words are both a dedication and a character sketch.

The Lady Burghley was a compassionate woman, whether she considered groups or individuals. Evidence appeared in a letter cited earlier; it was written not long after her death by a Dr. Richard Webster, who described her as ''the staff of poor chaplains'' and lamented that now he had no one to help him. Years later, men as different as an archbishop and Fulke Greville expressed appreciation for her help. Writing to Robert Cecil in 1601, Archbishop Whitgift thanked him for his kind words to ''my lord of London'' and acknowledged ''his great obligations to Cecil's father, by whose means, next to God and her Majesty, he is what he is; and also to Cecil's mother.'' The same year, Fulke Greville wrote Robert Cecil to ask help in getting permission to use some stone from a ruined house owned by the queen; he was quite willing to pay for the stone. He was sure Robert's father would have done more for him than this, he said, ''and that kind mother of yours, even in heaven where she is, if she can but remember that heavenly text of *Quare fremuerunt gentes,* with many other particulars of unoffensive familiarities between us, I assure myself would yet charge you upon her blessing not to refuse an old friend and courtier such a common courtesy.'' But he did not trust the generosity of Robert himself; hearing that courtiers now loved bribes more than they used to do, he offered to give him "the finest high-flying tercel" that he ever owned.

Mildred Burghley's compassion found an outlet in extensive educational and philanthropic activities, and she proceeded so modestly that even her husband did not know of them until he found the records in her handwriting after her death. The source of her funds for these benefactions is an interesting question. Since the law gave a wife's personal belongings—even her clothing, jewels, and adornments—to her husband and since he controlled her lands and houses while the marriage lasted, one might wonder where she found the money. Possibly her fee for the Fermor wardship and some other fees that she may have received, even though they are not in available records, were used for charities, though it seems that such sums might legally belong to her husband.

Another possibility exists. About 1555 her husband was making her an allowance of forty pounds a year. Noting that fact, Conyers Read merely wondered what part of the household expenses she was expected to pay with that sum. But perhaps the money was a personal allowance for the wife to spend exactly as she pleased, and she chose to spend a considerable part of it for her benevolences. More than a hundred years earlier, when Sir John Fastolf married a wealthy widow, he settled upon her "for her own use a hundred pounds a year" at a time when the local curate was serving for ten pounds a year. Other men may have made allowances to their wives in the fifteenth and sixteenth centuries, but no other examples are at hand. And to add another conjecture to the suggestion that the forty pounds for Mildred Cecil was a personal allowance, perhaps her husband increased her allowance as he prospered. No doubt exists about his prospering—from lands granted him by the queen, from his appointment as master of the Court of Wards, and from other sources.

Lord Burghley summarized his wife's benefactions as he struggled to make an adjustment to her death. Reading of her plans for the future, he said, "Now in conscience, this must be done according to her wish." As a result, the Cecil Papers at Hatfield House include records about the handling of her charities and other bequests after her death.

She had provided in perpetuity two scholarshps for students at St. John's College, purchasing lands for their support in the name of the Dean of Westminster. She assigned four marks yearly for four sermons to be delivered quarterly at St. John's College. Both these provisions honored her husband, who had attended that college. She gave money toward "a building for a new way at Cambridge to the Common Schools." She gave books in Hebrew to Cambridge University; Greek books to St. John's at Cambridge; books to Christ Church, Oxford; others to St. John's at Oxford; and still others to the college at Westminster. She named a sum of money to be given the master of St. John's, Cambridge, that he might provide fires on Sundays and holidays between the Feast of All Saints and Candlemas (November first to February second) when the college did not furnish fires. These sums, even the money for warmth, furthered education.

She provided for twenty poor people in Cheshunt, who were to have a mess of flesh and bread, with money for drink, on the first Sunday of each month. At various times of the year she had sent shirts and smocks to the poor in Cheshunt and in London. Four times a year she had secretly been sending money to all the prisons to London to buy bread, cheese, and drink for four hundred persons, and many times for more. In these provisions she seemed to be following neither the earlier Catholic doctrine (that all giving is worthy and that good works are essential to salvation) nor the extreme Puritan principles developed with capitalism (that poverty is sin and only those unable to work should receive gifts). Instead, she was a compassionate woman who wished to relieve suffering

She established loans to help those who were not in actual poverty but who might be given assistance without treating them as paupers. She assigned "a good sum" to the Haberdashers Company, so that every two years they might lend twenty pounds apiece to six poor men of certain occupations (such as smiths, carpenters, or weavers) in Romford, Essex; and another sum to provide twenty marks apiece to six other like persons, both in Cheshunt and in Waltham, to the sum of eighty pounds. She had been sponsoring a weaving project, giving wool and flax to women in Cheshunt and asking them to make it into yarn and then bring it to her so that she might see their manner of working. Sometimes she had them weave the yarn into cloth; and after paying them more for the weaving than it was worth, she gave the cloth to the poor. These projects, it might be said, were aimed at the deserving poor.

Shortly before her death she had bought much rye and wheat to be given to the poor in a time of scarcity when prices would rise. In this last provision she had no theories — only the realization that people might be hungry but lack the money to pay high prices for necessary food.

A few days after his wife died Burghley wrote a *Meditation,* thanking God for permitting her to spend many years with him and for the grace that enabled her to be sure of her salvation. His comments are

infused with religious feeling, including a firm belief in personal im-
mortality and a large measure of Christian resignation. Perhaps one
may disagree with Conyers Read (since each view is purely personal
opinion), who felt that the *Meditation* lacked what he called a cry of the
heart and that Cecil's attitude toward his wife had never been more
than complete respect. Burghley, one recalls, had never been given to
lyrical outcries, even about his feeling for Mary Cheke. As the years
passed, it would be normal for mutually shared ideas (moral, religious,
and political) to become stronger ties than youthful emotions.

By 1589 age, illnesses, the struggle to continue his duties to the
state and personal losses may have numbed him further against the
expression of feeling. Attacks of gout and other physical difficulties had
sometimes made it impossible for him to perform his official duties; in
later years he had himself carried to his post to deal with critical
situations. When it was possible to consult him, the queen refused to
proceed without hearing his opinion. Both Burghley and his wife had
been enduring the atrocious behavior of the Earl of Oxford, their son-in-
law; details about it were summarized earlier in the chapter. The earl
even refused to "cumber" himself with any care of his own children.
They became a part of the Burghley household; and though Lord
Burghley died in 1598 and the Earl of Oxford lived until 1604, it was
Burghley who arranged good marriages for the three daughters.

In 1587 Burghley's mother died. He had described her as his
earliest and his best friend. In June 1588 his favorite child Anne
escaped from an unhappy marriage into death. At one time he had said
that his wife and his daughter Anne were dear to him beyond the
whole race of womankind. In April 1589 the death of his wife followed.
One could scarcely blame him if he did not express a poignant, youthful
sorrow, or if he wished to escape into death himself instead of being
stretched out longer upon the rack of a tough world.

Men who were her contemporaries and also recent historians have
expressed appreciation of Mildred Cooke Cecil who became Lady
Burghley. One of them was her husband, who paid her an indirect
tribute in the precepts he wrote for his son, when he urged him not to
marry a fool: "For thou shalt find it, to thy great grief, that there is
nothing more fulsome than a she-fool." In the opening sentence of the
precepts he said:

> The virtuous inclinations of thy matchless mother, by
> whose tender and godly care thy infancy was governed,
> together with thy education under so zealous and excellent a

tutor, puts me rather in assurance of the hope that thou art not
ignorant of that summary bond which is only able to make thee
happy as well in thy death as life—I mean the true knowledge
and worship of thy Creator and Redeemer. . . .

B. W. Beckingsale, in writing the life of her husband, *Burghley:
Tudor Statesman,* said:

> Unlike her younger sisters, Mildred was a patient, quiet
> woman. Under her husband's watchful eye, she managed his
> great household. She could act independently of him, as she did
> in her well-known charities. . . . Her recreations ranged from
> archery to translating a Greek sermon. . . . But the character
> and intellect which were apparent in her long, severe coun-
> tenance won the respect and liking of men as various as Sir
> Richard Morison, Sir Christopher Hatton, and Sir Walter
> Raleigh.

Conyers Read concluded that she was "a wise, good woman,
devoted to learning of which she was herself a great exponent, devoted
to the welfare of scholars . . . devoted to the relief of the poor, par-
ticularly the deserving poor, as in the loan to artisans or the jobs for
poor women in spinning and weaving." He had also commented earlier
that she participated actively in her husband's political and intellectual
life.

*Family monument of Sir Anthony Cooke in the church of Edward the Confessor. Four daughters kneel behind the mother—Mildred Cecil, Anne Bacon, Catherine Killegrew, and Elizabeth Hoby.*

*Panel from an enameled glass window installed during the preparation of Gorhambury for Queen Elizabeth's visit in 1577.*

# CHAPTER TWO

# *Anne Cooke,*
# *Lady Bacon*
## 1527 or 1528-1610

Anne Cooke, probably the second daughter of Sir Anthony and Lady Anne Cooke of Gidea Hall, Essex, belonged without doubt to the new breed of intellectual women influenced by the Renaissance. She was given a thorough classical education by her father, so thorough that Latin and Greek quotations seemed to flow easily from her brain and her pen into her personal letters. She did not pursue wealth and status for herself and her family, waste time in idleness, or use her education as mere personal ornament. Without neglecting her family (and her mature sons may have wished for neglect at times, instead of her flow of advice), she had a major aim of contributing to the general welfare by her support of the Nonconformists. Using her personal influence and her knowledge of languages, she pursued this aim with fearless vigor and intelligence. Apparently she had little interest in economic or governmental problems unless they were connected with religion.

*Detail of the south entrance of Gorhambury, country home of the Bacons constructed during 1563-1568. Built on a simple plan and with local materials, it was modest compared to other great houses of that time.*

Compared with her sister Mildred Cecil, or with other outstanding women of the century, she was narrow but intense.

Anne Cooke became the second wife of Nicholas Bacon, probably through the influence of her sister Mildred, who had married William Cecil in 1545. By his first wife Bacon had three daughters and three sons — Nicholas, Nathaniel, and Edward. Anne gave him two sons, Anthony in 1558 and Francis in 1561. Anne's husband died in 1579, and she survived him about thirty years. Unlike many Tudor women, she did not indicate any concern about a second marriage. In her relationship with other people, apparently she was working for the good of their souls. And unlike her sister Elizabeth she did not busy herself in asking the Cecils, father and son, for personal favors. She used her classical scholarship to further religious beliefs and thus, as she saw it, to promote the welfare of England.

Anne Cooke, who did not become Anne Bacon, we may suppose, until 1556 or 1557, was with Queen Mary in 1553 when she was receiving the members of the Council for the first time. Why Anne was there is uncertain, since she did not usually take an interest in problems of government, and in later years, at least, she was violently antipapist. Perhaps she appeared because her sister Mildred had persuaded her to help intercede for William Cecil. His fears about involvement in the plot of Northumberland to put the Lady Jane Grey on the throne were discussed in Chapter 1. If that was Anne's purpose, her intercession, added to support from the Earl of Arundel and Sir William Paget, was successful. The queen allowed Cecil to make a full explanation, decided that he was "a very honest man," and later issued a formal pardon for him. The incident suggests another possible link between the Cecil and the Bacon families.

Anne Bacon and her husband Sir Nicholas Bacon had interests in common; both were concerned with education and with the classics. He had been educated at Corpus Christi, Cambridge, from 1523 to 1527 and, according to the author of *The Art of English Poesy,* he was an excellent orator who had based his skill on Quintilian. The author of this work praised both Cecil and Bacon for their ability in formal speaking but added a special tribute to Bacon:

I have come to the Lord Keeper, Sir Nicholas Bacon, and found
him sitting in his gallery alone, with the works of Quintilian
before him; indeed he was a most eloquent man, and of rare
learning and wisdom, as ever I knew England to breed, and one
that joyed as much in learned men and men of good wit.

Sir Nicholas made some excellent suggestions to further education.
He presented the government with a plan for using funds from the
dissolution of the monasteries to educate able young men as statesmen,
with emphasis upon French, Latin, and Roman or civil law. But the
funds from the monasteries were turned to other purposes. He formulated another complete plan for the education of minors under the
Court of Wards, with emphasis upon morals, physical development,
arts, and literature. Again, his ideas were not put into practice.

But acting as an individual, Sir Nicholas founded a free grammar
school at Redgrave, Suffolk, where he had lived as a boy and where one
of his country residences was located. He established six scholarships
for boys who needed help to get an education at Cambridge. He gave
books, presumably Greek and Latin ones and possibly some in Hebrew,
to the University of Cambridge. Just before his death he gave £200
toward the erection of a new chapel at his own college, Corpus Christi.

Both Anne and her husband used the classics in varied ways,
adapting ideas from them to their lives and using mottoes and other
details from them to decorate Gorhambury, their favorite country
home. The letters of Anne Bacon, including those to her son Anthony,
are filled with Greek and Latin phrases and quotations. The ideas of the
classics were important to her, and apparently she thought easily in
both languages. She wrote letters in Latin to religious leaders on the
Continent — to her, an essential use for her mastery of that language;
she translated the *Apologia* of Bishop Jewel from his Latin into English;
and with her English translation she sent him a letter written in Greek,
and he replied with one in the same language.

That Anne Bacon and her husband agreed also about simple living
is suggested by their housing plans. Their earliest home in London may
have been the building known to John Stow as Bacon House. He explained that it had been "new built by Sir Nicholas Bacon, lord keeper
of the great seal." We do not know whether Bacon built it for his first
wife or for Anne Cooke; but it was probably a modest place, since it
soon became a printing shop. When Bacon was appointed keeper of the

great seal, York House became his official residence. It was described
as a grand place, richly furnished, with beautiful tapestries and great
wall brackets holding many lighted tapers. Judging from what we know
of her entire life and character, perhaps Anne Bacon never felt at home
in York House.

By 1563 the Bacons were beginning to build a modest country
home in Hertfordshire near the place where the Cecils were erecting
the palatial Theobalds. They had bought the old manor of Gorham, part
of the revenue of the church of St. Albans ten miles away, and the work
of rebuilding it went on from 1563 to about 1568. Using local timber and
other materials near at hand, they kept the total cost under £4,000.
Chatsworth, which Bess of Hardwick completed about 1570, had cost
about £80,000; and Longleat, built by Sir John Thynne near the same
time, cost even more than Chatsworth.

The plan of the Bacon house, known as Gorhambury, was simple.
It was a quadrangle built around a large courtyard but without
corridors; hence members of the household had to cross the open
courtyard to get from one part of the house to the other. Two towers at
opposite ends of the building rose above the rooftops, with one bell
tower looming high above everything else. A bell, once used to call all
members of the household to prayers in the chapel and to meals in the
hall, is said to hang in the stables of the new house; an engraved
couplet reveals that the bell was made in 1563. The hall of Gorhambury
was only thirty-five by nineteen or twenty feet, with the ceiling about
twenty-two feet from the floor; it was certainly not planned for use in
entertaining a queen. At the entrance of the hall Latin verses stated
that the house had been finished by Nicholas Bacon when Elizabeth had
ruled ten years, that she had made him a knight and keeper of her great
seal, and that the middle way is a firm rule.

Inside the hall the decorations were emblematic paintings. Over
the fireplace a picture of an oak with acorns falling from it carried the
motto *Nisi quid potius,* or, *What is stronger?* On the wall behind the
dais was a picture of Ceres teaching mankind to grow corn, with a Latin
motto meaning *Instruction brings improvement.* The main decoration
was a painting representing the feast of the gods, "where Mars is
caught in a net by Vulcan."

In the orchard, according to John Nichols, was a small banqueting
house with the liberal arts pictured on the walls; over the pictures were
the names of learned men who had excelled in each art. For grammar,
one Englishman, William Lily, was named along with Donatus, Servius,
and Priscian; for arithmetic, a near contemporary, the French scholar
Budaeus, but not Cuthbert Tunstall nor Robert Record; and for

rhetoric, Cicero, Isocrates, Demosthenes, and Quintilian. Each of the men was honored with Latin verses, composed "by Bacon himself," it is said; but possibly Anne Bacon, the equal of anyone in England for classical scholarship, also made her contribution. Sir Nicholas added fine gardens to the estate, thus making the place famous.

Gorhambury was also provided with a good water supply. By "some force," said Ian Dunlop, the waters in the river Ver were raised, reservoirs were built in Prae Wood, and lead piping three-quarters of a mile long brought water to all parts of the house. Doctor Rawley, chaplain to Sir Francis Bacon, later made this statement: "When Sir Nicholas Bacon, the Lord Keeper, lived, every room in Gorhambury was served with a pipe of water from the ponds distant about a mile off. In the lifetime of Mr. Anthony Bacon the water ceased, after whose death, his Lordship coming to the inheritance, could not recover the water without infinite charge." Thus Gorhambury was built by a husband and a wife who liked cleanness and simplicity and who used their classical background as a part of their lives.

But about four years after the Bacons completed Gorhambury, they had reason to change their simple residence. The queen was visiting the Cecils (who were now Lord and Lady Burghley) at Theobalds in July 1572, and the Bacons heard rumors that she would come on to Gorhambury. Sir Nicholas became uneasy, behaving like a man who had never before had even a fleeting thought that the queen might visit them. What Anne Bacon thought is not recorded; but unless her intellectual interests had lifted her far above the normal reactions of a hostess, she may have been dismayed. On July 17 Burghley received this letter by a messenger from his brother-in-law:

> Understanding by common speech that the Queen's Majesty means to come to my house, and knowing no certainty of the time of her coming nor of her abode, I have thought good to pray you that this bearer, my servant, might understand what you know therein . . . and if it be true, then that I might understand your advice, what you think for me to be the best way to deal in this matter (for in very deed no man is more raw in such a matter than I myself).

Sir Nicholas added a postscript: "I have wrote because I would gladly take that course that might best please her Majesty, which I know not better to understand than by your help." Perhaps Burghley sent only oral advice; at least his reply is not available. Even John

Nichols, in *The Progresses and Public Processions,* says only that after three days at Theobalds the queen went on to Gorhambury. Perhaps she made a rest stop or a formal call.

But one bit of verbal exchange is recorded elsewhere. As the queen was being shown about Gorhambury, she said, "My Lord Keeper, what a little house you have gotten." Bacon answered, "My house is well, Madam, but you have made me too great for my house." Later Francis Bacon recorded the conversation in his *Apophthegms,* giving his father credit for the reply. As Francis was about eleven years old at the time, the words possibly came direct to his precocious ears.

The queen may have stopped again to call on the Bacons in 1573, though the evidence seems inconclusive. She may have been there briefly once or perhaps twice in 1574: she signed a charter of incorporation for Thetford, March 12, 1574, at Gorhambury.

However, the queen and her attendants came to Gorhambury on May 18, 1577, for a stay of five days, arriving before supper on Saturday and departing after dinner on the next Wednesday. This time they found a Gorhambury that had been greatly enlarged. It had been extended, with a magnificent gallery upon a Tuscan colonnade, the gallery being 18 by 120 feet and broken in the center by a front that projected slightly. Oak paneling had been added, and the compartments were adorned with Latin texts the Bacons had selected. The ground floor had open loggia, including three niches, with a gilded statue of Henry VIII in the center, and in the other two, busts of Sir Nicholas and Lady Anne.

The list of expenses for the hospitality offered the queen and her party is available; but one who wishes to see details itemized to the last penny may consult John Nichols, *The Progresses,* since only major items in round numbers will be given here. For wheat in the pantry and in pastry, the Bacons spent about £47; for beer and ale, £24; wine of all kinds, £57; fish, sea and freshwater, £36; veal, beef, mutton, and lamb, £74; spices of all sorts, £27; lighting, nearly £16; carriages to London and back, £10: loss of pewter, £6; loss of napery, about fifty shillings. The guests consumed twenty-five bucks and two stags; but since the cost for them was not listed, they were probably killed on the premises. Another item, "to them of the rach, £20," has been variously interpreted, but dictionaries of archaic and provincial words define *rach* as rushes. Large as the sum seems, it may have covered labor and material for fresh rushes on the floors, perhaps including the 120-foot gallery. If this interpretation of *rach* is correct, no dramatic entertainment was listed; and the reason for the omission may have been the conscience of Anne Bacon. In her later life, at least, she disliked dramatic performances of any sort and all extravagance.

The amount of food consumed seems enormous. Among the major items were eight oxen, sixty carcasses of mutton, eighteen carcasses of veal, and thirty-four lambs. Lists of poultry included two hundred and six capons, thirty-one dozen and eight chickens, ten dozen geese, and some of nearly all the other edible birds known to western man, including fourteen partridges, sixteen dozen quail, twenty-three mallards, twelve teal, and three dozen larks.

On this visit the queen received a cup as a gift, but it was listed without any mention of its cost. According to A. J. Collins, Bacon gave the queen three outstanding gifts at different times, but it seems unclear which one he gave her on her visit in 1577. One of the three was a cup of crystal ornamented with silver, gilt, pearls, and precious stones. It had "three emeralds, three rubies, and six pearls upon the brim of the cover, six rubies about the body, a rope of small pearls about the top, and a table ruby in the top of the cover." It must have cost a small fortune, though any cup given her was expensive, no doubt. Unless Anne Bacon's dislike of extravagance developed only in her later years, it seems possible that her husband omitted listing the cost of the cup to spare her feelings. But the gift of some cup in 1577, the amount of food furnished the queen and her retinue, as well as the enlarged Gorhambury suggest that the Bacons had become less raw about entertaining queens.

Today a newer Gorhambury, built in the eighteenth century and the seat of the Earl of Verulam, is standing less than two miles from the city of St. Albans. But in the park a little to the west of it one may find, "the Elizabethan porch and other remains of . . . the house . . . built by Sir Nicholas Bacon" and his wife Anne Cooke Bacon.

Simple living continued to be the pattern for the Bacons, when the queen did not influence them. An example appears in the cups he had made for his chief residences. By 1574 the great seal he had received in December 1558 when he became its keeper had become unusable. So he had the old seal, which must have been enormous (like the lord keeper himself), made into three silver cups and sent one to each of his three country residences—Redgrave, Suffolk; Stiffkey, Norfolk; and Gorhambury. Hertfordshire. Except for the place name on each cup, they were identical.

Anne Bacon's duties as wife, mother, and hostess seem simple in comparison with those of her sister Mildred Cecil. In the evidence available there is no indication of wards or other young men who were educated in the Bacon household, and two children were no great burden. Probably the family, like others in the period, sometimes migrated from one country residence to another to use food when it was available or to have the residence they were leaving made sanitary and habitable again. But Gorhambury, near the Cecils, seems to have been the favorite residence.

Besides being hostess to the queen at Gorhambury, Anne Bacon also entertained the Privy Council at times. The minutes of that body report that the Council met at "the Lord Keeper's House," in 1572, 1574, and 1577. Though the government followed the queen, it seems probable that all these meetings were at York House in London. A dinner or supper for the whole Council, including the queen and her attendants, would be a real undertaking for most women or for Anne Bacon, and good servants would change but not remove the responsibility of the hostess.

As a mother, Anne Bacon was affectionate, but domineering and desirous of guiding her sons long after they had reached maturity. Perhaps reasons existed that will help others to understand if not to justify her actions. She was intensely religious, with Puritanical reactions against extravagance, any theatrical performances, and even the mildest reveling; but she lived in an extravagant age. Since she survived her husband about thirty years, her long period as a widow may have intensified her concern for her sons. Her solicitude for Anthony was perhaps increased by his delicate health. When he was two or three years old, he had a dangerous fever; at fourteen he was threatened with blindness; when he and Francis were at Cambridge (with John Whitgift, later Archbishop of Canterbury, as their tutor), the lists of expenses often included sums "for Anthony being sick"; and for years he suffered from "the stone" and gout. In 1592 an attack of gout kept him form paying his respects to the queen when he had been expected to do so, and later he never found or made another opportunity.

Another reason, perhaps, for Anne Bacon's great concern about her older son Anthony was her long separation from him. When his father died in 1579, he was about twenty-one. He inherited property in Middlesex and Hertfordshire. Thus he became independent both legally and financially. He chose to spend some years on the Continent, gathering information about political intrigues and hoping to enter the service of his uncle, Lord Burghley. In his quest for useful information, he had to use both non-Catholics and Catholics. In his mother's letters to him in the later 1580s and the early 1590s, she expressed fears not only for his health and his finances but also for his religion.

His mother's actual interference is illustrated by an incident in 1588 or 1589 about Anthony's confidential servant Lawson. As he was suspected of sympathies with Catholics, Anne Bacon feared "papist" influence. When Anthony sent Lawson to England with political information, she persuaded Burghley to arrest him and keep him from returning to the Continent. A Captain Allen came to secure Lawson's release. Burghley would have yielded, but Anne Bacon was firm: "If there were no more men in England, and though you should never come home, he shall not come to you." Allen wrote Anthony that he could no more send Lawson than he could send him St. Paul's steeple. In August 1589 Francis wrote that Allen was in distress, but he did not dare help him because of their mother's displeasure. At the time Francis was about twenty-eight years old and Anthony about thirty-one.

When the mother wrote about 1591 to welcome her son Anthony home to England, she did not know which caused her more grief—that he was suffering from gout or that Lawson had stolen away to join him. After other admonitions in a letter loaded as usual with Latin and Greek quotations, she advised him to be sober and discreet of speech, courteous but not familiar. She added a postscript: "I trust you, with your servants, use prayer twice a day, having been where reformation is. Omit it not for any . . . your brother is too negligent, but do you well and zealously."

Anne Bacon's concern about the money her sons spent had a basis in fact, though she may have been wrong in blaming faithless servants and alleged friends. Like other young Elizabethans, including Sir Philip Sidney, Anthony and Francis Bacon may have thought they must live magnificently. But when they were in financial trouble, their mother helped them, though she was inclined to do it on her own terms. While Anthony was still on the Continent, Captain Allen, writing from England, told him his mother had called him a traitor to God and his country, had said that grief for him would shorten her life, that she had spent her jewels for him, and that she had to borrow from seven different people the last money she had sent him.

About 1593 or 1594 when the debts of Francis were troublesome, Anthony wrote his mother suggesting that an estate in which she had an interest be used to clear him and that for the purpose she sign a release. Her reply was forthright:

> If your brother desire a release to Mr. Harvey, let him so require
> it himself; and but upon this condition, by his own hand and
> bond, I will not: that is, that he make and give me a true note of

> all his debts, and leave to me the whole order and receipt of all
> his money for his land, to Harvey, and the just payment of all his
> debts thereby. And by the mercy and grace of God it shall be
> performed by me to his quiet discharge without cumbering him
> and to his credit. For I will not have his cormorant seducers and
> instruments of Satan to him vomiting foul sin by his coun-
> tenance, to the displeasing of God and his godly true fear.
> Otherwise, I will not, *pro certo.*

Her desire to warn Anthony against various people, even when he
was thirty-seven years old, must have been annoying. In April
1595 she wrote him that Lord Henry Howard (later the Earl of Northampton and an intimate friend of Essex) was a dangerous "in-
telligencing man" and no doubt a papist working secretly. The next
month she wrote to express her pleasure because two countesses,
sisters, were coming to live in his neighborhood. Both "feared God and
loved his word zealously." But he might watch the Countess of Warwick, for she would "search and sound and lay up for future use details
of conversation." In August of 1595 she was writing to Anthony expressing her regret at his moving to Essex House. He would be envied,
he would not be liked as he had been in his own house, and the lack of
quiet would make his gout worse. A few days later she complained that
Standen and Lawson would also be at Essex House, adding, "God keep
you from Spanish subtleties and popery." Anthony's replies, at least
the available ones, were usually controlled and kind. Once he went so
far as to remind his mother that she was not always as careful about
pleasing him as he was about his duty to her, but he suggested that he
would continue to be considerate of her as long as God gave him the
necessary grace.

Anne Bacon tried without apparent success to influence her sons
against the theater or any form of dramatic entertainment whatever and
all extravagant feasts. However, in earlier years she had taken her
place at feasts without protest. According to Henry Machyn's *Diary,*
the daughter of Master Bacon, "salter and brother to the lord keeper of
the great seal of England," was married at St. Dunstan's in the East,
April 20, 1562. After the great wedding a magnificent feast was held.
The lord keeper, most of the Council, and many ladies, including a
number of the queen's maids in gorgeous apparel, dined there. Though
Anne Bacon was not named, it seems that her absence would have been
a breach of etiquette. In July 1562 also, when the daughter of William
Harvey, Clarenceux king-of-arms, was christened, the godmothers
were Lady Cecil and Lady Bacon, the latter being identified as wife of
the keeper of the great seal. After the wedding the guests sat down at a

great banquet with many kinds of wine and food in abundance. Lady Bacon's aversion to feasts, other extravagance, and all dramatic entertainment may have increased as she grew older, lonelier, and more infirm in body and mind.

But as early as 1594 when Francis moved from Gray's Inn to a house in Bishopsgate, his mother wrote that she was unhappy because the move placed him near the Bull Inn where plays and interludes were acted. Also on August 5, 1595, she wrote to Anthony: "Alas, what excess of bucks at Gray's Inn, and to feast it so on the Sabbath: God forgive and have mercy upon England."

Anne Bacon registered her strong opposition even to the entertainment planned for December 5, 1594, at Gray's Inn where both her sons were members: "I trust they will not mum nor mask nor sinfully revel at Gray's Inn. Who were sometimes counted first, God grant they wane not daily and deserve to be named last." For some reason the revels there had been omitted for three or four years, and this year the members were determined to have something unusual.

Even while the mother was protesting, it is probable that her son Francis, who had a taste for such entertainment, was deeply involved in the coming revels with their strong intellectual tone. The members elected a Prince of Purpoole, giving him a privy council, officers of state, and attendants, and were planning to turn the whole place into a court and a kingdom. Thus they could present pertinent ideas about rulers and their counselors. James Spedding, a biographer and editor of Francis Bacon, believed that Francis helped develop the general plan and wrote most of the drama. The speeches of the six counselors are like him in both style and thought, he said; they enumerate "those very reforms in state and government which throughout his life he was most anxious to see realized." After the speeches of the counselors were over, the prince promised to deliberate on their advice but to act immediately on the advice of the sixth counselor, who had suggested that they turn to pastimes. He arose, chose a lady as his partner, and led revels that lasted through the night.

This drama on government remained in manuscript without an author's name for about ninety years. It was published in 1685 as a pamphlet of sixty-eight pages. A possible reason for not publishing it at the time was that Francis Bacon wished to shield his mother from discovering that he had a part in the revels. The suggestion is supported only by the fact that the sons at times seemed half afraid to disobey her wishes, even in their maturity, and that they were usually considerate of her. In 1599 when Francis appealed to the queen for help in clearing his estate, the first reason he gave for his request concerned his mother: "First, my love to my mother, whose health being worn, I do infinitely desire that she might carry this comfort to the grave, not to leave my estate troubled and engaged." When she died in August 1610, Francis asked his friend Michael Hicks to be with him at the funeral and to spend several days at his house, that he might "pass over this mournful occasion with more comfort." His brother Anthony had died in 1601. Even in the part of his will that had been written before he discovered a serious cause of alienation from his wife, Francis had implied a desire to be buried near his mother: "For my burial, I desire it may be in St. Michael's church, near St. Albans; there was my mother buried, and it is the only Christian church within the walls of old Verulam." In spite of the mother's domineering attitude, then, it seems that her sons were respectful and affectionate to the end. But unlike her sister Elizabeth Russell, Anne Bacon did not deplore the insolence of her sons and did not complain about their mistreatment of her. Though her forceful efforts to guide them might easily have alienated them, they seemed to realize that she was concerned with their welfare, both spiritual and temporal.

When Anne Bacon wished to place her sons in governmental positions, she weighed their qualifications with some objectivity and approached Lord Burghley and Robert Cecil with dignity. Commenting to Anthony in a letter of July 1596 on the appointment of Robert Cecil as secretary to the queen, she advised him to be careful, adding that he had wisdom but lacked experience in action. The lack, she said, had been caused partly by his indoor life and his ill health. When Anthony answered the letter a few days later, he thanked her for her wise and loving admonitions. When the position of solicitor-general was being debated about this time, she talked with Robert Cecil about the appointment of Francis. Though he had ability, she said, nothing was being done for him: "The situation is enough to overthrow a young and studious man, and he is considered fit to occupy a place." Thus she used understatement, not emotional demands. She approached Lord Burghley and his son, it might be concluded, not as if they were members of her family but as great officials in the government.

When Lady Anne Bacon reproached the Earl of Essex in December 1596 for his sexual conduct, she was doubtless acting from a strong sense of duty to other individuals and to the general public. Her letter to that nobleman was delivered to him by Anthony, who was then living at Essex House. Her letter, the reply of Essex, and her second letter appear in *Memoirs* by Thomas Birch:

> Hearing, my singular good lord, of your honor's return from the
> seacoasts this day . . . I am bold, upon some speeches of some
> and with some persons at the court, where lately I was, to
> impart somewhat to your honor because it concerned a party
> there more near to me than gracious to her stock. I will not deny,
> but before, this great suspicion of her unwife-like and
> unashamed-faced demeanor hath been brought to me even in
> the country, but loath to believe, I laid it up with secret sadness
> in my breast.

After saying that she had been glad to hear of his great martial
exploit and of improvement in the conduct of one who had been "inclined to work carnal dalliance," she had also learned from eyewit-
nesses of his recent backsliding. She continued:

> But you, my good lord, have not so learned Christ and heard his
> holy word in the . . . fourth chapter to the first epistle of the
> Thessalonians. It is written, This is the will of God, that ye
> should be holy and abstain from fornication, and every one know
> how to keep his own vessel in holiness and honor. . . . And
> more . . . That fornicators and adulterers God will judge and
> that they shall be shut out. . . . Good my lord, sin not against
> your own soul.

She had heard from Lady Stafford, she continued, that "the good
virtuous countess," his wife, was with child. He should not give her a
cause of sorrow and thus hinder the child's development. After another
paragraph of exhortation she closed with a Latin quotation.

The Earl of Essex answered her letter the same day with complete
courtesy, saying that he was not guilty of this charge, that he had never
been alone with the lady she had in mind, and that he had not been
guilty of such conduct with anyone since his return from Cadiz! Her
second letter, answering his, made no reference to her accusation but
expressed her appreciation for his taking time from his affairs to write
in his own hand a letter "to one almost forgotten in the world." Then in
vigorous and forceful language she wished him success, the protection
of God, a future in the heavenly kingdom, and the peace of God always.

Like all people of great moral and religious earnestness, Lady
Anne Bacon must at times have been a thorn in the flesh of the people
she tried to guide—her mature sons and the Earl of Essex. But she did
not complain about the way her sons treated her; she merely wished
them to live up to high ideals. And when she wrote the Earl of Essex,
she was trying to save him from himself.

Lady Anne Bacon's last years were clouded by an illness that
seems to have been physical and mental. Perhaps signs of this illness
appeared as early as 1594 when a servant wrote Anthony Bacon from
Gorhambury that she was becoming difficult, changeable, easily

angered, and inclined to fall out with her servants and associates. Or the report of one servant may have been only an attempt to justify himself in some situation. Certainly her letter to Anthony about his qualifications for an office, her talk with Robert Cecil about an appointment for Francis, and her letters to Essex, all of them written about 1596, indicate self-control, power of analysis and vigorous directness. In the letter to Essex she said also that she had recently been at court. But from about 1597 few letters are available, and during the last ten years before her death in 1610 it seems that she was silent.

The dignity and the character of Anne Bacon are suggested by the dedications of books to her from 1564 to 1596. The earliest of them was the tribute by Archbishop Matthew Parker in his preface to the 1564 edition of her translation *An Apology . . . in Defence of the Church of England:* "To the right honorable, learned, and virtuous lady, A. B. [Anne Bacon] M. C. [Matthew of Canterbury] wisheth from God grace, honor, and felicity." More will be said later of her work in this translation.

In 1566 T. Drant recognized Anne and her sister Mildred in the translations he published in one volume, *A Medicinable Moral . . . Two Books of Horace his Satires Englished. The Wailings of the Prophet Jeremiah. Also Epigrams.* He merely said: "To the Right Honourable my Lady Bacon and my Lady Cecil, favorers of learning and virtue." In 1578 *A Sermon Preached at Paul's Cross* carried a dedication to Anne Bacon from John Walsall when it was published.

A dedication that especially honored her appeared in *Christian Meditations upon Eight Psalms* by Theodore Beza, the famous theologian who succeeded Calvin at Geneva. Though the work was translated by John Stubbs Sceus, the dedication was by Beza and was addressed to her as the widow of Nicholas Bacon. He had prepared these meditations for a great princess, Beza said, but her sudden death stopped their publication; and they would still be lying among his papers if her son Anthony had not visited him and expressed interest in them. Since she had honored him with her letters in Latin, he believed that a dedication would not displease her. She was familiar with "the great and holy doctors, both Greek and Latin," he said, and she had the "Christianly high-minded courage" that he had noted in Sir Anthony Cooke when the latter had visited these parts during "those great calamities public to the realm and particular to him and his whole family."

A second dedication in the volume, dated May 1582 and signed by the translator, was addressed to a Lady Anne Bacon, "now wife to Sir Nicholas Bacon," that is, not a widow. This Sir Nicholas was the oldest son, by his first wife, of the husband of Anne Bacon; by chance he had also married a woman named Anne. Sceus hoped, he added, that the learned Lady Bacon would approve this dedication to the wife of her husband's son. The work was issued from Bacon House, mentioned earlier in the chapter.

In 1589 Thomas Wilcox dedicated *A Short yet Sound Commentary . . . on . . . the Proverbs of Solomon* to Anne Bacon, apparently meaning the widow of the keeper of the great seal. He said, "To the Honorable . . . and his very good lady, the Lady Bacon," he wished "all felicity, outward and inward, in this life, and afterward eternal blessedness through Christ in that life which lasteth forever." Few surpassed her in sound knowledge, steadfast faith, and other gifts of heaven, "considering her sex and position," he continued; she was born of "sanctified stock," had an education that was both learned and holy, was richly married, "with lawful and blessed seed," was beloved at home and reverenced in many foreign countries and churches. His comments were not conventional mouthings or romantic feminine flattery. Instead they were a character sketch of Anne Bacon. When the *Collected Works* of Wilcox appeared in 1624, this dedication, retaining the date 1589, was reprinted as the preface to the same *Commentary*.

About 1596 Andrew Willett published *Sacrorum emblematum centuria una,* one hundred Latin poems translated into English poems. Poem 39, a literal version in verse of Solomon's comment on the good woman, is dedicated to the "most learned and most prudent matron, Lady Bacon." If the authors of these dedications were trying to gain material rewards, they were at least adapting their ideas to the character of Anne Bacon, not indulging in fantastic flattery.

To Anne Bacon, her sound knowledge of Greek and Latin was not a decoration and not a means of gratifying her ego. Her first venture into publishing was her part in a volume, *Certain Sermons,* about 1550. The sermons had been written by Bernardino Ochino; six of them had been translated from the Italian by R. Argentine, it is believed, and twelve by Anne Cooke before her marriage. About 1570 twenty-five sermons by the same Ochino were published in an English version under the title, *Sermons concerning the Predestination and Election of God.* All of these had been translated by Anne Cooke Bacon. She dedicated the volume in these words: "To the right worshipful and worthily beloved mother, the Lady F., her humble daughter wisheth increase of spiritual knowledge, with full fruition of the fruits thereof." As her mother had been Anne Fitzwilliam before marriage, her daughter modestly used only the initial of her maiden name.

Whatever is good in the translation, Anne Bacon continued, had come from her ladyship's motherly goodness, acting as the minister of God, and from her many godly exhortations. She said, "it hath pleased you often to reprove my vain study in the Italian tongue, accounting the seed thereof to have been sown in barren, unfruitful ground. . . . I have at the last perceived it my duty to prove how much the understanding of your will could work in me toward the accomplishing of the same." That is, she has finally used Italian for a godly purpose. Her mother's chief delight was in destroying the glory of man and exalting the glory of God, "which may not be unless we acknowledge that He doth foresee and determine from without beginning all things, and cannot alter or reward after our deserved works, but remain steadfast according to his immutable will." So she had dedicated to her ladyship these sermons, treating of the "election and predestination of God," and proceeding from "the happy spirit of the sanctified Bernardine." Thus the preface reveals the character and the religious beliefs of both Anne and her mother and emphasizes her desire to use all her knowledge in spreading religion.

Anne Bacon's most important work as an author was her translation from Latin into English of *An Apology . . . in Defence of the Church of England* by Bishop John Jewel of Salisbury. He had aimed his Latin version at the Continent; hers was directed to the people of England. She sent one copy of her work to the author with a letter in Greek, and he replied in Greek. She sent another copy to Matthew Parker, Archbishop of Canterbury. Both men approved her work without the change of a single word — a fact that seems to confirm both her theological knowledge and her linguistic skill. Apparently the archbishop considered her English version so important that he rushed it into print at once; as he said, he "returned it to her printed." A version without a preface appeared in 1562, and a version with a preface and a dedication to her (mentioned earlier in this chapter), in 1564. Again the translation proved her command of Latin and her desire to use it in spreading religious ideas in England.

Anne Bacon made a determined effort to support and to spread her religious views about 1584 when she secured an interview with Lord Burghley to plead the cause of the Nonconformists. At this time John Whitgift, who had become Archbishop of Canterbury, wished to stop any conflict that might arise from opposition to the Act of Uniformity or the Book of Common Prayer. To attain this objective he drew up articles forbidding all reading, preaching, or catechizing in private houses and requiring all the clergy to take an oath to support the royal supremacy, the Book of Common Prayer, and the Thirty-nine Articles. The House of Commons opposed the ideas of Whitgift, and the people presented a petition to the queen. During the Christmas recess the bishops and the Nonconformists held a conference about these differences of opinion.

The day after Anne Bacon had her interview with Lord Burghley, she wrote him a letter pleading that the Nonconformists might have the right to assemble, consult, and then explain their views, not to the bishops, but either to the queen or to the queen and her Council. She added her personal experience:

> . . . I confess as one that hath found mercy, that I have profited more in the inward feeling knowledge of God his holy will, though but in a small measure, by such sincere and sound opening of the scriptures by an ordinary preaching within these seven or eight years, than I did by hearing odd sermons at Paul's wellnigh twenty years together. I mention this unfeignedly the rather to excuse my boldness to your lordship, humbly beseeching your lordship to think upon their suit, and as God shall move your understanding heart, to further it.

The day before Anne Bacon wrote this letter the cause of the Nonconformists had already been defeated. In this situation she was opposing forces she could not reasonably be expected to control. Again she did not write to Burghley as if he were a member of the family and an intimate; she addressed him as a powerful official in the government of England.

Anne Bacon never realized what her greatest gift to the world was — her younger son Francis; but that gift she could neither have planned nor foreseen. Perhaps it was fortunate that she never knew the end of his marriage, indicated by his revoking all special gifts to his wife in his will, leaving only her rights by law, and that she never knew the end of his public career — his trial before the House of Lords, his confession that he was guilty of ''corruption and neglect'' although he had never changed a verdict because of a gift, and his sentence to be fined and imprisoned during the king's pleasure. But it was unfortunate that she never realized his intellectual influence. To use his own words, he "rang the bell which called the wits together," and thus he made a contribution to the thought of the world.


Anne Cooke, Lady Bacon, was no status-seeker and no egotist about her own attainments. Thus she was unlike Elizabeth Russell but like her sister Mildred Cecil. But unlike Mildred she was neither quiet nor patient — she was intense. Through her life she was not interested in securing for herself rank, wealth, idleness, or a second marriage. So far as one can judge, she was a good wife in the conventional sense, but she gave no sign of interest in secular government or in her husband's work as a government official, though she was clearly his equal in the formal education of the period. Being affectionate but domineering, she seemed at times to view her sons as clay to be molded into Puritan Christians assured of salvation, not as individual human beings. Long after they were mature men, she admonished them as if they were adolescents, trying to save them from extravagance, theaters, and "popery." She peppered her letters with quotations from Greek and Latin because she thought in those languages and she was writing to people who also understood them. Her letter in Greek to Bishop Jewel perhaps complimented him rather than exalted herself. Her Latin letters to Beza were a ready means of communicating with another scholar on the Continent. When she translated the sermons of Ochino and the *Apology* of Bishop Jewel she was making available to the English people ideas that she considered vital. She was not self-centered enough to plan an elaborate funeral or monument for herself. If she had a sense of humor, a sense of proportion, or the ability to enjoy wholesome secular activities, she tended to conceal such qualities under a thick cloak of religious zeal. Her major aim was to further Calvinistic Puritanism not only in her sons but in all England. She worked toward her aim with persistence, vigor, integrity, and intelligence supported by profound classical scholarship.

*Right: Portrait of a youthful Bess of Hardwick, perhaps commissioned by her third husband William St. Loe. It now hangs in Hardwick Hall.*

*Below: Facsimile of seal and signature, "E Shrewsbury."*

*Above: Detail of Hardwick Hall showing the E S monogram in the fretted scrollwork of the towers. The many windows gave rise to the saying "Hardwick Hall, more glass than wall."*

*Left: Described as "the most beautiful room in all of Europe," the high presence chamber in Hardwick Hall contains detailed plaster friezes of forest scenes, vast bay windows, and a magnificent fireplace.*

# CHAPTER THREE

# *Bess of Hardwick,*
# *Countess of Shrewsbury*
## 1518?-1608

The well-known portrait of Bess of Hardwick is that of a woman past middle age, with a hard angular face, a mouth that is too firm, and eyes that are close-set and wary. Her great ruff and the magnificent strands of pearls she is wearing do nothing to soften the features. This portrait, reproduced from one at Hardwick Hall and used in a biography by Ethel Carleton Williams, may picture her as she was in later life. But art experts now say that another portrait at Hardwick Hall with a wrong label "has a good claim" to be a portrait of Bess. Painted about 1550-1555, when she was in her thirties and happily married to her second

COUNTESS OF
SHROESBURY

*A later portrait of Bess by an unknown artist also hangs at Hardwick Hall.*

59

husband, it presents a woman who is young, attractive, vivacious, even seductive. The two portraits illuminate the life of the girl in modest circumstances who became the Countess of Shrewsbury.

Bess lacked many qualities possessed by other women presented in this book. She was not intellectual; she had no classical learning, no literary interests, no struggle to decide religious beliefs or to further them in others, and no apparent interest in abstract ideas. She had little concern for the general welfare. Judging by her actions, her major aim was to secure status and wealth for herself and her children. She became a wealthy woman and a countess through four marriages, but her last marriage ended in bitterness and separation. She established four dynasties, three of them existing today. She tried to place a granddaughter on the throne of England; but opposed by the royal power of Queen Elizabeth (the woman most like her in Tudor England), she failed. She was the great woman builder of the English Renaissance, with one of her three structures standing almost intact today—Hardwick Hall in Derbyshire. Though not an intellectual, she had a triple measure of shrewdness, representing or even surpasssing the materialism of her age.

Elizabeth Hardwick, usually known as Bess of Hardwick, began her life in comparatively humble surroundings. Born about 1518 or 1520, she was the third daughter of John Hardwick and his wife Elizabeth Leake, who lived in a small country home, Hardwick Hall, near Chesterfield in Derbyshire. When her father died in 1528, he was able to leave each daughter only forty marks as a portion—hardly a sum to entice an ambitious young man into marriage. Thus Bess faced an uncertain future. The education she had in her own home was probably limited—reading, writing, keeping accounts, but no music or dancing, no French or Latin. All her later life indicates that she was no literary woman. She named only three books in her will, all of them in English and all about religion: the Proverbs of Solomon, Calvin's discussion of Job, and a book of meditations. Her lack of status among literary men, even after she acquired property and became a countess, is suggested by the fact that only one book is known to have been dedicated to her, and it is limited and utilitarian. Published in 1567 by Thomas Harman, its title was *A Caveat or Warning for Common Cursetors*. The author's aim was to warn his "singular good lady, the Countess of Shrewsbury," who had a "most tender, pitiful, gentle, and noble nature," against the poor in her own parish and those from other parishes who came to get relief at her gates. That Harman thought her tender and gentle is a surprise!

Another surprise, with literary connections, is that Bess was a friend of the gracious Margaret Parker, wife of the archbishop. In the Lambeth Library (Edith Weir Perry reported) is a copy of Parker's metrical version of the Psalms with this inscription in Margaret's handwriting: "To the right virtuous and honorable lady, The Countess of Shrewsbury, from her loving friend, Margaret Parker." One question remains unanswered: why the book is still at Lambeth Palace and not at Hardwick Hall.

The first chance for Bess to enter a larger world came when Lady Zouche offered to take into her London household a girl from the Hardwick family. Whether Lady Zouche chose the girl, the mother decided, or Bess volunteered, we do not know. But Bess went. In the residence of the Zouche family she probably learned fine cooking, perhaps wine-making, embroidering, sewing, the use of herbs in food or as medicine, and the management of a great house with many servants.

Bess made the first of her four marriages while she was in the Zouche household. Young Robert Barlow came as a guest, became ill, lingered, and developed a desire to marry Bess. The Barlows were willing; and since the young man belonged to a good family with property, the girl's mother would have been unlike most Tudor parents if she had objected. Young Robert was either the oldest child or the oldest son of the Barlow family but was not of age; hence the property settlement known as the assent of the father was apparently arranged to provide a jointure for the widow if her husband died. Robert Barlow did die on February 2, 1533, after only a few weeks or months of marriage. If Bess was born in 1518, she became a widow when she was about fifteen. She inherited property that included lands, forests, and lead mines. Though she had done nothing but accept what fortune offered her, she now had a solid position in life.

She remained a widow fourteen years, living quietly in Derbyshire and maintaining with the Barlow family the friendly relations that continued while they and Bess lived. Meantime the sisters of Bess had married, and her brother James had taken over the old home, Hardwick Hall. Compared with the later career of Bess, these fourteen quiet years seem unusual.

When Bess married Sir William Cavendish on August 20, 1547,

she advanced in property and status, but the marriage was also companionable and happy. As he was a friend of Henry and Frances Grey, the parents of Lady Jane, the ceremony was at their home, Bradgate in Leicestershire. In his memorandum book Cavendish noted that he and Bess were married at two in the morning, but he gave no reason for the odd hour. He had been the king's agent for monastery lands, had received some of the spoils himself, was treasurer of the royal chamber under Henry VIII, had been appointed acting auditor of the Court of Augmentations in 1541, owned good properties himself, and was knighted in 1546. After his marriage to Bess, Sir William disposed of scattered holdings in other counties and acquired properties, mostly in Derbyshire but partly in Nottinghamshire nearby.

Sir William and his new wife had common interests — country living, social life, children, a desire for more property, and a zest for building. In 1549 he bought the estate of Chatsworth, where a sister of Bess, Alice, had been living until 1547 when the place was sold. In 1549 it came on the market again and became a joint enterprise of husband and wife. Though they had intended to do no more than make repairs, by 1551 they had fully realized its dilapidation and had in mind a new structure. Roger Worth, "my master's mason," drew plans and by Christmas husband and wife were studying them together. The house they built was a quadrangle of Derbyshire stone with a central gatehouse flanked by towers. It was four stories high "with large transomed windows extending for two stories on the upper floor . . . suggesting that there were two long galleries in the house." The interior was probably dark, since the panes had more lead than glass. In later building projects Bess corrected that error. The work moved slowly. Five years later they could see little more than a foot of the outer wall. But the career of Bess as a builder began with Chatsworth.

As the wife of William Cavendish, Bess gave birth to eight children in ten years, three sons and five daughters. Frances, the first child, was born in 1548; a second daughter, Temperance, born the next year, died early; Henry (whose godmother was the Princess Elizabeth and who died in 1616 without legitimate issue) in 1550; and William, who became his mother's favorite, in 1551. Two years later Charles was born. Then came Elizabeth in 1555, Mary in 1556, and Lucrece, who lived only a short time, in March 1557. Six of the eight lived to be married, all of the six except Henry produced one or more children, and five of the eight outlived their mother. The record was unusual. Among upper-class families in the period (where more complete data exist), two of every five who were alive at birth died during the first year, and at least one more was likely to die before reaching maturity. Bess did not have children by any other husband.

In August 1557, while Bess was in the area of Chatsworth, she had word that her husband was alarmingly ill in London. She ordered her traveling litter prepared and started as soon as she could on a journey that took three nights and four days. Footmen who accompanied the litter ran ahead whenever they approached a town, and when necessary, spoke for rooms at an inn. Dangers included poor roads, floods, and robbers. At St. Albans four extra men were hired to be an armed guard for the litter as it moved into London. Sir William was still living when his wife reached him, but in the next two months he gradually failed. When his widow recorded on October 25 that her "most dear and well-beloved husband" had died, she had perhaps proved in ten years of her life that her adjectives were sincere. He was buried in the church of St. Botolph, Aldersgate, with a stately funeral, described by Henry Machyn in his *Diary:* Sir William Cavendish had two white branches, twelve staff torches, three great tapers, and escutcheons suitable for him as a knight.

Bess apparently acquired considerable property from him. Though he had been married twice before and had five children by these earlier marriages, only two daughters had survived. Thus when he married Bess, he had no direct male heirs. No doubt he and Bess had arranged a jointure before the marriage; and though his will seems to be unavailable, the bulk of his considerable property must have come into the hands of Bess to use for the children, all under ten years of age, and herself.

Bess did not wait long for her third marriage. In 1559 she became the wife of Sir William St. Loe, a man older than she, it is said, and a semi-invalid. Though he had been married before, his daughter or daughters were well settled with good jointures, and he also had no direct male heirs. He had served the queen well when she was still Princess Elizabeth, during Wyatt's rebellion. He carried her reply when Wyatt sent her word to move away from London as far as she could; and though he was imprisoned in the Tower for possible complicity, St. Loe avoided making any statement that might incriminate her. As queen, she rewarded him "for his service," making him captain of the guard and chief butler of England and Wales, with an annuity of a hundred marks. Because St. Loe was a friend of the queen, Lady St. Loe became a lady of the bedchamber—her first position at court.

St. Loe's devotion to his wife was ardent and lasting. He showed it not only by words of affection in his letters but also by unusual gifts of money. For instance, when the accounts of William Cavendish as treasurer of the queen's chamber were found to be in chaos, not by dishonesty but by neglect, and when the new treasurer insisted that the wife and the oldest son must help make good the shortage, St. Loe parted with £ 1,000 to secure a final settlement. And when a daughter of Cavendish by a previous marriage needed help, St. Loe undertook to support her until she married; to find her a suitable husband or pay her a thousand marks; or if she rejected the husband he provided, to pay her six hundred marks. An indenture covering the agreement exists, according to Ethel C. Williams, a biographer of Bess; but she did not give its source. Cavendish had by his first wife two daughters, Catherine and Anne, who lived to be married, and by his second wife three children who died early, in addition to the eight Bess bore. A man who had been the father of thirteen children by three different wives and who was careless about his accounts for the queen, might have been careless about a portion for a daughter. As his daughter Catherine had been married earlier, it was apparently Anne who benefited by the generosity of St. Loe.

When St. Loe died in 1564 or 1565, all his property came to Bess. Probably a jointure had been arranged at the time of the marriage, but his will is available and it leaves no doubt. St. Loe assigned nothing to the church or to charity, made no provision for servants, left no gift to' any other relative or friend, and named no other person in his will, not even a witness. God, the earth, and his wife were remembered. He bequeathed his soul to Almighty God and his body to the earth of which it was made, knowing that it would be raised up in the latter day to join his soul. And "for and in consideration of the mutual affection, mutual love, and assured good will which I have ever . . . found in my most entirely beloved wife, Elizabeth St. Lowe, I do give and bequeath unto her, the said Elizabeth . . . my houses, farms, plate, jewels, hangings, implements of household . . . and [all] catalles whatever. To have, hold, use . . . to her own profit and behoof. . . ." He added that the "said Elizabeth, my wife, I do make and ordain my whole and sole executrix of this my last will and testament, in witness whereof, I . . . have subscribed my name and put my seal. . . ." Thus he left no doubt about his wish to give his wife all his worldly possessions.

When Lady Elizabeth St. Loe married for the fourth time about three years later, her rise in the world was phenomenal. Accepting George Talbot, sixth Earl of Shrewsbury, after hesitation — real or apparent — she became a countess. Her new husband was considered one of the wealthiest men in England, with large holdings in the counties of York, Nottingham, and Derby and with seven great houses: Wingfield Manor, Worksop Manor, Sheffield Castle, Sheffield Manor, Rufford Abbey, Buxton Hall, and Tutbury Lodge. He also held Tutbury Castle on a lease from the queen. As a part of the total bargain Bess arranged good marriages for two of her children: her oldest son Henry married the earl's daughter Grace, and his son Gilbert married her youngest daughter Mary. The double wedding of the children took place in the parish church of Sheffield (now the cathedral) on February 9, 1568. It has been said that she did not marry the earl until their children had been married, but no record of the parental ceremony appears. However, when Harman dedicated to Bess his *Caveat or Warning,* calling her his "singular good lady, the Countess of Shrewsbury," the publication date was 1567.

For six or seven years the Earl of Shrewsbury seemed unusually happy in his new marriage. Until 1574 or so he wrote Bess letters of affection and trust, calling her by his special name for her, None. A typical example, published by Joseph Hunter, was written in 1573 or 1574:

> My Dear None: Of all joys I have under God the greatest is yourself. To think that I possess [one] so faithful, and one that I know loves me so dear, is all, and the greatest comfort this earth can give. Therefore God give me grace to be thankful to him for his goodness showed unto me, a vile sinner. . . .

But in October 1574 the Earl of Shrewsbury began to lose confidence in his wife because of her part in managing the marriage of her daughter Elizabeth to Charles Stewart, younger brother of Henry, Lord Darnley, who had married the Queen of Scots. As the grandson of Margaret Tudor, Charles had a valid claim on the English throne after the murder of his brother Lord Darnley in Scotland — a claim made somewhat greater by his birth and residence in England. When he married without the queen's consent, he was guilty of treason. Bess, aided by Lady Lennox, the mother of Charles Stewart, had taken a calculated risk, hoping to put a grandchild on the throne of England. The Earl of Shrewsbury had a strong sense of duty, a timidity that had been growing with age and illness, and an unusually strong loyalty to his queen. Perhaps he had enough imagination to see himself in the Tower, with all his great properties confiscated, for possible complicity with his wife. But the queen ordered a thorough investigation and then acted with justice. She ordered the mothers and the newly married pair to come to London, confined the mothers in the Tower, and sent the bride and groom to their house in Hackney with orders not to talk to any person without the permission of the Council. The mothers and their servants were questioned for weeks but were released in the spring. The Earl of Shrewsbury kept his estates, his freedom, and the confidence of his queen.

Among other factors that led to the destruction of the fourth marriage of Bess, a minor one may have been the earl's health. Reports about his illness had been circulating; in 1574 the English ambassador to France asked about a rumor that he was unlikely to regain his health. But ten years later, when the earl wished a vote of confidence from the Council, he seemed to be in complete command of his faculties. If his wife's conduct in 1574 had not undermined his belief in her, probably his illness alone would have increased his dependence on her.

Another minor cause of the rift in the marriage was the earl's growing dislike of the time and energy his wife spent at Chatsworth. All told, the project took twenty years or more — six or seven when Bess and Cavendish worked together, several years while St. Loe encouraged her with his amused tolerance and addressed her as ''My dear Chatsworth,'' a space of time when she was a widow again, and then several years as the wife of Shrewsbury. For perhaps thirteen of the years Bess had planned and supervised the building and then had completed the inner decoration and the furnishings. She experimented with the plaster frieze that was becoming popular, and when she failed to get a plasterer from John Thynne, builder of the famous Longleat, she discovered a competent local worker, Abraham Smith. She tried her hand at elaborate decorations — curtains of black damask edged with gold lace, a bed covered with black velvet and ornamented with gold lace and gold fringe, and hangings she and the members of her household made together. Perhaps she was learning about decoration from her royal prisoner, for Mary Queen of Scots (who came into their charge about 1569) had good taste, years of experience at the French court, and an interest in needlework. For some years she and Bess were friendly, perhaps until Bess boasted that her granddaughter Arabella would succeed to the throne of England. They had worked together embroidering a large panel with the design of a hand pruning a vine and with the initials M. R. and E. S. intertwined. Thus Bess was getting complete experience, both theory and practice, in erecting and furnishing a great house. In the earlier years of her work after she married Shrewsbury, his attitude was friendly to Chatsworth. In 1569 he had brought the Queen of Scots there briefly, and in 1570 he urged that she be brought to Chatsworth because it was secluded. Then he began to resent the absence of Bess when he was told that she had gone to Chatsworth.

An important cause of the estrangement between Bess and her husband was the strain placed upon them by their position as custodians of Mary Queen of Scots. That strain, lasting from 1569 (about a year after their marriage) to 1584, was physical, financial, and psychological. The physical strain came from overcrowding, from placing a second large household into a castle or manor intended for one. When Mary first came to them at Tutbury Castle, she brought thirty-six personal servants and a half-dozen carts overflowing with her luggage; her entire staff had 140 people. In addition, soldiers were on guard duty; and at any hint of a plot the number of guards was increased. The need for moving from one residence to another increased the physical strain—moving for sanitation, for relief from dampness and overcrowding, and for security of the prisoner. Each move meant taking some things that belonged to the custodians and transporting the staff and furnishings used by the prisoner. Bess, rather than her husband, probably took the brunt of the physical strain.

But the Earl of Shrewsbury carried the financial burden. The allowance of £52 a week was inadequate, and even that amount was not always paid promptly. Two letters from the Earl of Shrewsbury to Burghley, when he heard that the queen was planning to cut down the sum, clarify the problem. (Both were published by Edmund Lodge.) In the first letter on July 26, 1580, he said the sum he had been receiving did not cover the cost of food. In addition, he was spending £1,000 a year for wine, spices, and fuel; and he was forced to spend another £1,000 to cover the loss of plate, pewter, and "all manner of household stuff which by them [Mary and members of her household] is exceedingly spoiled and willfully wasted. . . ." He was paying more than £400 a year in added annuities to his servants to prevent corruption and get better service. In the second letter of August 9 he said that he had not reckoned the cost of the soldiers he had to keep; the queen allowed him sixpence a day for each, but they were costing him more. Recently he had the added expense of bringing the queen to Buxton for her health. The disgrace of a cut in the allowance would hurt him more even than the loss of the money.

The cost of providing for Mary was greater because she insisted on living like a queen, with wines from France and other luxuries. If she did not get what she wished, she complained, often managing to reach Queen Elizabeth with her complaints—and Elizabeth also expected Mary to live like a queen. Mary's staff included a master of horse, a surgeon, a secretary, three cooks, a baker, a pastrymaker, and ten maidservants. She kept royal state, using a great chair covered with cloth of gold and red velvet, silver plate at meals, and silver toilet articles, with a Turkey carpet on the floor instead of mere rushes.

The psychological strain of being a custodian to the Queen of Scots came largely from the plots aimed at putting her on the throne of England. At one time the earl had 500 extra men on guard, and he had to see that they were paid. When an early plot became known, the queen sent additional help, and the earl and his wife rushed Mary from Tutbury to a better defended Coventry. The Ridolfi plot, developed about 1569 to 1570, ended two years later with the execution of the Duke of Norfolk for treason. The plan furthered by Francis Throckmorton, to have the Duke of Guise invade England and put Mary on the throne with the help of English Catholics, led to the execution of Throckmorton in 1584. By the time the plot of Anthony Babington that led to Mary's execution was uncovered, the Earl of Shrewsbury and his wife had been freed of their responsibilities.

Such tension, lasting for about fifteen years, must have been a nightmare. Besides being almost a congenital plotter, Mary was a vivid complainer. She had real illnesses, and when displeased, she had imaginary ones. The many comments of other people, especially when made to Queen Elizabeth, were annoying. If Bess did needlework with Mary, the queen heard that she was too friendly with her prisoner; if she stayed away, Mary was unhappy and might reach Elizabeth with her complaints. As custodians, the earl and his wife had little freedom to travel, quarrels between the two groups of attendants were inevitable, tempers grew short from overcrowding, problems of sanitation developed quickly, exhaustion at times was inevitable, and the earl's health suffered. Perhaps few marriages could have survived all these problems.

But the final breakup of the Shrewsbury marriage was apparently triggered by Bess. She tried a desperate means of setting them free from their situation. With the help of her sons William and Charles and a servant, she circulated rumors that her husband and the Queen of

Scots had carried on an illicit relationship. Of course the reports did not decrease as they spread. That Bess was really trying to save her husband from being drawn into a plot to connive at the escape of his prisoner, as Ethel Carlton Williams suggested, seems improbable on the basis of the evidence. When Queen Elizabeth heard the rumor she sent for the earl and talked with him about its possible origin, satisfying herself that he was not guilty. The Council summoned Bess and her sons; they denied knowing the source of the stories they had been spreading and asserted that Mary had lived honorably since entering England. The Council accepted their submission.

But the Earl of Shrewsbury had been deeply wounded. When he was called to the next meeting of the Privy Council, he would not take his place in that body until all the members had agreed on a long, formal statement ending with the words "that he had faithfully and honorably discharged the service committed unto him." He also appealed to Walsingham for a public retraction from his wife. He brought suit for slander against William and Charles Cavendish and the servant who had a part in spreading the rumors. The queen intervened; and with the help of the lord chancellor, Leicester, and Burghley, she worked out articles for a settlement. But charges and countercharges continued. The earl applied for a formal separation from his wife, asking to have all her property except a small allowance for her living expenses, or by some accounts, permitting her to keep Chatsworth and some other land for the other two sons. The earl also began collecting rents from the properties Bess owned. At one time he tried to seize Chatsworth, but William and Charles Cavendish repelled him with threats of violence.

When the property dispute came before the lord chancellor and two other justices in January 1585, the three decided that Shrewsbury must return all the rents he had seized, that he might have an income of £ 500 from the lands in dispute, and that his wife and her Cavendish children were free to enjoy all her other property. One would expect these legal experts to favor the man if they could find any reason for doing so; Leicester and Burghley were the earl's friends, and the queen had trusted and often favored him. To Shrewsbury their verdict was bitter.

Efforts to reconcile Shrewsbury and his wife began early after the breach and continued to the end of his life — efforts by the queen, asking him to let his wife visit him, at least, efforts by Lord Burghley and by Lord Chancellor Bromley. Bishop Overton appealed to him in a letter as late as October 12, 1590:

> But some will say . . . that the countess is a sharp and bitter
> shrew. . . . Indeed, my good lord, I have heard some say so, but
> if shrewdness or sharpness may be a just cause of
> separation . . . I think few men in England would keep their
> wives long; for it is a common jest, yet true in some sense, that
> there is but one shrew in all the world, and every man hath
> her. . . . My honourable good lord, I doubt not but your great
> wisdom and experience hath taught you to bear some time with
> a woman as with the weaker vessel.

The earl and his countess might have been equally surprised to
learn that she was the weaker vessel! But probably she never saw the
letter, and perhaps he never fully realized its contents. For some time
before his death he had lived in a small manor house at Sheffield Park
in a "degrading connection" with a woman named Eleanor Britton. As
his perceptions failed, she and a nephew of hers began systematically
robbing him, taking jewels, other small articles of value, and even
larger furnishings that had been assigned to the son and heir, Gilbert
Talbot, for his future use. The earl died November 18, 1590.

Bess, who had continued to make gestures of reconciliation over
the years, was probably not surprised if and when she learned that her
mention in her husband's will was brief. He used no term of affection.
He did not use her Christian name. Instead, he stated mere facts about
"lands, tenements, and hereditaments assigned for the jointure of my
wife," adding a direction that would be needed if she survived him. But
Gilbert Talbot was not only surprised but shocked to discover how much
of his father's property remained in the hands of his stepmother and to
learn that his father, who had earlier been considered one of the
wealthiest men in England, was comparatively poor at death. Though
other causes — general inflation, the custody of the Queen of Scots, and
Gilbert's own extravagance — had diminished the estate, Gilbert
recognized the visible cause nearest him, his stepmother. He had been
her friend, siding with her against his father. Suddenly he was her
bitter enemy.

The death of the Earl of Shrewsbury in 1590 brought his wife, it is
said, an additional annual income of £2,000 as her jointure. With this
sum added, a writer in the *Dictionary of National Biography* (under
Talbot, Elizabeth) estimated that she had an income of £60,000 a year,
but without indicating how he reached that figure. At least it seems safe
to conclude that she had become a wealthy woman.

During her marriage to the Earl of Shrewsbury Bess had been
carrying on business affairs as if she were a feme sole (a widow or a
single woman) and not a feme covert with all her property under the
control of her husband. (See the Introduction for details about the legal

rights of a husband to manage or to dispose of his wife's property.) The work of Bess on Chatsworth is evidence that she continued to operate as if she were a free-wheeling single woman. She completed it after her marriage to Shrewsbury; she must have paid many bills then on its construction and all the bills for the magnificent furnishings. Its total cost has been estimated at £80,000, almost as much as Sir John Thynne had spent on Longleat. At one time, presumably while she was still the wife of the earl, she stated that she owned 8,000 sheep. Also, she purchased the old family homestead, Hardwick Hall, in 1576, some time before the final break in her marriage, and she had done so after the earl refused to put any money into the venture.

Bess had clearly manipulated an unusual settlement with Shrewsbury before she married him, one that allowed her to keep under her control much or all of the property from three previous husbands; it must have been a settlement in writing. Such arrangements did not become common until the seventeenth century. But no other supposition seems to explain either the actions of Bess or the decisions of the queen, Burghley, Leicester, and the three judges who made the final decision in 1585 allowing Bess to keep and enjoy most of her property.

The year 1590, when the Earl of Shrewsbury died, seems the appropriate time to survey the life of his countess, Bess of Hardwick, though she may have been too much the woman of action to stop for such a survey herself. If born in 1518, she was then about seventy-two years old. She had by this time demonstrated enormous powers of survival. She had outlived four husbands; and though the fourth was perhaps ten years younger than she was, she survived him by eighteen years. She had borne eight children in ten years of marriage to Sir William Cavendish, six of them had lived to be married, and five of them were still living when she died. She had survived fifteen years as one of the custodians of Mary Queen of Scots. She had survived six years of active bickering with her fourth husband, and she was destined to survive future quarrels with Gilbert Talbot (the new Earl of Shrewsbury), with her son Henry, and with her granddaughter, Arabella.

Earlier, she had survived one plot against her life and another against her character. The plot against her life (which seems to rest on reasonably sound evidence) developed after she married William St. Loe. His brother had expected to be his heir, but he either feared or learned that the property would be willed to Bess. Shortly after the marriage Bess had a strange illness, leading to rumors that she had been poisoned and that she had died. A letter from St. Loe's mother to Bess offers some reason to believe that the brother had tried to poison Bess and then had accused her of trying to poison her husband. St. Loe's refutation of the last charge is said to be in the Muniment Room at Chatsworth.

The plot against her character was developed while she was the widow of St. Loe. A former fellow of Merton College, Henry Jackson, whom she employed as a tutor for her younger children, began spreading scandal about her. The queen issued for her protection a directive, September 29, 1567 (reprinted in the *State Papers*), to the Archbishop of Canterbury and the Ecclesiastical Commission:

> We understand that you have examined the pretended contract devised by Henry Jackson against Lady St. Loe, who has long served with credit in our court. As such a slanderous device should be severely punished, we require you . . . to proceed to extreme punishment — by corporal or otherwise, openly or privately, and that speedily, that our servant may be restored to her good fame.

But the records of their decision are not extant; probably we shall never know what punishment Henry Jackson received, nor what scandal he started.

Bess had also survived two periods of imprisonment in the Tower. Each time she was released without visible signs of loss. In the first episode she was innocent of any wrongdoing, but she was imprisoned from August 20, 1561, to March 25, 1562. Catherine, younger sister of Lady Jane Grey, a maid of honor at court with a claim on the throne, had no right to marry without the queen's consent. The frightened girl stopped Bess and made her confession: she and Edward Seymour, Earl of Hertford (and son of the Protector by his second wife, Anne Stanhope), had been secretly married, their child would be born in a few weeks and her husband was on the Continent. The girl had hoped that her own mother would persuade the queen to consent to the marriage, but the mother had died before that could be done. Bess refused to take action. Then the Lady Catherine went to Leicester, who refused to intercede but hurried to the queen with the story. Somebody told the queen that Bess had been a confidante. So the queen sent her, with Catherine, to the Tower and kept her there while she tried to discover the facts, especially the name of the clergyman who performed the marriage ceremony. As Bess was innocent, it is said that she never forgave Catherine Grey for involving her.

When Bess went to the Tower on December 27, 1574, because she had furthered the marriage of her daughter Elizabeth to Charles Stewart, she was clearly guilty. He had a claim to the throne, no one had asked the permission of the queen for the marriage, and to marry without her permission was treason. This time Bess was in the Tower until sometime in the spring of 1575.

If Bess had stopped in 1590 to think over her life, she might have congratulated herself on her wealth, her survival from various crises, and the fact that her children were well settled in life—though it was not evident till later how well some of them were settled. Bess was the founder of four dynasties, three of them still in existence. She had either remarkable foresight or excellent luck or perhaps a combination of the two. About 1567 or 1568 she had arranged the marriage of her daughter Mary to Gilbert Talbot, at a time when his brother Francis was the oldest. But Francis died in 1582. When the sixth earl died in 1590, Gilbert and Mary became the Earl and the Countess of Shrewsbury. Their daughter Althea married Thomas Howard and thus became a founder of the family of the present Duke of Norfolk.

Frances, the oldest of the Cavendish children, married Sir Henry Pierrepont of Home-Pierrepont near Nottingham and became an ancestor of the Earls and Dukes of Kingston in the seventeenth century. But that line has become extinct.

Henry, the oldest son, died without legitimate issue in 1616. Elizabeth, who became the wife of Charles Stewart in 1574, had one child, Arabella, who died childless in 1615. The third son, Charles, was succeeded by his son William, who first inherited from his mother the title Baron Ogle. Later he was created Marquess and then Duke of Newcastle. His line continues to the present time.

William, the second son and his mother's favorite because they shared the same attitude toward property, inherited the whole landed estate after the death of his older brother Henry without heirs. Thus he finally owned "three of the most splendid seats ever raised by one hand in the same county"—Chatsworth, Old Cotes, and Hardwick Hall, all in Derbyshire. William became Baron Cavendish in 1605, and the first Earl of Devonshire in 1618. His second son William succeeded as the second Earl of Devonshire. William's oldest son became the first Duke of Devonshire, and from 1697 to 1706 rebuilt Chatsworth almost in its present form, with one wing added later. The Dukes of Devonshire are descendants of William Cavendish, the second son of Bess of Hardwick.

But when Bess played for higher stakes and tried to place her granddaughter Arabella, on the throne of England, fortune deserted her. Arabella's father, Charles Stewart, had died in 1576 when his daughter was about a year old; her mother Elizabeth, who did not bear another child, died in 1582. Bess managed before long to get Arabella under her control. She began giving Arabella an education fitting her for an exalted position, she tried to get the Lennox family jewels for the girl (but they had been taken to Scotland in an effort to reclaim the family lands), and she petitioned the queen to grant funds for her upbringing. She also tried to arrange a suitable marriage for her. When Arabella was about nine, she was formally betrothed to the two-year-old Lord Denbigh, son and heir of Leicester by his wife Lettice Knollys. But the "noble impe" (as he was called in his epitaph) died when he was about three years old. Other marriage plans came to nothing.

In August 1587 when Arabella was about twelve, Queen Elizabeth invited her to court, asked her to dine with her, and seated her at her own right hand. Later the queen said to the wife of the French ambassador, "Look at her well, for she is not as simple as you may think. One day she will be . . . mistress here, but I shall have gone before her." On the same day, if these accounts are correct, Lord Burghley asked Arabella to dine and spoke of her with praise. Either the queen and Burghley were taking her succession seriously or they were administering indirect discipline to the son of Mary Queen of Scots. But the effect on Arabella of this attention was unfortunate: she became arrogant, servants found her difficult, and the Venetian secretary, Giovanni Scaramelli, reported that she was claiming first place at court and refusing to yield even when asked to do so by the master of ceremonies.

Bess suffered through a plot in 1592 by English Catholics and the pope to seize Arabella, take her to Flanders, and marry her to Rainutio, a son of the Duke of Parma. As the girl had been living for a time with Gilbert and Mary Talbot in London; and as Mary had Catholic sympathies, Mary was suspected of a part in the plot. Arabella was ordered back into the firm hands of her grandmother. She was guarded night and day, not allowed to speak to strangers nor to leave the grounds alone, and forced to sleep in a small room connected with the bedroom of Bess. Of course she resented the restrictions.

Some actions of her overzealous relatives, with her own behavior, continued to diminish her chances of succeeding Queen Elizabeth. And after two women rulers, strong tides of feeling were developing in favor of a king. Arabella paid visits to the court in 1596, when she was about twenty-one and presumably at her best in appearance and manners, and again the next year. During the second of these visits Mary Talbot suggested that her own two daughters act as maids-in-waiting to her. The queen replied that such maids were only for a princess who was heir presumptive to the throne. Perhaps that answer was final.

In these years Henry Cavendish was welcoming any chance to annoy his mother and was sometimes using Arabella as his means. He was carrying on a well-developed plot early in 1603 to have Arabella proclaimed queen at the death of Elizabeth. Only the grim watchfulness of Bess was able to keep the girl from leaving on March 10, and a little later going to prison and perhaps death. After this episode, Bess wrote to Sir Henry Brounker, who had been investigating these affairs, asking that Arabella be removed from her care and put elsewhere into safekeeping. Other details in the life of Arabella, either earlier or later, are not relevant here. Her grandmother's long struggle to put her on the throne of England had failed through circumstances beyond her control: the lack of character in Arabella and the royal power of Queen Elizabeth.

For Bess of Hardwick, 1590, the year she became Dowager Countess of Shrewsbury, was also a year of decision in her career as a builder. With the earlier property she had apparently kept under her control and with the additional income of £ 2,000 a year as her jointure from the estate of Shrewsbury, she quickly saw that she might do much more than remodel Old Hardwick Hall. That structure, which she had bought herself in 1576 when the earl refused to put any of his money into it, was only a good farmhouse. She decided to build a grand new Hardwick Hall. She had the money. She had twenty years of experience at Chatsworth; and for perhaps thirteen of those years she had worked alone in completing and then furnishing the great structure. For this new venture she may have had someone draw a plan for her, as Roger Worth, "my master's mason," had drawn one about 1551 for her and Sir William Cavendish to study. If she did, one might guess that the ideas were largely her own. Though Robert Smithson was the most likely person to make a drawing with some ideas of his own, her careful accounts do not show any payments to him. Also, it seems that an architect, in the modern meaning of the term, did not exist in the sixteenth century. Bess was probably her own architect, as much so as Burghley (with some suggestions from his wife) had been at Theobalds.

From Chatsworth, too, she had knowledge of the furnishings and decorations mentioned earlier: the uses of the new plaster frieze, the hangings, the bed, and the needlework that she, members of her household, and Mary Queen of Scots had worked on together. She had masons and craftsmen whose skills she already knew. Abraham Smith, mason, plasterer, and carpenter at Chatsworth was one of them. She had building materials at hand: stone from quarries by her own stables and lead in the mines she had inherited from her first husband. At places near, she could buy iron, black marble, and alabaster.

In herself, Bess had the important asset of remarkable vigor. At seventy-two she needed an outlet for creative energy. She had another asset in knowing how to handle workmen. She demanded good work, she could be blunt and direct in ridding herself of the incompetent, but she was not high-handed enough to take the law into her own hands. Her basic attitudes are clarified by an early letter, perhaps to her bailiff or steward, while she was building Chatsworth:

> Crompe, I do understand by your letters that Wortly saith he will depart at our Ladyday next. I will that you shall have him bounden in an obligation to avoid at the same day, for sure I will trust no more to his promise. And when he doth tell you that he is any penny behind for work done, to Mr. Cavendish or me, he doth lie like a false knave. . . . And for Thomas Mason, if you can hear where he is, I would very gladly he were at Chatsworth. I will let you know by my next letters what work Thomas Mason shall begin one [on?] first when he doth come. And as for the other mason which Sir James told you of, if he will not apply his work, you know that he is no meet man for me.

The letter was written from the court and signed, "Your Mistress, E. Seyntelo."

In the Bagot letters (now in manuscript at the Folger Shakespeare Library) conflicts with tenants or workmen appeared, but Bess appealed to officers of the law. In September 1594, during the building of Hardwick Hall, she wrote to Richard Bagot, a justice of the peace, thanking him for his favor about Tuft, "a lewd workman who has not carried out his contract," but she left the final decision to him and the other justices and promised to abide by their arbitration. Between 1600 and 1604 she wrote Walter Bagot, sheriff, asking his help in evicting a widow who was holding a farm unlawfully. Though this case cannot be judged without more information, at least Bess had not taken the law into her own hands.

When Bess began building Hardwick Hall she had perhaps been shrewdly observing great houses and their furnishings for more than forty years. Her scrutiny may have begun when she and Cavendish were married at Bradgate, the home of Henry and Frances Grey, for some details of Bradgate appeared in the structure of Chatsworth. But in 1591 she made a trip to London, staying for several weeks in her house on Cheyne Walk, Chelsea. The trip was mainly for furnishings, but since it is said that the shell of the new Hardwick Hall was not up before 1593, she may have been noting details of construction. Making detours when necessary, she visited Holmby, which had been the residence of Sir Christopher Hatton; Holme-Pierrepont, where her daughter Frances and her husband were living; and Sir Francis Willoughby's great mansion at Wollaton. This last structure had new and interesting details, and Robert Smithson had carried out much of the work. When Bess returned to her work on Hardwick Hall, no doubt she had her head full of shrewd observations on furnishings and at least small details of construction.

Among other things, she had bought thirteen pieces of Brussels tapestry with the story of Gideon from Sir William Newport, the nephew of Sir Christopher Hatton. Having inherited his uncle's estate, he was taking the name Hatton. She had paid a little more than £326 for the tapestries, but she secured a rebate later of £5 because they carried the Hatton arms in the border. Then she sewed pieces of cloth with the Hardwick arms over the Hatton arms and added horns to the Hatton does, changing them to Cavendish stags. Thus she proved to be the same thrifty woman who had furnished Chatsworth. At that time she had in her possession some copes probably acquired by Cavendish from Lilleshall Abbey; she removed the heads of the saints from the copes and substituted the heads of classical gods and goddesses.

The new Hardwick Hall, as Bess completed it, is a symmetrical structure with six towers of equal height. The windows, increasing in length with each added story, make the whole building seem taller than it is. Many windows, with little lead and much glass, give the effect of light; from this came the popular saying, "Hardwick Hall, more glass than wall." The initials E. S. are used in the fretted scrollwork of the towers. The elevations, said James Lees-Milne, are almost free from the "Flemish fuss and detail" of other great houses. He added:

> Ornament has been reduced to a minimum, pilasters and niches have been eliminated, and in place of the disturbing swirls and jags of the Wollaton skyline, quiet balusters, over the main block, and scroll devices of exquisite delicacy have been substituted. The same refinement and reliance upon the horizontal emphasis, in sharp bands of cornice and frieze, as at Longleat, have been repeated.

A visitor enters the building through a plain porch, coming into a hall with a stone fireplace. "The hall . . . is as perfect a piece of work in the Tuscan order as any other in Elizabethan days. . . ." Some needlework on a black background, perhaps done by Mary Queen of Scots, pictures the vices and the virtues. The first floor has a number of rooms with low ceilings, much old furniture, many portraits, and the bedroom used by the countess, with hangings of scarlet velvet embroidered in silver and gold. Here also is the ladies withdrawing room; from it one may easily step into the chapel and sit in the gallery for the service, while the servants use the lower floor of that plain and simple room.

But the remarkable parts of Hardwick Hall are the long gallery and the high presence chamber (the latter sometimes known as the great chamber or state room). Going up the stone staircase hung with tapestries about Hero and Leander, one may enter the long gallery, "all but two hundred feet in length." Light floods the room. The thirteen pieces of Brussels tapestry with the story of Gideon—the ones Bess had bought on her trip to London in 1591—hang on the walls. The draftsmanship in them is said to be excellent, with the colors as clear and beautiful as they were when the tapestries were first woven.

In the long gallery Bess placed pictures of her associates and the members of her own family. Mary Queen of Scots, her parents, her husband (Lord Darnley), and her son, who became James I of England, are there. Pictures of the family of Bess include three of her husbands; perhaps she had none of her first husband, Robert Barlow. Pictures of two sons Henry and William, of two daughters Elizabeth and Mary, and two quite different pictures of Arabella (one showing her as a baby and the other as a girl about thirteen) are also displayed. In the gallery also (according to Sacheverell Sitwell) is a picture of Queen Elizabeth wearing a stiff farthingale "patterned, incredibly, with birds and fishes, a sea horse, or serpent, and even a spouting whale." Perhaps the picture was a gift from the queen to the countess for attending her at court.

Another door leads to the presence chamber. Of this room Sitwell has said:

> It is . . . in our opinion, the most beautiful room, not in England alone, but in the whole of Europe, with a great frieze of parget work, ten or twelve feet deep, of coloured plaster, representing a stag hunt and a boar hunt, the court of Diana, and the story of Orpheus. There are forest scenes of men and dogs hunting under the trees; and in a corner, Diana and her court. Above the window bays are panels of Spring and Summer. Spring is whipping Cupid with a birch of flowers; while

Summer, crowned with corn, sits naked on a heap of corn
stooks, to watch the harvest. This noble room—but the plaster
frieze is so beautiful it dwarfs all else—has a magnificent and
plain fireplace, set flat, so that it does not interrupt the eye, and
the floor has the Hardwick or rush matting laid upon it.

About 1597 Bess moved into her new Hardwick Hall, though many
details may have been completed later, and was able to enjoy it eleven
years before she died. During these last years the fires of old family
quarrels smoldered or became extinct. Sometime in 1605 Arabella
ventured to visit her grandmother, and though she was not reinstated in
the will, she was given later a sum of money and a gold cup. Bess
enjoyed the help of her son William in business affairs and the company
of his children in Hardwick Hall or at Old Cotes nearby. When a
grandson of Gilbert and Mary Talbot was to be christened, Bess sent a
gift; as a result, she was asked to be godmother, but she did not act in
that capacity only because the king and queen offered to be godparents.
In December 1607 Gilbert and Mary Talbot and Charles Cavendish
were invited to Hardwick Hall. Gilbert reported later to Robert Cecil
that there had been no word or hint about the former unkindness. On
New Year's Day 1608 Mary sent her mother a handsome gift. Bess
mellowed enough to add a codicil to her will giving her son William
£100 to use for keeping in repair forever the almshouses she had
established earlier in the city of Derby and listing other gifts for various
members of the family.

Hardwick Hall stands today almost as Bess left it when she died.
She was shrewd enough to have both house and furnishings entailed, so
that they could be willed to her heirs only, not alienated, devised or
bequeathed to any other person. Situated in Derbyshire on a hill between Chesterfield and Mansfield, the Hall is nearer Mansfield. Unfortunately, it is off the beaten track for tourists or for English people
who are driving their own cars, and it is not easy to reach by public
transportation. Though it is one of the architectural glories of the Tudor
Age, not merely a memorial to Bess of Hardwick, comparatively few
people visit the place. It is now administered by the National Trust of
Great Britain.

In estimating the work of Bess as a builder, some have credited her
with five structures, including Bolsover and Worksop; but these two
belonged to the Earl of Shrewsbury, and no evidence appears to indicate that she did any work on them. In her will and in the inscription
prepared for her tomb she named only three: Chatsworth, Old Cotes,
and Hardwick Hall.

Little remains today of the Chatsworth Bess completed while she was the wife of the Earl of Shrewsbury. It was doomed when the William Cavendish who became Duke of Devonshire in 1694 began to remodel it about 1686. Soon he decided on a new structure. About 1707 he completed the present building except for a wing added early in the nineteenth century. The unusual beauty of the situation remains, of course, also a piece of stone wall and a building in the garden known as Mary's bower. A moat had been formed around this building; perhaps it was used briefly for the royal prisoner. But the real work of Bess at Chatsworth is gone.

Bess built Old Cotes about two miles from Hardwick Hall for her favorite son William, it is said. In her later years, after he brought his family, with two sons and a daughter, to live at Hardwick Hall, he sometimes supervised the building at Old Cotes; he audited the last of the building accounts for Hardwick Hall; and he was her right-hand man in other business affairs. Perhaps Old Cotes was completed by 1599, or at the latest by 1603. It was pulled down about 1708, and stone from it was used to build a farmhouse on or near the same site. Probably Old Cotes did not equal her other two structures in cost or interest, but Bess valued it enough to name it among her achievements as a builder.

To the end of her ninety years, Bess of Hardwick, Countess of Shrewsbury, kept her mental abilities, including her keen wit and her memory. In her will she asked that her funeral should not be "over-sumptuous" with "too much vain and idle charge." Apparently her request was honored more in the breach than the observance. The total cost, cited by Lawrence Stone from records at Chatsworth, was £3,257. That sum was greater than the cost of a funeral for Lord Burghley, for the Earl of Leicester, or for Robert Cecil, Earl of Salisbury. Of thirty-two funerals for aristocrats and other people of importance between 1489 and 1651, only that in 1632 for the Earl of Rutland cost more than the funeral for Bess of Hardwick.

She had arranged to be buried in the church of All Saints in Derby, now the cathedral for the diocese, and had planned her own tomb. In her will she had said, "It is appointed . . . that my tomb and internment shall be erected and built, which at this present is finished, and wanteth nothing but setting up." Under a canopied arch she had arranged for a fine monument with an effigy of herself. The long Latin inscription, perhaps completed by her son William, calls her a magnificent builder (the wording in her will had been modest); names as her work Chatsworth, Old Cotes, and Hardwick Hall; lists the six children who lived to maturity; and names her four husbands, with the titles of the three who had titles. She is reclining with her head resting on a cushion, and her sculptured form wears a black gown with a red cloak. A stag, the symbol of the Cavendish family, lies at her feet.

It seems fitting that she should lie there alone.

# CHAPTER FOUR

# Catherine Willoughby, Duchess of Suffolk

## 1520-1580

Catherine Willoughby was a vigorous individualist, as Bess of Hardwick was. But they wore their individualism with a decided difference. Bess used her drive and business shrewdness to establish herself and her family. Catherine was concerned with abstract ideas of religion and had the major aim of spreading religious information, according to her views, to promote the general welfare. She worked toward her aim with vigor, persistence, and intelligence and with a reasonable degree of success. She proved her integrity when she refused to compromise but risked property and life in exile.

Catherine was not famous as a classical scholar. She did not specialize in writing Greek and Latin epigrams; she published no translations and no other books. But she was an educated woman, sure of her religious views. According to Lawrence Stone, she owned a theological library so subversive that "it was kept locked up in a chest under the seal of the Bishop of Lincoln." She had a quick wit, straightforward honesty, fortitude, and the ability to think clearly; as a result, she made her own decisions instead of following conventional thinking.

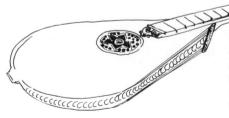

*Catherine's education with the daughters of the Brandon household included instruction in music. She may have learned to play the cittern, a popular instrument of the time.*

Miniature of Catherine Willoughby, after Holbein, at Grimsthorpe Castle.

Stone effigies in the church at Spilsby, not far from Eresby and Grimsthorpe, with an inscription in Latin (reproduced at right) stating that here are buried "Richard Bertie and Catherine, Duchess of Suffolk, Baroness of Willoughby and Eresby."

Catherine's Spanish mother, Maria de Salinas, was an attendant of Catherine of Aragon, who remained loyal during years of humiliation and poverty and in 1509 began enjoying again with her mistress the gay life of the court. In 1516 when Henry was still encouraging English-Spanish marriages, Maria became the wife of Lord Willoughby at Parham Old Hall near Framlingham in Suffolk. The king named a ship the *Mary Willoughby,* and his grant of land to the couple included the reversion of Grimsthorpe in Lincolnshire, later the favorite home of their daughter Catherine, who was named for the queen. Maria continued to spend some of her time at the court as long as Catherine of Aragon remained there as queen. In 1536 when the former queen was dying at Kimbolton Castle, again in poverty and loneliness, Maria returned. She gained entrance in spite of the guard's orders to admit no one, and once inside she went straight to the queen's rooms. Catherine of Aragon died in her arms.

Even with this heritage Catherine Willoughby did not seem an individualist in 1533 when she was married to Charles Brandon, the Duke of Suffolk. But she was only fourteen then, and circumstances were against her. Her father had died about 1526, leaving her as his only direct heir to receive all lands not entailed to male heirs. Because she became Baroness of Willoughby and Eresby, with much property, she was a ward of the crown. The king sold the wardship to the Duke of Suffolk for more than £2,666 on March 1, 1528, according to the practice of the time, giving him a chance to make a profit from the management of her estate. But Sir Christopher Willoughby, her father's brother, began making complaints and accusations in an effort to take over Catherine's property (the common law having developed the principle of preferring male over female heirs); hence the duke appealed to Wolsey to support his ward's claim. Thus he probably saved most of the estate for her, though a few details were not finally settled until 1565. When the duke bought the wardship, perhaps he planned for Catherine to marry his son.

Catherine came to live in the household of the Duke of Suffolk according to a custom of the time. The Duchess of Suffolk then was Mary Tudor, the younger sister of Henry VIII; by her first marriage to Louis XII she had been Queen of France. Catherine continued her education with the Brandon daughters, Frances and Eleanor. The girls learned to read and write, keep accounts, manage a great estate, direct many servants, use herbs as food or medicine, play one or more musical

*Holograph of a letter signed "K Suffolk."*

instruments, spin, weave, and do fine needlework. Probably they had Latin and other literary subjects. It would be strange if the duchess did not teach them all she had learned from both English and French courts about the manners used in royal life.

In June 1533 Mary, Duchess of Suffolk, died. In September 1533 Charles Brandon, Duke of Suffolk, forty-seven years old, married his ward Catherine Willoughby, then about fourteen. Since she became the second peeress of the realm, excepting royalty, the marriage was brilliant by standards of the time. The difference in their ages was not unique. How Catherine felt about the marriage we shall never know. Her recent biographer, Evelyn Read, assumes that she was happy, but no evidence exists. In accepting the situation, Catherine followed conventional thinking of the time; and probably no fourteen-year-old girl who had been living in the home of her guardian and had become accustomed to obeying him could have waged a successful battle against the standards of the age and the brilliance of the marriage.

In March 1534 the son of the duke and the former duchess (the one probably meant by the original plan to become Catherine's husband) died.

Charles Brandon and Catherine had two sons: Henry, born in September 1535, and Charles, born early in 1537. The duke died in 1545, naming his widow first among the several executors of his will for his vast properties. Of course Henry inherited the title. While Catherine was supervising the education of her sons at Cambridge in 1551, both died of the sweating sickness within an hour of each other. Frances Brandon and her husband Henry Grey then inherited the title, becoming Duke and Duchess of Suffolk.

In 1553, after she had been a widow some eight years, Catherine married Richard Bertie, her gentleman usher but also her friend. The Berties had two children: Susan, born in 1554, and Peregrine, born in Wesel in October 1555. After the accession of Queen Mary, they spent about four and a half years in exile on the Continent, leaving England January 1, 1555, and returning in the spring or the early summer of 1559.

As a mature woman Catherine, Duchess of Suffolk, was a many-sided individualist—in supervising the education of her sons, in her choice of Grimsthorpe with all its responsibilities as her favorite place of residence, in her consistent belief that individuals should choose their own partners in marriage, in her decision for herself about her religious views, and in her desire to give others the means for making their decisions.

In supervising the education her sons received, she was an individualist. Holding the wardship and marriage of her older son after his father's death, she allowed him to be tutored for a time at court with Prince Edward. Perhaps the fact that her friend, Queen Catherine Parr, reorganized the royal school and selected the excellent tutors for it influenced her decision. She took the younger son Charles to Grimsthorpe with her, where she provided excellent tutors under her direct supervision. In the autumn of 1549 when Henry was fourteen, both boys entered St. John's College, Cambridge, the college of Ascham and Cecil. Here standards were high and life was Spartan, with a long day begining at four or five in the morning and continuing till nine at night. After supper the boys attended lectures or carried on discussions, mainly in Latin. Their tutor Thomas Wilson, author of *The Art of Rhetoric,* soon recognized that the boys were unusual in mind, character, and response to learning. Instead of leaving her sons while she lived at court or pursued a second marriage, Catherine took a house at Kingston only five or six miles away, so that she might keep in touch with their education. Whenever they had meals with her, it is said, one of them read aloud a chapter in the Greek New Testament, and the other interpreted it in English.

In the summer of 1551 Catherine met the tragedy that tested both her faith and her fortitude. The sweating sickness, a disease with no known cure at the time, stalked into Cambridge. The two boys were sent to Buckden in the hope they might escape it. Both were stricken shortly after they reached the place. As soon as Catherine learned that they had gone, she followed. When she reached Buckden, Henry was dead and Charles was dying. She plunged into shock so deep that she seemed not to hear questions and made no response to expressions of sympathy. When friends could not get her to make plans, they buried the boys quietly in Buckden where they died. The unusual abilities of both boys emerge from the book of tributes edited by Thomas Wilson, including Greek and Latin epigrams by Ascham, who taught Charles his Greek, and by Lawrence Humphrey, Nicholas Udall, Martin Bucer, Wilson himself, and others. Perhaps the grief of Catherine was greater because of the talents and the promise of her sons.

Catherine returned to Grimsthorpe when she became capable of making any decision. It had become her favorite residence in 1536 when her husband was commanding troops against the rebellion called the Pilgrimage of Grace, and she had chosen to remain there instead of moving to London for safety. At that time, when she was seventeen but had been a wife three years, she had learned to manage the whole estate, overseeing the plowing, sowing, and other outdoor activities and supervising a large household. Grimsthorpe continued to be her favorite residence while the duke was living; she carried all the responsibilities when the duke was at court, or acted as warden of the marches against Scotland in 1542, or went to France with the king in 1544. She had continued this double duty after the duke's death in 1545.

But after the death of her sons she returned to Grimsthorpe alone. While she managed the estate and the household, she fought a battle with herself, testing her resources, finding if she had the faith in life and the religion she professed to carry her through her crisis. About December 7 she wrote to her trusted friend, William Cecil:

> I give God thanks, good Master Cecil, for all the benefits which it hath pleased Him to heap upon me; and truly I take this last (and to the first sight most sharp and bitter) punishment not for the least of His benefits, inasmuch as I have never been so well taught by any other before to know His power, His love and mercy, mine own weakness, and that wretched state that without Him I should endure here. And to ascertain you that I have received great comfort in Him, I would gladly do it by talk and sight of you. But as I must confess myself no better than flesh, so I am not well able with quiet to behold my very friends without some part of these vile dregs of Adam to seem sorry for that whereof I know I rather ought to rejoice.

She closed with thanks to Cecil for his lasting friendship. Apparently she was achieving a subdued victory over her personal tragedy.

When she was ready to try human companionship again, at the end of the year she went to spend the Christmas holidays with Frances and Henry Grey, who had become Duke and Duchess of Suffolk when the male line had failed with the death of her sons. Their oldest daughter, Lady Jane Grey, was a precocious fourteen years of age. It has been said that a special warmth of feeling existed between her and Catherine, and the idea seems reasonable.

Later the Grey family brought Catherine other griefs and losses—lesser ones compared with the death of her sons, but some of them called for fortitude. In 1553 she endured the uncertain queenship of Lady Jane for nine days, followed by her imprisonment and her release through Mary's clemency. Then Henry Grey was drawn into Wyatt's rebellion. As a result, he and his brilliant daughter Lady Jane were both executed in 1554. The strange marriage of Frances Grey to Adrian Stokes, master of her horse, a young, uncouth man with an attractive physique, followed hard upon the execution of Henry Grey. At the news of this union, it is reported that Queen Elizabeth exclaimed, "What! Has the woman so far forgotten herself as to marry her groom?"

Later, after Catherine had returned from her exile on the Continent, the two sisters of Lady Jane were frustrated into creating their own tragedies. Lady Catherine, a maid of honor and a possible heir to the throne, was secretly married to the Earl of Hertford, son of the Protector, Edward Seymour. When her pregnancy became apparent, she and her husband were both sent to the Tower with orders to keep them apart. After they managed to have a second child, they were sent to different places; but both were kept in custody until her death in 1568.

The third sister Mary also came into disgrace while she was a maid of honor. In 1565 she secretly married Thomas Keys, the queen's sergeant porter. For objective onlookers the situation may have had comic elements. The difference in rank was appalling to aristocrats, he was a widower with a flock of children, and he had been chosen for his position because he was huge, but Mary was so tiny that she was called a dwarf. Mary was kept under supervision. From 1567 to 1569 she was with Catherine, Duchess of Suffolk, who appealed to Cecil for financial aid in her care, describing Mary's shabby and inadequate furnishings and her shame and sorrow about her situation. After two years Mary was transferred to the custody of Sir Thomas Gresham but was never allowed to see Keys again. After he died, Mary was given her freedom.

Eleanor Brandon, Catherine's younger stepdaughter, seems to have brought her no special grief or concern. Married to Henry Clifford, who became Earl of Cumberland in 1542, she had one surviving child, Margaret, who became the wife of Henry Stanley, Earl of Derby. Though Margaret was put under restraint about 1590 as a possible heir to the throne, and her son Ferdinando exposed a treasonous group who wished to make him king, Catherine had died years before these developments. Thus her concern for members of the Brandon family apparently ended about 1569, when Mary Grey Keys was removed from her household.

As a mature woman, Catherine, Duchess of Suffolk, was individualist enough to resist the conventional ideas of the age about marriage. Her chance to respond with her opinions came about May 1550 when Edward Seymour, Protector, and then the most powerful man in England, wished to negotiate a contract of marriage between his daughter Anne and her older son Henry. As she held the wardship and right of marriage for him, she had the legal right to negotiate such a contract between the two young people. Her friend, William Cecil, had been asked to consult Catherine. She answered him as follows:

> And now . . . as they be yet without judgment to give such consent as ought to be given in matrimony, I cannot tell . . . wherein we might work more wickedly than to bring our children into so miserable a state not to choose by their own liking. . . . This I promise you I have said for my lord's daughter as well as for my son . . . I know none this day living that I rather wish my son than she, but I am not . . . therefore desirous that she should be constrained by her friends to have him whom she might not like so well as I like her. . . . And so, my good Cecil, being weary, I leave you to the Lord.

Her younger son, Charles, was apparently not considered for marriage negotiations before his death at fourteen. As he had been the Duke of Suffolk less than an hour, he had no time to become a prize in the matrimonial market. If he had lived, no doubt Catherine would have made the same kind of answer about him.

Catherine gave her greatest proof of being an individualist in her views on marriage in 1553 when she accepted Richard Bertie as her second husband. She had remained single about eight years, spending her time in the hard work of managing Grimsthorpe and in supervising the education of her sons. With her rank, property, and personality she might have married any eligible peer in England. Instead, she chose to marry a man without rank or wealth, but one with education and character, one who shared her religious views and had been giving her loyal support and companionship. Richard Bertie had been her gentleman usher. A man holding such a position in the household of a great lady or gentleman came of a good family and had the special duty of walking before the master or mistress in formal processions. Bertie had become Catherine's friend and advisor. When she wrote to Cecil two or three months after the death of her sons, saying, "you may use him that I send you as if I stood by," she was almost certainly referring to Bertie. Thus the relationship had been tested in depth before the marriage. The ages of the two helped make the marriage appropriate;

born about 1517 or 1518, he was two or three years older than Catherine.

Richard Bertie's education and intellectual interests also made his marriage to Catherine suitable. He had entered Corpus Christi College, Oxford, in 1534 and was granted the B.A. degree in 1537. Those who knew him considered him an intelligent man with a gift for repartee. He spoke French, Italian, and Latin well. He demonstrated some capacity for intellectual work when he answered John Knox and his *First Blast of the Trumpet against the Monstrous Regiment of Women,* pointing out its inconsistencies — though the queen probably never saw the work and it was never published. His honorary degree, an M.A. conferred in August 1564, may not be evidence of intellectual attainment, but at least he was in distinguished company: the Duke of Norfolk; the Earls of Sussex, Warwick, and Oxford; and Sir William Cecil received degrees at the same time. Bertie was attending the queen on a state visit to Cambridge. Better evidence, perhaps, of his intellectual grasp lies in the fact that he and Hugh Latimer became friends in Catherine's household. Latimer had spent time there as her chaplain, preaching his seven sermons on the Lord's Prayer; he also probably officiated at the marriage of Bertie to Catherine.

When Catherine's children by Richard Bertie, Susan and Peregrine, reached the age of marriage, it seems that she wished them also to choose their own partners in marriage. Susan was married to Reginald Grey during the winter of 1570-1571 when she was about seventeen; perhaps her mother considered her mature enough to make her own choice. At least no conflict is recorded. Catherine did bestir herself, though, about the title of her new son-in-law; she wrote letters to Cecil and to the queen and arranged interviews with the queen. The title had clearly belonged to Reginald Grey's father, but he had never assumed it because the estate was impoverished. Her efforts seem to have succeeded; before the end of 1571 Reginald became the eighth Baron Grey de Ruthven and also the Earl of Kent.

When Catherine's son Peregrine was about seventeen, problems developed; but each time Peregrine seems finally to have made his own choice. Plans had been made at one time for him to marry Elizabeth Cavendish, daughter of the vigorous Bess of Hardwick. This marriage was given up, apparently because Peregrine decided that he did not wish to marry her.

About 1577 when Peregrine was twenty-two, he and Mary de Vere, sister of the brilliant but unscrupulous Earl of Oxford, developed an ardent mutual attachment. The situation was difficult because the earl had married Anne Cecil in 1571, with results that were becoming tragic.

He accused his wife of being unfaithful, disowned one of his children for a time, refused to live with his wife, accused Lady Burghley of alienating his wife's affection from him, and treated Burghley with insolence. Catherine and Burghley had been friends for years. Since Mary de Vere was a maid of honor, Catherine was reluctant to tell Bertie all the facts for fear his opposition would impel the young people into action without the queen's consent. This time, Catherine did not want to appeal to Burghley for help.

But with all her explanations and pleadings, she could not talk Peregrine out of the marriage. Finally she acted on the principle she had expressed years earlier by agreeing that he must make his own choice. She went further: she helped him by writing to Burghley more than once, asking him to use his influence in getting the queen's consent to the marriage of her maid of honor to Peregrine. As a result, the two young people became husband and wife some time in 1578. For several years the marriage was unhappy, giving support to those who believed in letting older and wiser heads make decisions about marriage for young people. But about two years after the death of Catherine, Peregrine and Mary achieved a settled relationship.

Catherine was an individualist with integrity in her loyalty to her chosen religion, in contrast to the thousands who meekly followed the opinions of any ruler who gained the throne. She had been baptized as a Catholic, with Stephen Gardiner as her godfather and presumably Catherine of Aragon as her godmother. She chose her later religious principles for herself. Listening to the sermons of Hugh Latimer at court, she accepted the ideas held by him and other reformers. In the late 1530s (as Evelyn Read has said) she and her husband were appointing men with reforming sympathies as chaplains in their household. It seems highly probable that she would have been the decisive influence in such appointments. Alexander Seton, a Scot, who fled to England after preaching against "the corrupt doctrine of the papacy," was one of them. John Parkhurst, who chose exile when Mary became queen, was Seton's successor in 1542. In one of his many Latin poems he paid a high tribute to Catherine. When Anne Askew was being racked after she had been condemned for heresy (a fact confirmed by others in addition to John Foxe), the purpose was to question her about ladies of the court who were likewise suspected of that crime. Catherine was one of the half dozen or more named in this connection. By early 1547, if not earlier, her religious views were known outside

England; Chapuys, writing from Louvain to Mary of Hungary, reported that Henry VIII was favoring heretics and was influenced by his queen, who was "instigated by the Duchess of Suffolk" and by others. Thus Chapuys gave indirect support for the idea that Stephen Gardiner was watching both Catherines with hostility in the last years of Henry's reign and that he watched the Duchess of Suffolk after he came into power again under Queen Mary.

The integrity of Catherine Bertie about her religious beliefs was proved when she went into exile instead of recanting to escape death. The main events of the exile were published by John Foxe in *Acts and Monuments;* and though modern readers may well ignore his denunciations and his rhetoric, he checked facts with care. He probably had every chance to learn the facts about the Berties. Catherine had been his friend and protector in 1550: when he was answering questions about himself for the official register on June 24 of that year, the day before he was ordained a deacon, he said that he was living in the London household of the Duchess of Suffolk. Though the Berties came back from exile in 1559, their story did not appear in the first edition of the work by Foxe in 1563. It did appear in the two-volume edition of 1570, the one-volume edition of 1576, and in the following editions in substantially the same form. Thus Foxe had plenty of time to check his story before publishing it; and the Berties, who lived till 1580 and 1582, had every chance to deny it or any of its details. It is possible also that the narrative Foxe published was written by Richard Bertie himself. The relationship of Foxe and Catherine, the education of Bertie, and the vivid details of the narrative make the conjecture probable.

Catherine's fears must have begun stirring when Queen Mary released Gardiner from imprisonment in the Tower and made him her chancellor. She probably knew also that her well-known witty comments in safer days had made Gardiner her enemy. During Lent 1554 Richard Bertie was summoned to appear before Gardiner and was questioned about his wife's remarks years earlier and about her attitude to the Mass. After Bertie had discussed with Catherine the details of the talk, he asked Gardiner for a second interview: in this one he was granted permission for a journey to the Continent to collect debts that the king of Spain and others had owed to the Duke of Suffolk. As his wife was chief executor of the estate, she had authorized him to take this action. Of course he meant also to find a safe place on the Continent for Catherine and their baby Susan. Catherine was to wait at her London house in the Barbican until she received notice of the time and other arrangements for an escape. Though the statute for the burning of heretics was not reenacted till mid-January 1555, it must have been foreseen like a slow-gathering storm. The brief account that follows is based on Foxe.

In the thick early morning fog of New Year's Day 1555 Catherine, with the baby and six servants, slipped from the London house in the Barbican, separated for safety, and barely escaped a guard who had heard them. Catherine and two women reached the barge waiting at Lion Key; and the oarsmen, reluctant to move in the heavy fog, finally landed them at Leith. There a Master Cranwell told them the flight had been discovered, but he arranged the disguise of a merchant's daughter for Catherine, and she was taken to visit her supposed father. Bertie was able to join her there, and she rested while they were awaiting a favorable wind for the Continent. Once on the ship, they thought they were safe, but they were blown back twice when the winds changed suddenly. The second time, a seaman who had to go ashore for food and water was sharply questioned, but he swore that only a common merchant's daughter was on board—and he probably believed his statement. Finally the party landed at Brabant, the women changed to the long hooded cloaks worn in the Netherlands, and all made their way to the small town of Xanten.

Xanten was peaceful, the villagers were shy but friendly, and the Berties lived simply. But one February day a man approached Bertie and told him that many of the villagers thought he and his family were people of importance; the Bishop of Arras, who had heard rumors, was planning to seize them and examine them about their religion. That afternoon, with the baby and the two servants, they started as if for an ordinary walk; but when they were well out of the town, they walked faster. Cold rain began, the air was raw, and the ground became slushy. It took them nearly four hours to cover the five miles of their journey.

About seven o'clock that winter evening they passed through the gate into the fortified town of Wesel, where they knew many Protestants were living. It was a destination they had planned, but they had been waiting in Xanten to hear from a Master Perusell. He had received much kindness from Catherine while he had been minister of a French refugee church in London. But after they were in the town, finding him was difficult; they were turned away from inn after inn, no matter how much they offered to pay. Perhaps innkeepers thought Bertie was a common foot soldier of Germany, traveling with his woman—a type of person they detested. Finally Catherine began crying. Leaving her and the baby under the shelter of a church porch,

Bertie hurried to find help. When he heard two boys speaking Latin, he offered them coins if they would take him to the house of someone who spoke French. They did. When the door of the house opened, they made the man who faced them understand that they were looking for Perusell. A moment later Perusell stood before them; he was a guest at supper in the house. He found the Berties a place to live, they were with people of their own religious faith, and their fears gradually subsided. They stayed in Wesel nearly a year. Foxe does not mention the birth of their son there on October 12, 1555, but it is verified by other records. They named him Peregrine.

But happy days did not last. Sir John Mason, stationed at Brussels as English ambassador to the Emperor Charles V, was usually kind to other Englishmen on the Continent without asking them about their religion. He sent word that Lord William Paget, a member of Queen Mary's Privy Council, with the help of the Duke of Brunswick, was planning to seize the Berties and charge them with heresy. They said farewell to Wesel and to security.

Weinheim in the Palatinate was their destination. They knew that the ruler, Otto Heinrich, was a Protestant. He and his brother had been associated with Martin Bucer, whom Catherine had befriended while she was living near Cambridge and supervising the education of her sons. But Weinheim was 150 miles across country as a bird flies—and much farther by the ways they must travel. Gradually they moved from the flat country up the Rhine valley, perhaps traveling part of the way by boat. Two small children made the trip both difficult and dangerous. But at the end of the journey they were housed in a strong castle belonging to the ruler. Here they lived safely for about a year, but their security vanished when they realized that they were coming to the end of their finances.

This time help came through John à Lasco, the son of a Polish nobleman. He had adopted the reformed religion, and about 1550 he had been superintendent of a church of alien Protestants in London. As he was a friend of Martin Bucer and visited him in Cambridge, Catherine may have met him there. Catherine is credited with helping to establish a church for aliens in London, so he would have had every reason to seek a meeting with her. In his travel from England back to Poland, he heard of the Berties and their journeys from place to place. He told King Sigismund of Poland about them. The king offered them a house, lands, and a secure income. But Bertie wished official assurance. He secured it through another English exile, William Barlow, who traveled swiftly alone, interviewed the king, and brought back a formal offer under the king's seal.

After another wearing journey, with one encounter that nearly cost

Bertie his life, they reached their destination. The king received them with honor and gave them a large house in Samogitia (territory on the Baltic Sea that is now Lithuania) and the right to rule over that area as long as they lived within its boundaries. With the executive ability that both Catherine and her husband seemed to possess, they were useful and secure until the reign of Mary came to an end on November 17, 1558. Elizabeth was proclaimed queen on the same day. In the late spring or early summer of 1559 the Berties reached England again, ending a long, dangerous odyssey.

Catherine's properties, seized after their escape from England, were returned to them, though irreplaceable personal belongings were doubtless gone. She wrote a little later that she had scarcely enough furnishings left for Eresby and Grimsthorpe. Peregrine, born at Wesel, was given denization, August 2, 1559. He was described as the son of Richard Bertie, "who left the realm by license of Queen Mary." But the miseries and dangers of exile were embedded in their memories. Nearly ten years later, when Catherine was writing to remind William Cecil about the suit of a poor Dutchman who wished to cross the Channel and bring his belongings and his wife back to England, she commented with sympathy on the sufferings of those who became exiles for their religion.


With her uncompromising individuality, Catherine was unhappy when she discovered that Queen Elizabeth was not establishing immediately a clear-cut Protestant regime. But the queen liked form and ceremony; she realized that the common people found comfort in the ritual and the vestments of the priest; she was unwilling for priests to marry; she supported her bishops in exercising a central control; and she distrusted, equally perhaps, religious radicals and democratic procedures in the church. She was also willing to move slowly; thus she kept foreign governments guessing while the country settled into acceptance of her reign.

Catherine disagreed. In her first enthusiasm she had written the queen: "For if the Israelites found joy in their Deborah, how much more we English in our Elizabeth. . . ." She was bitterly disappointed to find that her firm friend, William Cecil, had the same ambivalent attitude. In March 1559 she answered a letter of his, one that apparently has not survived:

> The hand within the letter seems to be my lady your wife's, the
> superscription Sir William Cecil's; but howsoever it be, it is all

> one, yea, and so I would to God all our whole nation were one in
> Jesus Christ, as behooveth. . . . Wherefore I am forced to say
> with the prophet Elie, how long halt ye between two
> opinions? . . . If the Mass be good, tarry not to follow
> it . . . but if you be not so persuaded, alas, who should move
> the queen's majesty to honour it with her presence, or any of her
> counsellors? Well, it is so reported here that her majesty tarried
> but the gospel and so departed. . . .

Catherine never accepted what Cecil realized fully — that he could
not urge the queen strongly because her Tudor stubbornness might
drive her even more sharply toward her conservative position.
Catherine had not been able to compromise but had chosen exile; Cecil,
putting his love of England above dogma, had stayed and taken
communion at Mass. But this difference did not destroy a friendship
furthered by the fact that they had been neighbors of a sort for years.
Grimsthorpe, Lincolnshire, was about twenty miles northward from
Cecil's paternal home, Stamford Baron, which lay across the Welland
River from Stamford in Northamptonshire. When Cecil came to the area
for a time, Catherine might send him the gift of a buck or invite him to
Grimsthorpe for deer hunting. She also asked Cecil for advice or for
help with personal problems. When she disagreed, as she did with
Cecil's attitude about religious compromise, she was frank; when he
gave comfort and aid, she was grateful; and from the available evidence
she was never small or nagging. He did many favors for her. Later, he
may have taken her son Peregrine into his household for a period of
training, but evidence for the possibility, stated by Evelyn Read, is
elusive.

Catherine's disapproval of the queen's compromise in religion was
part of a larger pattern in her relationship to her ruler. Very likely she
and the queen were never firm friends. When Bertie was in Parliament
about 1563 to 1567, it is possible that he gave support to certain
religious measures that he and his wife desired but the queen abhorred,
with a resulting chill in the relationship. The queen granted titles to
Reginald Grey, the husband of Susan Bertie, after persistent pleas from
Catherine; she refused to let Richard Bertie become Baron Willoughby,
though Cecil probably added his pleas; later she gave the title to his son
Peregrine. But in all these requests about titles, the queen was acting
from accepted principles.

Catherine also complained to Cecil that the queen changed from
gracious friendliness to coldness from one audience to another, or even
within the same audience, and she did not understand the reason for
these shifts. Perhaps the basic reason was a difference in temperament.

The queen was devious; she needed to be when she was dealing with foreign ambassadors. She could lie royally, intending to deceive, or she could lie with laughter, suggesting that her statement was a huge jest but making it difficult for her listener to protest. Catherine was straightforward, almost incapable of twisting the truth even a little.

After their return from the Continent in 1559 with their children Susan and Peregrine, the Berties continued to use Grimsthorpe as their chief residence. Though it was comparatively isolated and life was not idleness, Catherine remained an individualist who preferred the country to London and the royal court. The household had probably a hundred people in addition to the family—forty persons in the livery of the duchess, forty household servants including cooks and maid-servants, and about twenty more for the farming operations on the estate. Since all were members of the great household, the mistress did not limit herself to directing work and paying wages. Her larger responsibilities included their illnesses and their small operations at need; their marriages; the christening of their children; and especially for Catherine, an influence on their religious education.

The Berties lived well at Grimsthorpe with apparent content and happiness. Their account books for about two years are available, and biographer Evelyn Read has examined them in detail. Sums spent for clothing include the cost of expensive furs, silks, satins, velvet, fine linens, and sheer lawns, much of the clothing being made at home. Bread was baked at home, but strong beer and double beer were listed at seven shillings a barrel, and small beer at four shillings sixpence. The cellar had a variety of wines and such cordials as hippocras and jubilate; these were often shipped by sea freight from London to Boston and then brought overland to Grimsthorpe. Spices they bought were expensive, cinnamon being ten shillings, sixpence a pound; cloves, eleven shillings; and mace, fourteen shillings. Their purchases in-cluded other spices also—ginger, pepper, aniseed, and cumin seed. The herb garden furnished peppermint, thyme, verbena, lavender, and sage. Food, as usual, meant huge amounts of fish and meat. Though raisins, figs, and oranges were purchased, other fruits and vegetables were seldom listed.

The household accounts included rewards and gifts. At New Year's Day 1561 the Berties gave the queen a piece of jewelry that had cost about fourteen and one-half pounds; but they spent nearly five pounds more because it was "not well wrought" and had to have "extra work and extra gold.'' A man called a doctor received a silver cup valued at more than five pounds for treating the duchess and Susan. An Italian not called a doctor had five shillings for recommending medicine when the duchess had a light case of smallpox. Expenses included many small tips to the servants of friends who sent them gifts.

Entertainers came often and were rewarded. The waits of Lincoln (a small group of singers or players on wind instruments, probably maintained at the public charge) were often given small sums for entertaining the household. A fencing master once brought his company. A group of puppeteers stayed two nights to give performances. In January 1561 musicians from Godmanchester, Huntingdonshire, played and were rewarded with twenty shillings. Traveling players came in January and July 1561; the Queen's Players performed in July of 1562 and were given twenty shillings. Master Bertie entertained himself, especially at holiday seasons, with risking small sums at cards, sometimes losing two or three shillings an evening. In the summer, members of the household lost small sums at rovers, a kind of archery contest.

The Berties often went to Eresby or Boston, to London, and to the court at Greenwich. If Bertie traveled to London alone, he went quickly by horseback. But when Catherine journeyed there, with the escort usual for a duchess, she spent three days with two stops overnight. When she paid a visit to court, she had a large group of attendants dressed in her livery; once at the Swan in Charing Cross she paid for the suppers of twenty-four people who had ''attended upon her Grace at court.''

Members of the household were paid on the quarterly basis. The treasurer received twenty-five shillings; gardeners, fourteen or fifteen shillings each; and two cooks, twenty-five shillings each. Accounts for 1561, when Peregrine and Susan were about six and seven years old, included threepence to buy ''birch for rods.'' Hence it seems that the children were not handled by the advice of the classical writers on education but by the counsel of Solomon. Mr. Coverdale, ''the preacher,'' was paid five pounds a quarter. He seems to have acted also as a tutor: he received twelve shillings for the cost of Elyot's *Dictionary,* four shillings for copies of Lyly's grammar, and more than two shillings for four *Dialogues,* perhaps those of Erasmus.

Mr. Coverdale, the preacher and apparently the tutor of the children mentioned in these accounts, was almost certainly Miles

Coverdale himself, though it seems that Catherine has not been credited before with this service to religion. In publishing the household accounts, Evelyn Read merely wondered whether he was a relative of the great translator of the Bible.

That Catherine would have been happy to help Miles Coverdale seems to need no proof, since she was concerned with getting an English version of the Bible into the hands of the common people. The Berties had some contact with Coverdale while they were all in exile. Coverdale was the pastor at one time of a hundred or more Protestants gathered at Wesel, though it is not quite certain that he and the Berties were in that city at the same time. But after Coverdale had left Wesel for Bergzabern, a certain Conrad Huber wrote to him, asking him to investigate a report that Catherine had many debts. Coverdale replied, saying that he had talked at Frankfort with the "very distinguished husband" of the duchess, who assured him that she had no debts at all. He promised to look into the report further when he went back to Wesel to bring his wife from there.

After Coverdale returned to England late in 1558 or early in 1559, he was certainly in need of financial aid. As he had been bishop of Exeter from 1551 to 1553 but had left England after Mary became queen, Queen Elizabeth named him by letters patent to take part in the consecration of Matthew Parker as Archbishop of Canterbury in December 1559. Coverdale was not appointed again to his former bishopric; and though he may have been offered but refused the bishopric of Llandaff, he held no ecclesiastical position for several years.

Some time in 1563 he was offered the living of St. Magnus in London. In January 1564 he was writing Sir William Cecil and Archbishop Parker, explaining "how destitute I have been of a competent living ever sith my bishopric was violently taken from me . . . and how I never had pension, annuity or stipend of it these ten years; how unable I am either to pay first fruits or long to enjoy the said benefice. . . ." So he was asking the queen's warrant to exempt him from payment of the first fruits. The queen granted his request, and he held the living of St. Magnus until 1566. Later, between November 1, 1567, and January 18, 1568, he preached eleven sermons at the church of the Holy Trinity in the Minories.

Since the accounts from Catherine's household with references to Mr. Coverdale the preacher are dated from 1560 to 1562, they belong within the time when Miles Coverdale needed financial help. Possibly he lived at Grimsthorpe from late 1559 or early 1560 to 1564. He remained active as a preacher until 1568; hence he was physically able to teach two small children of a friend — or even to use the birch rods if an occasion required. He may have known Greek and Hebrew, he certainly knew French, he was expert in both German and Latin, and he had an unusual knowledge of theology and the Bible — subjects extremely important to Catherine, Duchess of Suffolk. Hence he was well qualified to teach her children.

Through the chapter we have followed Catherine as she shaped her mature religious views for herself by listening to the sermons of Hugh Latimer, as she chose exile instead of compromise about her firm beliefs, and as she accepted into her household at different times Latimer, John Foxe, and probably Miles Coverdale.

The dedication of Latimer's sermons to her was no empty gesture. *The First Sermon of Master Hugh Latimer . . . before the King's Majesty* in 1549 was addressed to her because of her virtuous behavior, her love of God, "and also godly charity toward the edification of every member grafted in Christ Jesus. . . ." Another volume, *Seven Sermons Made upon the Lord's Prayer* by Latimer, published in 1571 or 1572, honored her because the sermons were preached at her house at Grimsthorpe by one whom she had nourished and whose doctrine she had adopted. The writer of the dedication praised her also because her "princely spirit" had caused her to leave "possessions, lands, and goods, your worldly friends and native country . . . to become an exile . . . to choose rather to suffer adversity with the people of God than to enjoy the pleasures of the world. . . ." She had been allowed to come home agan, he continued, that she might be "a comfort unto the comfortless and an instrument by which his holy name should be praised and his gospel propagated and spread. . . ."

In his introduction to the *Selected Sermons by Hugh Latimer,* 1968, Allen G. Chester reported that Latimer preached only one sermon at court in 1550 and that for several years following "he was an honored guest at Grimsthorpe in Lincolnshire" in the household of Catherine, Duchess of Suffolk, now his patroness in reality. During his stay there, in spite of illness and age, he preached two sermons a Sunday and usually began working at his book by two in the morning. Besides the sermons on the Lord's Prayer, addressed to the servants of the duchess in her private chapel, he preached twenty-one other sermons either at Grimsthorpe or in parishes nearby. Authority for many of these facts was Augustus Bernher, a Swiss servant and friend of Latimer who edited his sermons for publication.

Many services of Catherine to the religion she cherished may remain unknown, for she must ave acted quietly at times when it was neither possible nor desirable to leave written records. But a few others are known. About 1549 and 1550 while she was living near Cambridge to help in the education of her sons, she had close connections with Martin Bucer. He came to Cambridge in November 1549, and in the following January he began a series of lectures on Paul's Epistle to the Ephesians. Catherine's two sons studied with him; she also attended many lectures and had discussions with him about religious ideas. When his family joined him that winter, she provided such practical helps as a cow and a calf for their use. When Bucer became ill, she helped to nurse him. After he died, she comforted the widow and gave her practical aid. About this time she was also extending courtesies and aid to Master Perusell, minister of the French refugee church in London. Professor Roland Bainton has stated that Francis Berti, possibly a relative of Catherine's husband, persuaded her to help Perusell; and as a result, Edward VI assigned the dilapidated church of the Augustinian monks to two pastors of refugee churches. Thus the "Church of the Strangers" was founded. Since John à Lasco visited Cambridge to see Bucer, it seems likely that Catherine met him at this time and extended to him any help within her power. Details earlier in the chapter indicated that both Perusell and John à Lasco helped the Berties in their exile; and Otto Heinrich, who gave them a secure home at Weinheim, had been a friend of Martin Bucer.

Other services to religion are credited to Catherine. When Hugh Latimer, Nicholas Ridley, and Thomas Cranmer were imprisoned after the accession of Queen Mary, Catherine sent them alms as long as she remained in England. She probably heard of their fiery deaths while she was in exile; and because of her personal associations with Latimer, she must have been especially grieved at his execution. John Old, translator of various books of the Bible for the second *Paraphrase* of Erasmus, was among those who paid tribute to the work of Catherine; in one of his prefaces he mentioned the Visitation of Lincolnshire in 1547 and "the helping forwardness of that devout woman of God, the Duchess of Suffolk." Conyers Read summed up her influence by calling her "an indomitable lady who might almost be accounted the mother of English Puritanism."

Catherine's integrity led her to further the religious life of the common people who lived on her estate or near her property. She saw to it that every little church in the area had its own copy of the Bible in English, it is said, and that families had the gospel, the ten commandments, and the Lord's Prayer in their own language. She also did what she could to see that preachers in their sermons used simple words and ideas to reach people and influence their lives.

Perhaps the power of her personality is suggested further by the fact that neither her contemporaries nor those who have written about her since have tended to call her the Dowager Duchess of Suffolk, though that was her title from 1545. Nor did people writing of Frances Brandon Grey, either then or later, trouble themselves often to call her the Duchess of Suffolk, though from 1545, she actually held the title. Most of those who read the life of Catherine Willoughby now would probably agree that she was an outstanding woman — if they are willing to judge her, not by their agreement with her religious views, but by the zeal and integrity with which she supported the views she had chosen and used them to advance the general welfare. Though her aim was limited compared with the many interests of Margaret Beaufort, Catherine of Aragon, or Mildred Cecil, within her aim she succeeded.

Catherine Willoughby died September 19, 1580. Though her health was never good after the years of exile, she survived until she was about sixty years old. Less than two years later, her second husband followed her in death. In family affairs she was not always fortunate. Her brilliant sons by the Duke of Suffolk had died nearly thirty years earlier. She did not live to see her other son, Peregrine Bertie, achieve a settled married life after his initial unhappiness; she never knew that he won the affectionate gratitude of Queen Elizabeth by his work as a military commander. Leaving her daughter Susan a widow, she never learned of Susan's second happy marriage. She never saw any of her grandchildren. Her personal achievement was the maintaining of her integrity without compromise. Her service to England was the part she had in establishing the religion she cherished.

She and Richard Bertie were buried in the church at Spilsby, not far from Eresby and Grimsthorpe. One may see there the stone effigies of the two, with the simple monument and the Latin words telling us that here are buried "Richard Bertie, and Catherine, Duchess of Suffolk, Baroness of Willoughby and Eresby."

*Engraving of Mary
Sidney Herbert, made
in 1618 and considered
to be the only
authentic likeness of
her.*

*Facsimile of signature,
"M Pembroke."*

*The Tudor gatehouse, a feature
of the vast structure at Wilton
Park. Mary Sidney Herbert
welcomed writers and scientists
to Wilton House, making it
into "a little university."*

# CHAPTER FIVE

# *Mary Sidney Herbert, Countess of Pembroke*
## 1561-1621

Mary Sidney Herbert was perhaps the most self-effacing of the women included in this volume. She devoted her energy to helping others; her influence did not have breadth, but within her area of influence she was unusually effective. She was not actively concerned with extravagant entertaining, political affairs, exerting an influence at court, or promoting religious views in others though she was a devout woman herself. Her contribution was the encouragement of literature, not as a goddess inspiring writers from a throne above, but as a human being offering them a home at Wilton House (her chief residence during her married life) with chances to discuss problems and learn literary forms. Men of science were also longtime residents there; some of the latter may have been brought in by her husband, but it seems evident that both writers and scientists were welcomed by husband and wife. It is said that she made Wilton House into a college or a "little university," and we need not depend upon John Aubrey for the evidence.

She contributed to literature in other ways. She encouraged her brother Sir Philip Sidney to write and to begin his *Arcadia* in a period when he needed an outlet. After his early death she edited and published his works. She did literary work of her own, including translations from Italian and French, and she transformed more than a hundred of the Psalms into Elizabethan lyrics. Perhaps she was the only woman of the period with poetic talent—though the evidence is mainly in her work with the Psalms. Either she wrote no other poems or they were never published under her name. She seemed content to remain "Sidney's sister, Pembroke's mother." She was also remarkable in her personality—generous, desirous of helping many people, courteous, and gracious. As others said, she was fair, good, learned, and wise. Perhaps she deserves even more recognition than she has received.

Mary Herbert's place in the period owed much to her own personality and much to her family connections. By birth she was entitled to the badge of the great Dudley family, the bear and the ragged staff, and also to the crest of the Sidneys, a porcupine. Her mother, Mary Dudley, was a daughter of the Duke of Northumberland and his wife Anne Guildford. As *de facto* ruler of England for a brief period ending with the death of Edward VI, the duke tried to put his oldest unmarried son Guildford on the throne as the husband of Lady Jane Grey. After the execution of the duke in 1553 and of Guildford and Lady Jane in 1554, the other sons were held in prison. Their mother was refused an audience when she wished to plead to Queen Mary for them, but she secured the support of the Spanish gentlemen who were attendants of Philip. As a result her sons were pardoned and set free. The three who remained fought valiantly for Spain at St. Quentin in 1557. Henry was killed in battle; the survivors, Robert and Ambrose, were rewarded by the removal of their attainder. These stirring events occurred only a few years before Mary Sidney Herbert was born.

The Dudleys brought the Sidneys connections with other great families. Catherine, the sister of Mary Dudley Sidney, was married in 1553 to Henry Hastings, Earl of Huntingdon. In 1565 Ambrose, who held his father's earlier title of Earl of Warwick, took as his third wife Anne Russell, daughter of Francis, Earl of Bedford. They were married in the chapel at Whitehall with the queen present. On the accession of Elizabeth, Robert Dudley became master of the queen's horse and, later, the Earl of Leicester. He influenced events in the life of his niece Mary perhaps more than all the other Dudleys together.

The Sidneys, for our purpose here, began with William, an esquire in the household of Henry VIII; he was knighted for bravery at Flodden and became steward, chamberlain, and tutor to Prince Edward. His son Henry, born in 1529, was eight years older than the prince and was educated by the same masters. In 1547 Henry became one of the four principal gentlemen of the bedchamber to Edward VI. In 1551 he was knighted; he married Mary Dudley; and possibly in recognition of this connection with the Dudleys, he was licensed to retain fifty servants wearing his livery in addition to menial servants. About this time he was being sent on diplomatic missions to Scotland and France. In 1552 the little king gave Penshurst in Kent to William Sidney; and when he died in 1554, his son Henry inherited the property. The *Calendar of the Patent Rolls* for the reign of Edward VI lists many offices and properties granted by the king to Henry Sidney. They include his appointment for life as the king's "otterhunter," with pay for himself and a groom and funds for their dogs. But these rewards, some of them valuable, soon came to an end. On July 7, 1553, Edward VI died in the arms of Sir Henry Sidney.

Under Queen Mary, Sidney escaped punishment for any possible involvement in Northumberland's plot to put Lady Jane Grey on the throne and continued to serve the ruler. In 1555 his sister Frances became the bride of Thomas Radcliffe, Earl of Sussex. Thus the Sidneys had another connection with the peerage, and Sir Henry's daughter Mary grew up with a background of service to the state and of relatives among the peers.

Under Queen Elizabeth in the first year of her reign, Henry Sidney became the lord governor of Ireland, and in 1559 or early in 1560, lord president of the council in the Marches of Wales. In 1578 he was recalled from his post in Ireland, but he was reappointed twice in Wales and held the office there until his death. Historians seem in surprising agreement about the faithfulness and efficiency of his service in both positions—and about the failure of Queen Elizabeth to give him any adequate reward.

The Dudleys and the Sidneys differed in temperament and in values. "The Dudleys were gamblers, opportunists who played for high stakes," as James M. Osborn said; "they were usually either on top of the game or were heavy losers. With this trait they combined a shrewd practicality and a belief in education, both in books and in practical skills. . . . The Dudleys were also personally attractive and brave in battle and in court politics." The Sidneys believed in education, with slightly more emphasis on books; they were no gamblers; they had dignity rising from self instead of rank alone and a large share of personal integrity. They were also a close-knit family with more parental affection than was usual in Tudor times.

Sir Henry Sidney gave sufficient evidence of integrity by his conscientious service in Ireland and Wales, without appreciation from the queen and with a minimum of financial recompense. He continues to receive praise from successive generations of historians. Though his wife Lady Mary was a Dudley, she seemed unlike the Dudleys except for a certain political astuteness. After her marriage perhaps she became more and more like the Sidneys, and her daughter Mary had a way of seeming all Sidney.

The character of Lady Mary Sidney is suggested by the fact that the queen chose her in 1559 as intermediary to deal with Quadra, the Spanish ambassador, and also with the ambassador to Emperor Ferdinand I (successor to Charles V) in negotiations about a possible marriage to the Archduke Charles. This position called for coolness, quickness, and swift decisions about the amount to say or to leave unsaid. The reports of the Spanish ambassador about his talks with her, from early September to mid-November 1559, are available in the *Calendar of State Papers, Spanish.*

Again Lady Mary suggested her worth when she cared for the queen through an attack of smallpox in 1562, contracted the disease herself, and was disfigured for life. Writing to Walsingham in 1583, her husband said: "When I went to Newhaven, I left a full fair lady, in mine eyes at least the fairest; and when I returned I found her as foul a lady as the smallpox could make her . . . scars of which since . . . remain in her face . . . so as she liveth solitarily. . . ." It is said that she went to court only when the queen commanded.

Lady Mary Sidney acted with courage and reason when she wrote Lord Burghley May 2, 1572, pleading that her husband might not be elevated to the peerage because the title had been offered him without added income to support the honor. Several letters written by Sir Henry make clear that the lack of money was a continuing reality. In one from Dublin Castle to Mr. Secretary Cecil, February 24, 1569, he said that no servant in Christendom endured greater toil of mind and body than he and no deputy of a prince was more familiar with penury, since he was "forced to borrow, yea, almost to beg for my dinner."

Lady Mary's letters about lodgings at court have been interpreted as if they were mere feminine whining. But her explanations to Sussex, who was her brother-in-law and also the lord chamberlain, seem reasonable. She asked for hangings because the place was cold and windy and she feared a return of a recent illness. In a second letter she said she had lost her accustomed lodgings, and if the queen sent for her she had to go out through the open cloister. Again, when she wrote her husband's secretary Edward Mollineux in October 1578 that he must find them better rooms, her reasons seemed sound. Her illness kept her in bed much of the time, the queen expected access to her at any time, and her husband required space where men could come to talk business. In a second letter to Mollineux she told him that he must do even better: she named certain people for him to consult, adding that she had never known Hampton Court to be without spare rooms, even when three times the present number were in residence. Again she mentioned her husband's need for space to receive Irish and Welsh callers. It seems safe to suggest that lodgings at court not only involved practical necessities but were also signs of the queen's favor. When

Simier told the queen that Leicester was married and she flew into a rage in July 1579, Mendoza reported to his government that "a sister of Leicester's of whom the queen was very fond" lost her lodgings at court. Apparently he considered that loss worth reporting, and the sister must have been Sir Henry Sidney's wife. It seems reasonable to conclude that when Lady Sidney did battle for better lodgings at court, she was fighting for ordinary physical comforts and also defending her husband's prestige against his political enemies.

The true quality of Lady Mary appears also in a letter her son Philip wrote to his father April 25, 1578, after the father's recall from his position in Ireland. The son advised him not to return at once and not to refuse to return, but merely to use the time till Michaelmas in doing the things he had been asked to do before he came home. Thus his time "comes fully out," and his enemies could not assume they had procured his fall. Meantime his friends at court would be working in his interest. He added: "Among which friends, before God, there is no one that proceeds either so thoroughly or so wisely as my Lady my Mother. For mine own part I have had only light from her." His letter and the other facts given above concerning her suggest that she was an astute, courageous woman fighting her husband's political battles.

Philip Sidney's mature integrity appeared in his defense of his father, *Discourse on Irish Affairs,* in 1577. Integrity motivated him in an encounter with the Earl of Oxford who ordered him off a tennis court because he wished to use it himself. Sidney refused to act on the queen's suggestion that he humble himself to the earl. He told the queen that rank did not justify wrongdoing, that Oxford was a lord but not a lord over him, and that her father had encouraged the gentry to appeal to their ruler against the wrongs committed by noblemen. Again, integrity impelled Philip Sidney to risk the queen's resentment by wording and signing a formal protest against her marriage to Alençon after a number of prominent men had met and discussed the reasons for their opposition. According to Mendoza, the meeting was at Baynard's Castle, a London house of the Earl of Pembroke. As a result of the protest, Sidney was an exile from the court for some months.

To the heredity and environment of the Sidneys, the daughter Mary added qualities of her own: generosity, a sense of equality with any struggling writer, and pleasure in helping others develop.

The facts of Mary Sidney Herbert's life can be summarized briefly as a basis for the analysis of her character and her achievements. The first child recorded for Sir Henry Sidney and his wife Mary Dudley

Sidney was a son Philip born at Penshurst in 1554. Then came three girls: Margaret and Elizabeth, who died early, and Ambrosia, who was born at Hampton Court in 1560 and died in 1574. Mary, the only daughter who survived to a mature life of some years, was born in Worcestershire, Wales, at Ticknell Castle near Bewdley, October 27, 1561. (Henry VII had enlarged Ticknell when he sent Prince Arthur to Wales as nominal head of the government there. With Ludlow Castle it was used as another residence, and Sidney and his successor used it in the same way.) Two sons came after the birth of Mary: Robert in 1565, who survived Mary five years; and Thomas, born in 1569, who lived to be married but died in 1595.

No definite facts are known about the education of the daughter Mary, but no one has reason to doubt that she was educated. Private tutors may have been employed for her and Ambrosia, but not for her and Philip, since he began to attend Shrewsbury when she was three years old. Probably she had a good training in Latin because it was implied in the standards of the time and of the Dudleys and the Sidneys. Her translations in her mature life proved her sound knowledge of Italian and French. She may have learned some Greek, studying it with Philip; for when Estienne dedicated an edition of the New Testament to him, he commented that Philip's knowledge of Greek made a translation for him superfluous. But no evidence indicates that Mary ever used Greek.

Since the family was in Ireland about 1570 and 1571 and probably for another period later, spent time at Ticknell and Ludlow in Wales, and lived part of the time at historic Penshurst in Kent, it would be interesting to know how these places affected Mary's development. But we have no details.

Possibly her mother made a great contribution to her education, though the statement must rest on conjecture, not fact. However, the mother's astuteness and general character offer some evidence. When Lady Sidney was acting as the queen's intermediary in 1559, Quadra reported that she could converse in Italian with him. M. W. Wallace noted that Thomas Hoby sent to her husband, presumably for her use, *An Epitome of the Italian Tongue* (his own compilation, used in translating Castiglione's *Courtier*); that the greetings she sent in April 1573, in a letter to Burghley, to three Cooke sisters (Mildred, Anne, and Elizabeth) suggest a strong friendship for women of learning; and that Geoffrey Fenton's dedication to her, in 1557, of *Certain Tragical Discourses* may indicate that she was interested in the literature of her own time. The quotations she and her husband wrote in their copy of Edward Hall's *Chronicle* (the copy now owned by the Folger

Shakespeare Library) imply a knowledge of French and Latin and a concern with philosophical ideas. Since Lady Mary Sidney lived "solitarily" whenever she could after her attack of smallpox about 1562 (when her daughter was less than two years of age), it seems likely that a close relationship existed between mother and daughter until Mary was about fourteen and left for the queen's court. And the mother certainly had the time, the learning, and the wisdom to plan the daughter's education.

Important dates in the life of Mary Sidney Herbert were 1574 to 1577, 1586, and 1601. About 1574 her sister Ambrosia died. Apparently Leicester called the queen's attention to the charm and beauty of the only remaining daughter of the Sidneys. In February 1575 the queen wrote one of her gracious letters of condolence on the death of Ambrosia; if Sir Henry wished to remove his other daughter from the "unwholesome air" and send her to court, she would give the girl her special care. So Mary came to court. By December 1576 rumors circulated about a marriage between Mary Sidney and Henry Herbert, Earl of Pembroke. Again Leicester furthered plans for the union and is said to have paid part of the portion. Pembroke had "stipulated" £3,000, an extremely large sum for the time, and her father had some difficulty in arranging for it. He paid £1,500 on December 5, 1577, according to one authority, £1,000 on December 18 (borrowing for the purpose from his brother-in-law James Harrington), and he made the final payment of £500 on February 3, 1578. If these facts are correct, the marriage was solemnized before any of the portion was paid, April 21, 1577. The bride was about sixteen years of age.

Of course the relatives of Mary Herbert became frequent visitors at Wilton House. In June 1577 Leicester paid a visit to his niece. From August 21 to September 5, her brothers Philip and Robert were there, and Philip was writing from Wilton, it is said, about December 18. Again in 1580, from March to August, Philip spent much or all of his time at Wilton House, though he and his sister may have gone occasionally to Ivychurch, a smaller residence in Wiltshire. In 1580 Philip felt himself an exile from the court. Under the urging of his sister he began *Arcadia*.

The first child of the Herberts, born April 8, 1580, was named William. The queen was his godmother; the Earls of Warwick and Leicester were godfathers, with Philip Sidney acting as a deputy for Leicester. Catherine, born October 15, 1581, died at Wilton on October

16, 1584, the day after her third birthday. A second daughter, Anne, was born March 9, 1582; the exact date of her death does not appear in the available records, but the last mention of her presence at any public event was in 1603. A second son, Philip, born October 10, 1584, and apparently named for his uncle, survived to inherit the title from his brother in 1630. All four children were born within a period of about four and a half years. The Herberts were more fortunate than the Tudors in the survival of sons.

The year 1586 was one of great losses for Mary Herbert. Her father died May 5, her mother August 11, and her brother  Sir Philip Sidney died of his wound at Zutphen on October 17. We have no record of her personal grief, but some suggestions will be made later about its possible relation to the use of her time in the years that followed and to the subjects stressed in her translations. Other deaths followed soon after: in 1588 the Earl of Leicester; in 1590 the Earl of Warwick. With their deaths she lost her close links with the Dudleys. Perhaps it was easier for her to reconcile herself to the death of her parents because of their disappointments and her mother's chronic illness. But her brother Philip, after two or three years of marriage to Frances Walsingham, with no sons and one daughter, had died at thirty-two, leaving his literary work unpublished and his genius unfulfilled.

After the death of Sir Henry Sidney, Mary's husband, the second Earl of Pembroke, succeeded him as head of the government in Wales. During his service he wrote letters from Ticknell Castle, Bewdley, Cardiff Castle, and Ludlow. In 1589 he was complaining because he had been ordered to spend half the year at Ludlow. Whether his wife joined him in Wales seems uncertain.

From about 1586 or at least from 1588 to 1590, Mary Herbert began a period of literary work, translating from the French and the Italian, completing the Psalms which her brother had begun to turn into Elizabethan lyrics, and editing and publishing all the work, both prose and poetry, that her brother Sir Philip had left unpublished. The details of that work will be discussed later as a part of her literary contribution to the world. There is no evidence that she did any publishing, translating, or writing before her brother's death or after 1600.

From about 1595 Mary Herbert must have been concerned with problems of her own and her husband's health. Details appear in letters written by Rowland Whyte to Robert Sidney, Mary's brother. About 1595 Whyte wrote that when the earl paid a visit to court, the queen "used him very well at his departure," and sent "my lady your sister a jewel." If "my lord of Pembroke, who is very 'pursife' [asthmatic] and 'maladif' [sickly] should die, the tribe of Hunsdon do lay wait for the wardship of the brave young lord.''

On November 22, 1595, Whyte reported that Lady Pembroke had been dangerously ill from a swelling in the throat, and Dr. Goodrich, it was said, "went down" to lance it. In June 1598 Pembroke was petitioning the queen to let him retire from his office in Wales because of his infirmities. On September 8, 1599, Whyte wrote that Pembroke was sick again, "I fear of his old disease''; on September 12 he was dangerously ill, but the next day he was out of all danger. At Michaelmas he wrote that Goodrich had brought about a great cure. Though it seems clear that Dr. Moffett was the physician in residence for the family, possibly Goodrich was summoned from London at his request. On January 5, 1601, the older son William was writing Robert Cecil about his father's illness, and on either January 18 or 19 Pembroke died. William, not twenty-one till the following April, succeeded his father as Earl of Pembroke.

Whether Mary Herbert remained at Wilton House after the death of her husband until the marriage of her son William in 1604 seems uncertain. As he came of age about three months after his father's death, he could then legally take over his share of his father's property. She is said to have been there in 1603 when the king came, but evidence seems uncertain. But sometime between 1601 and 1604 she ceased to be mistress at Wilton, and if her "little university" had not ended sooner, it must have been terminated within those years.

After James came to the throne, the Dowager Countess of Pembroke and her daughter Anne attended the Feast of the Garter about July 9, 1603. William Herbert, Earl of Pembroke; Henry, Prince of Wales; and three other young noblemen became members of the order. The daughter had been provided for in her father's will but was never mentioned after 1603. She was about twenty-one at that time and unmarried; perhaps she was frail or had some other handicap or, as the daughter of a wealthy earl, she would probably have been married by sixteen or earlier. At the same feast the countess and her daughter did homage to the new queen. The Countess of Pembroke, with several other countesses, was in the procession when the king, queen, and prince went from the Tower to Whitehall on March 15, 1604. But two items of 1605 and 1606, indexed under her name by John Nichols in *The Progresses,* clearly belong to her daughter-in-law Mary Talbot Herbert. The first noted that the Lord and Lady Pembroke appeared at court; the second, in a letter to the father of the young countess, described her beautiful dancing in the presence chamber.

Both sons of Mary Sidney Herbert were married in 1604. William's wife Mary was the daughter of Gilbert Talbot, Earl of Shrewsbury, and his wife Mary Cavendish and hence the granddaughter of Bess of Hardwick. During the same year Philip was secretly betrothed, "without the knowledge of his or her friends," to Susan de Vere, the granddaughter of Lord Burghley. In a letter to his own father-in-law, William Herbert reported that Robert Cecil had been much troubled over the betrothal, but the king had intervened (perhaps because Philip Herbert was one of his favorites) and had brought the affair to an amicable settlement. On December 27, 1604, Philip Herbert and Susan de Vere were formally married.

From 1609 to 1615 Mary Sidney Herbert held a lease from Lord Northampton on the famous Crosby Hall, then in Bishopsgate, London. In reporting the lease, Charles W. F. Goss said that her residence in Aldersgate, Pembroke House, was not then appropriate for her use. In 1615 King James granted her Ampthill Park in the southern part of the parish of Houghton Conquest about six miles from Bedford. Using a beautiful situation on top a hill, she erected a mansion, Houghton House, known for a time as one of the finest in the county, but later a ruin. Inigo Jones is said to have been her architect. In the center of the west front "a bear and ragged staff . . . and a collared and chained porcupine" made clear its connection with the Dudleys and Sidneys. Her son Philip is said to have inherited from her a reversionary interest in the place but surrendered it to the king about 1623.

Mary Sidney Herbert spent much of her time in 1615 and 1617 at a spa on the Continent in the hope of improving her health. Dr. Matthew Lister may have attended her there as her physician, thus leading to a false rumor that the two had been married. Perhaps the rumor grew also from facts about the acquisition of Ampthill Park. Early in the reign of James I the property was held by Sir Edmund Conquest as keeper. "In 1615 he made over his interest in it," said Daniel Lysons, "to Matthew Lister and Leonard Walstead, trustees for the celebrated Mary, Countess of Pembroke, . . . who holding the park under the crown . . . built a splendid mansion. . . ."

Mary Sidney Herbert died at her house in Aldersgate, London, in 1621, probably on September 25, though authorities name different days of that month for her death. John Chamberlain reported that she died of smallpox and that the body was carried toward Wilton "with a great show of coaches and torchlight," but whatever he said of her may need verification. However, she was buried in Salisbury Cathedral along with other members of the Sidney and Herbert families, probably "in the choir . . . directly above the steps leading up to the high altar."

To sum up facts about the life of Mary Sidney Herbert is comparatively easy. The next task is more difficult and may be a form of rushing in where angels fear to tread — an evaluation of her life in terms of the satisfaction or even the happiness she found. But the task may be undertaken without dogmatic conclusions.

By Tudor standards, in an age when the premarital emotions of the bride and groom were not considered important, probably the marriage of Mary Sidney to Henry Herbert was satisfactory and may even have been happy. By conventional standards Mary was making a brilliant marriage: she became a countess with financial security or even affluence. The age difference between a bride of sixteen and a bridegroom who was probably in his early forties and physically vigorous was not then considered important. He came of a good family, being the son of William Herbert and his wife Anne Parr, the sister of Queen Catherine Parr. The available record of his personal life contains no excesses in conduct. He had been married twice before, but in an age of many marriages that fact would seem unimportant. His first marriage, to Catherine Grey, sister of Lady Jane, had been a political arrangement; after the failure of the plot to put Lady Jane on the throne and the executions that followed, he pleaded that the marriage had never been consummated and secured an annulment. His second wife, Catherine, daughter of George Talbot, Earl of Shrewsbury, had died in 1575 without issue. Thus he had no direct male heir — another practical Tudor consideration.

Sir Henry Sidney's eagerness for the marriage suggests that it gave promise of being desirable, since he was a man of the highest integrity, and he and his wife apparently had more parental affection than was usual in the period. Though in difficult financial circumstances, Sidney borrowed money and is said to have accepted a gift from Leicester to meet the large portion Herbert had stipulated. Sidney's letter to Leicester, February 4, 1577, was filled with gratitude; he was so happy at his dear child's advancement, he said, "that I would lie a year in close prison rather than it should break." And if God and all the powers of earth "would give me my choice of a husband for her, I would choose the Earl of Pembroke."

Henry Herbert and Mary Sidney had enough interests in common to make some basis for a good marriage. He was a man of culture, having been educated at Peterhouse, Cambridge, and perhaps at Douay. He was a patron of antiquaries and a collector of heraldic manuscripts, it is said, and from about 1589 to his death in 1601 he had under his protection a group of players. Perhaps he sponsored the university education of Philip Massinger, whose father Arthur had for years been a confidential agent in the household. Although no evidence indicates that his wife had an active interest in English romantic drama or the stage, it might be said that her literary interests came within speaking distance of his fondness for plays, even in an age when plays were not considered literature.

Pembroke must have given both his approval and his financial support to any activities his wife carried on at Wilton House, or she could not have engaged in them at all. In legal theory a wife had no property at all under her control. Occasionally a man gave his wife an allowance to spend as she wished, but the practice does not seem to have been general. Financially and legally a wife was under the guardianship of her husband.

The Earl of Pembroke indicated in his will that he had full confidence in his wife and consideration for her future. The details of his will refute the statement of John Chamberlain (who sometimes sank to the level of a male gossip) that he left her ''as bare as he could.'' Of course she had her dower rights — one-third of her husband's great landed estates. From an inquisition taken at the death of her son William in 1630, Frances B. Young listed the lands held by the Lady Mary, widow of Henry, Earl of Pembroke, ''for her life in satisfaction of her dower.'' A widow could continue to hold such lands, even if she married again. Her husband also left her many special gifts in the will, naming plate, jewels, and ''household stuff'' to the value of 3,000 marks (1,000 marks in each of the three classes of objects) on condition that she be bound to ''my son William and to any two of four persons named hereafter . . . in the sum of 6,000 marks for the safe re-delivery thereof or their value, at my now dwelling house at Wilton . . . within six months after her decease or re-marriage.'' If he had made no such provision, these chattels would have gone to his son, not to his wife. A day or so before he died, he added a codicil to the will, providing that only her own surety should be required for the return of these properties. He also left her a small residence in Wiltshire known as Ivychurch, with all his lands and tenements there for as long as she lived or remained unmarried. It seems to have been a favorite place where she spent occasional periods of time. It was not a part of her dowry, or it would have been hers during her life even if she had remarried. At the close of the will he left to ''the Lady Mary, my well-beloved wife,'' for the period of her life, Devizes Park in Wiltshire. It is not clear whether this was an extra gift or whether he wished to make sure that it became part of her dower. All these detailed provisions indicate thoughtfulness for her, and the change about the surety provisions suggests that his confidence in her increased in his last years.

Even if her married life was comparatively happy because of her husband's conduct and character, she had other sorrows beyond her control. One daughter died the day after she was three years old; the other lived to be twenty-one and made public appearances with her mother in 1603, but it seems that no marriage had been arranged for her. As the daughter of the Earl of Pembroke, who could afford to allow a generous portion, she would have been married at fifteen or sixteen under normal circumstances. To repeat an earlier suggestion, perhaps she had fragile health or some handicap that prevented a desirable marriage. For Mary Herbert, the untimely death of her talented brother Sir Philip was without doubt a tragedy.

The two sons who survived the death of her husband in 1601 were not unmixed blessings. The older son William matriculated at New College, Oxford, about 1593 when he was thirteen, an age that was not unusual in the sixteenth century. But he grew tired of university life and settled in London. Eventually he entered into an illicit relationship with Mary Fitton, then a maid of honor at the court. When the girl's pregnancy became obvious, William admitted his responsibility but refused to marry her. The queen sent him to the Fleet for several months of imprisonment. When the child was born, about two months after William fell heir to the family property and the title, it did not survive.

William's mother must have approved some of her older son's interests. At the first of every year he gave Ben Jonson twenty pounds to use in buying books, as Jonson himself said in his *Conversations with Drummond.* He also bought 251 Greek manuscripts, known as the Barocci collection, and presented them to the Bodleian Library. The man who did these things was not completely unworthy of his mother, as Francis Davidson apparently thought in 1602 when he dedicated to him his *Poetical Rhapsody,* describing him as a worthy son of a peerless mother. His mother surely approved his friendships with other literary men and his patronage of them, in addition to Ben Jonson. The list included John Donne, Samuel Daniel (who had been his tutor), George Herbert (a distant relative), William Browne, Philip Massinger, George Chapman, and John Davies of Hereford. Others dedicated works to him; he became known as a generous patron of many writers.

William Herbert also wrote poems, but they were not published until 1660; then the younger John Donne edited and issued them, thirty years after the writer's death and nearly forty years after the death of his mother. The editor had part of them from the Dowager Duchess of Devonshire and others from musicians Henry Lewes and Nicholas Lanier. In his address to the reader the editor stated that many of the other poems and all of the sonnets had been set to music, the sonnets by the greatest masters of music. The 1660 volume includes poems by Sir Benjamin Rudier (*DNB*, Rudyerd) and poetical debates between him and William Herbert. It seems probable that William's mother knew of some of his poems, since William was about forty years old when she died.

If Mary Herbert's younger son Philip had any interests similar to those of his mother, they were an alleged concern with pictures and a known concern with architecture. But he was certainly not intellectual nor literary. He went to New College, Oxford, with his brother at nine years of age and matriculated at that time. After a brief period he apparently renounced books and universities for the rest of his life. He loved hunting and field sports, he knew dogs and horses intimately, and he was handsome physically. As a result he became one of the early favorites of King James. He continued to receive property grants and other honors (including the title Earl of Montgomery) as long as the king lived. His surly manner never seemed to offend his ruler. Apparently he sometimes flaunted convention by bringing his mistresses into his home, and it was rumored that he became notorious in another way when a page of the king's household switched his face and he did not retaliate; but the rumor does not fit with his reputation for being both foul-mouthed and quarrelsome. Perhaps his second wife, Lady Anne Clifford, described him accurately when she said he was no scholar but was quick of apprehension, crafty, and by nature choleric.

Apparently Mary Herbert's life was reasonably happy. Half her children survived her—not a bad average in that period. One son shared her literary interests. Her husband aided her in creating an intellectual and literary center at Wilton. She received praise from able contemporaries for her translations (especially for her poetic versions of the Psalms) and for her personality; she had expressions of respect and gratitude from the writers she assisted; these tributes seem warmly sincere.

Mary Sidney Herbert, Countess of Pembroke, made an important contribution to the literary life of her period when (with the support of her husband) she developed Wilton House as an intellectual and literary center. It seems impossible to find out how and when she began this service. It may have been a gradual evolution, or she may have thought of the plan after the death of her brother to help her adjust to the loss and to honor his memory. She received dedications before 1586, such as the one from Thomas Howell in 1581 and the one from

Gervase Babington in 1583. But neither suggested that she had helped his literary development, and the work of Babington was theological; so far as we know it did not include poems, plays, or other secular work. But Howell had by some means discovered that she had an urge to help many people. Writers who dedicated work to her because they lived and studied at Wilton House usually dated their work in 1588 and later. Though these statements do not prove that she opened Wilton House to other writers because of her brother's death, they do suggest the interesting possibility.

The earliest available statement about Wilton House as a place where writers learned their craft is that of Samuel Daniel, who probably became a resident there about 1590. He made the statement in 1603 when he dedicated his own work, *A Defense of Rhyme,* to Mary's son William, then Earl of Pembroke, and was explaining how he began to use rhyme:

> Having been first encouraged or framed thereunto by your most worthy and honorable mother, receiving the first notion for the formal ordering of those compositions at Wilton, which I must ever acknowledge to have been my best school, and thereof always am to hold a feeling and grateful memory.

Another contemporary, Walter Sweeper, made the most reliable and definite statement of all about the activities at Wilton House when he published his *Brief Treatise* in 1622. He described Thomas Moffett as a physician, his own worthy friend, and one of the "distinguished guests" that had made Wilton House "a little university." His statement is broad enough to cover scientists and literary men of all kinds and the interests of both Mary Herbert and her husband. From other sources we learn that Moffett had studied medicine in Basel, became a member of the College of Physicians in England, was a pioneer in chemical medicine and in entomology, though his *Insectorum . . . theatrum* was not published for some years after his death. One might suppose that the Earl of Pembroke persuaded him to come to Wilton House because he wished to have a resident physician; but if so, Moffett soon became concerned with other interests of the family. At the end of 1592 he was writing *Nobilis,* a life of Sir Philip Sidney intended to inspire to virtue the older son William — though it seems doubtful whether he completely succeeded in that aim! At the close he added, "At Wilton, the Calends of January . . . 1593." He gave the biography in manuscript to William Herbert as a New Year's gift, and it remained in that form until 1940. In it Moffett paid a rare compliment to William's mother when he discussed the reactions of Sir

Philip not long before his death in 1586. Sidney could have borne the news of his parents' death, Moffett thought, if he had received no other bad news; but it was reported to him also that his sister was mortally ill—"such a sister . . . as no Englishman, for aught I know, had ever possessed before."

In 1599 Thomas Moffett dedicated *The Silkworms and their Flies* to Mary Herbert, using a three-stanza poem for the purpose and characterizing her as a noble nurse of learning and a renowned patron. He began:

> Vouchsafe a while to lay thy task aside:
> Let Petrarch sleep; give rest to sacred writ;
> Or bow or string will break if ever tied.
> Some little pause aideth the quickest wit.

In the third stanza he begged her, humorously or seriously, to give aid to his subjects:

> I sing of little worms and tender flies,
> Creeping along or basking on the ground.
> Grace't once with thy heavenly-humane eyes,
> Which never yet on meanest scholar frowned . . .
> Deign thou but breathe a spark or little flame
> Of liking, to enlife for aye the same.

Though Moffett published his work in 1599, it is not possible to deduce with certainty that Mary Herbert was translating Petrarch and working on the Psalms in that exact year; probably the dedication was written about that time or a little earlier. Neither is it possible to assert with no shadow of doubt that Thomas Moffett, physician and entomologist, turned poet because of his association with her, but it seems likely.

When the Earl of Pembroke made his will about 1601, he left Moffett an annuity of a hundred pounds, twenty pounds a year for a livery gown, and an additional sum for medicines if he continued to act as a physician for members of the family. Aubrey stated, without citing evidence, that Moffett spent his last years at Bulbridge, a manor house owned by Pembroke. After the earl's death in 1601, Moffett survived him till 1604.

Years later, John Aubrey was following the lead of informed contemporaries Sweeper and Daniel; and thus his statements, taken with a grain or two of salt, may deserve consideration:

> In her time Wilton House was like a college, there were so
> many learned and ingenious persons. She was the greatest
> patroness of wit and learning of any lady in her time. She was a

> great chemist and spent yearly a great deal in that study. She
> kept for her laborator in the house Adrian Gilbert . . . half-
> brother to Sir Walter Raleigh, who was a great chemist in those
> days. . . . She also gave an honorable yearly pension to Dr.
> Moffett. . . . Also one . . . Boston, a good chemist . . . and she
> would have kept him but he would have all the gold to himself
> and so died, I think, in a gaol.

While other direct evidence is lacking for Mary Herbert's interest in chemistry, indirect evidence is available because her brother studied it. In *Nobilis,* Moffett said of him: "Astrology alone . . . he could never be so far misled as to taste, even with the tip of his tongue." But "with Dee as teacher and with Dyer as companion, he learned chemistry. . . ." John Dee also recorded in his *Diary* two visits of Philip Sidney to himself—on January 16, 1577, with Leicester and Dyer; and on June 15, 1583, when a Polish prince came to honor Dee and was attended by Sidney, Lord Russell, and others. Mary Herbert may have provided a "laborator" and equipment for her brother years earlier, and she may have become interested in the science herself.

Aubrey also records that Mary Herbert brought together at Wilton House "a noble library of books." It has also been said that they included books of history and polity as well as the chief Italian poets. These statements all seem reasonable; they are in part supported by her literary interests, her translations from Petrarch, and perhaps by the interest of Abraham Fraunce in Tasso. Later, the books were dispersed, and one might be tempted to point a finger of suspicion at Philip Herbert, who inherited the title in 1630 from his brother William. But instead, the great fire of 1647 at Wilton House may have consumed the books; for it destroyed all the structure except the east front and most of the contents of the building.

Writers who were helped by Mary Herbert and lived for a time at Wilton House included Gervase Babington, Nicholas Breton, Samuel Daniel (whose comment was mentioned earlier), and Abraham Fraunce.

In 1583 Gervase Babington dedicated to her *A Brief Conference betwixt Man's Frailty and Faith.* He had been sent from Cambridge as a tutor, he may have been a chaplain first, and he became a friend of the whole family. His works, published after his death in 1615, carried a dedication to the sons, but he praised the lady mother and also the father for the way he had governed the family.

Nicholas Breton's dedications, like many others, expressed friendship, personal attachment, and gratitude. In 1592 he addressed her in *The Pilgrimage of Paradise Joined with the Countess of Pembroke's Love.* Her noble virtues, he said, "the wise no less honor than the learned admire, and the honest serve." He likened her to the Duchess of Urbino, describing himself as "your poor unworthy named poet, who by the indiscretion of his youth, the malice of envy, and the disgrace of ingratitude, had utterly perished (had not the hand of your honor revived the heart of humility)." He felt sure that "the judgment of the wise and the tongues of the learned" would clear him of any suspicion of flattery. In the second part of his work he emphasized the idea that the real love of the countess was heaven with eternal life.

Breton was almost certainly speaking of Wilton House in *Wit's Trenchmour,* 1597, in his comparison of the home of a lady to a little court with "God daily served, religion truly preached, all quarrels avoided, peace carefully preserved, swearing not heard of, where truth was easily believed, a table fully furnished, a house richly garnished, honor kindly entertained, virtue highly esteemed, service well rewarded, and the poor blessedly relieved."

In 1597 and in 1601 Breton addressed other brief dedications to Mary Herbert. In *A Divine Poem,* 1601, he again characterized her as one whom "the wise admire, the learned follow, the virtuous love, and the honest serve." He closed by saying "in all humble thankfulness for your bountiful undeserved goodness, praying for your eternal happiness, I take my leave." About this time Pembroke died and his wife ceased to be the real mistress of Wilton House; though Breton lived till about 1626, his connections with Mary Herbert apparently ended.

Samuel Daniel, who went to Wilton House as a tutor for William, possibly about 1590, became a protégé and dedicated a number of works to the countess. In 1592 an edition of his sonnets, *Delia,* had a prose dedication to her, and a second edition adding an ode and *The Complaint of Rosamond* repeated the dedication. He said in part, "I desire only to be graced by the countenance of your protection, whom the fortune of our time hath made the happy and judicial patroness of the Muses. . . ." A 1594 edition carried also a dedicatory sonnet to her. When he published his tragedy *Cleopatra* in 1594, he prefaced it with a long dedicatory poem beginning, "Lo, here the labour which she did impose"; he added that her "well-graced *Antonie*" had long remained alone, desiring the company of his *Cleopatra.* In his introductory fourteen-stanza poem he predicted that she would be known for her work on the Psalms after Wilton House had been leveled to the ground; this dedication was repeated in an edition of 1623, *The Whole Works . . . in Poetry.*

Daniel dedicated to Mary Herbert a prose work also, *The First Four Books of the Civil War between the Two Houses of Lancaster and York,* concluding his remarks by stating that he had been revived by her goodness, held himself ever bound to her and her noble family, and would labor to do them honor and service. His expression of gratitude to Mary Herbert for training him in the use of rhyme, with his admission that Wilton had been his "best school," was mentioned earlier.

Abraham Fraunce was aided by several members of the Sidney-Herbert families, including the countess. He attended Shrewsbury School, but some years after Philip Sidney had been a pupil there, and apparently with Sidney's help, he entered St. John's College, Cambridge, where he resided for perhaps five years. Called to the bar at Gray's Inn, he practiced in the court of the Marches of Wales, doubtless with the help of the Sidneys. After the death of Sir Philip, he came under the patronage of Sidney's sister and thus dedicated most or all of his poetic work to her. As he was one of those who tried to use classical meters in English verse, his poems are in hexameters. They seem awkward and unreadable today, but his contemporaries placed a high value on his work.

Though Fraunce lived until 1633, his poetic work was published about 1587 to 1592, apparently about the time when he was being assisted by Mary Herbert. His dedications to her began in 1587 with *the Lamentations of Amintas for the Death of Phyllis,* a work he described as "paraphrastically translated out of Latin into English hexameters." At this time he said, "Mine afflicted mind and crased [diseased, infirm] body, together with other external calamities have wrought sorrowful and lamentable effects in me that for this whole year I have wholly given over myself to mournful meditations." Then he continued to give reasons for making his translations and for using the meter he had chosen. In 1588 he addressed to her his *Arcadian Rhetoric* signing his Latin lines, "Your honor's most affectionate, Abraham Fraunce." In 1591 he dedicated *The Countess of Pembroke's Emanuel* "To the right excellent and most honorable Lady, The Lady Mary, Countess of Pembroke," closing with the same phrasing. Also in 1591 he published *The Countess of Pembroke's Ivychurch* . . . and in 1592 *The Third Part of the Countess of Pembroke's Ivychurch entitled Amintas Dale,* again dedicating to her.

The Earl of Pembroke, having succeeded Sir Henry Sidney in the government of Wales, recommended Fraunce to Lord Burghley for appointment as queen's solicitor in the Court of the Marches, but he was not given the position. Sometime in the early 1590s Fraunce entered the service of the Earl of Bridgewater. The reason for his leaving Wilton House remains uncertain.

In addition to the preceding comments concerning activities at Wilton House, Mary Herbert received an amazing number of other tributes to her writing or her personality. Some were informal comments within articles not devoted to her exclusively, and one was in a letter; others were formal dedications. They were usually in restrained language, not romantic flattery; they have a way of seeming sincere; instead of soliciting future favors, they convey affectionate gratitude for what she had already done. Exceptions, perhaps, were Nathaniel Baxter and Robert Newton. In 1606 Baxter (Philip Sidney's tutor in Greek twenty-five years or more earlier and known to him as Tergaster) dedicated to her *Philip Sidney's Ouranis,* with metrical addresses to other members of the Sidney and Herbert families. And in 1620, Newton, author of *The Countess of Montgomery's Eusebiae,* referred to Susan de Vere Herbert in his title; but on his title page he named Mary Herbert first and added names of others connected with the family. Possibly Baxter and Newton hoped for rewards. In some instances we do not know why an author (for example, Thomas Morley, who published *Canzonets,* songs for three voices, in 1593) chose to address his restrained dedication to Mary Herbert.

Interesting comments that were not formal dedications include those by Thomas Nashe, Gabriel Harvey, Francis Meres, and Sir John Harington as well as a poem by Sir Benjamin Rudier on her picture. Nashe's comment appeared in the first edition of *Astrophel and Stella,* in a prefatory article with the title "Somewhat to Read by them that List" and was signed by him. His wording is not typical of the tributes to her, but it illustrates comment within an article. He spoke of the many goodly branches that overshadow grief at the loss of Philip Sidney: "amongst the which, fair sister of Phoebus and eloquent secretary of the Muses, most rare Countess of Pembroke, thou art not to be omitted; whom arts do adore as a second Minerva and our poets extol as the patroness of their invention; for in thee the Lesbian Sappha with her lyric harp is disgraced. . . . Learning, wisdom, beauty, and all other ornaments of nobility whatsoever, seek to approve themselves in thy sight and get a further seal of felicity from the smiles of thy favor."

For once, Nashe seemed to realize that his rhetoric was getting out of control, for after a one-line Latin quotation he said, "I fear I shall be counted a mercenary flatterer for mixing my thoughts with such figurative admiration, but general report that surpasseth my praise condemneth my rhetoric of dullness for so cold a commendation."

Gabriel Harvey praised her in *Pierce's Supererogation* in 1593. He said, "though the furious tragedy *Antonius* be a bloody chair of estate, yet the divine *Discourse of Life and Death* is a restorative electuary of gems.'' He did not expressly name her, he added, ''not because I do not honor her with my heart, but because I would not dishonor her with my pen, whom I admire and cannot blazon enough.''

Francis Meres, in *Palladis Tamia* in 1598, described her as ''learned . . . liberal unto poets; and besides, she is a most delicate poet. . . .'' He may have seen manuscript copies of some of her Psalms, or perhaps she wrote other poems that were never published with her name attached. Sir John Harington, writing to Lucy, Countess of Bedford, December 19, 1600, sent her ''the divine and truly divine translation of three of David's Psalms done by that excellent countess, and in poesy, the mirrois [sic] of our age.'' He tactfully added that she and the countess he was addressing were alike in blood and degree and were not unlike in appearance and those gifts of the mind that clothe the nobility with virtue. Harington also wrote an epigram on women named Mary, beginning with his wife and ending with Mary Herbert.

Sir Benjamin Rudier, who may never have known her personally but was an associate of her son William, entitled a poem ''On the Countess of Pembroke's Picture.'' His poem appeared in the 1660 edition of poems by William Herbert and also some by Rudier.

> Here (though the lustre of her youth be spent)
> Are curious steps to see where beauty went;
> And for the wonders in her mind that dwell
> It lies not in the power of pens to tell.
> But could she but bequeath them when she dies,
> She might enrich her sex by legacies.

Among others who paid tribute to Mary Herbert, but not in formal dedications, were Charles Fitzgeoffrey in *Affaniae* in 1601 and Sir John Stradling in *Epigrammatum* in 1607; each devoted to her an epigram in a collection of them. William Smith, probably in the late sixteenth century, wrote a poem as a tribute to her; and he added poems to make a ''posie'' of flowers from her ''devoted servant'' to the ''right noble, honorable, and the singular good lady, the Countess of Pembroke.'' His ''posie,'' still in manuscript, was noted by Frances B. Young in the British Museum. Daniel Rogers, poet, diplomat, and man of scholarly tastes, addressed lines to her picture before his death in 1591; but his poem is not available.

John Taylor included her as the subject of sonnet five in a series of sonnets, *The Needle's Excellency*. The date of his first edition is unknown, but in speaking of her he used the past tense. His sonnet to her· began:

> A pattern and a patroness she was
> Of virtuous industry and studious learning.

It ended:

> She wrought so well in needlework that she
> Nor yet her work shall ere forgotten be.

William Browne (1591-1643), who lived at Wilton House presumably when her older son was master there, wrote an elegy on Mary Sidney Herbert some time after her death if the first line is a literal statement: "Time hath a long course run since thou wert clay." Though Browne was praised by such contemporaries as John Davies of Hereford and Ben Jonson, his elegy is a long, pedestrian poem. Reading it impels one toward accepting Ben Jonson as the more probable author of the well-known epitaph — the most beautiful poem written about her.

From the formal dedications to Mary Herbert a few will be selected for brief discussion. Others are listed in *The Index of Dedications* by Franklin B. Williams, Jr. The earliest was *Devices* in 1581 by Thomas Howell, appearing when she was nineteen or twenty years old, the year after the birth of her first child. Howell mentioned her desire to benefit many people, her virtuous life, rare wisdom, honorable courtesy, and sweet behavior. Similar qualities were often mentioned in future comments on her, not because others copied Howell, it seems, but because they observed her.

John Davies of Hereford honored Mary Herbert in several different publications. In *Microcosmos* in 1603 he added, at the close of his volume, poems addressed to leaders of Scotland and England, several poems addressed to other members of the Herbert family, and one addressed jointly to Mary Herbert and her daughter Anne. In *Other Essays* Davies published two sonnets honoring "the right noble and well-accomplished lady, the Dowager Countess of Pembroke." In the first of the two he wrote:

> If aught be fair or right in me, it is
> Not mine but thine, whose worth possesseth me;
> If I be all amiss, I all assign
> To shame and sorrow, sith no part is thine.

Davies also addressed three women in *The Muses' Sacrifice* in 1612 as "the most noble and no less deservedly renowned ladies, as well darlings as patronesses of the Muses, Lucy, Countess of Bedford, Mary, Countess-Dowager of Pembroke, and Elizabeth Lady Carey (wife of Sir Henry Carey), glories of women.'' He added pages of quatrains for ''the heavenly three.''

Other outstanding writers praised and thanked Mary Herbert. When Edmund Spenser published the first three books of the *Faerie Queene* in 1590, he directed to her one of the seventeen sonnets at the close of the work; the memory of her brother, he said, commanded him to worship that ''goodly image in her face,'' but she embellished the resemblance with her own special virtues. In 1591 when he dedicated to her ''The Ruins of Time'' in *Complaints,* he admitted that he was bound to her ''by many singular favors and great graces.'' In his elegiac poem for her brother, *Astrophel,* he complimented her as the sister Clorinda, ''The gentlest shepherdess that lives this day.'' He also included what he called her doleful lay, though he probably wrote that part of the poem himself. However, he dedicated the whole poem to Sidney's widow, who had become the Countess of Essex. Again in *Colin Clout's Come Home Again,* Spenser praised Mary Herbert as Urania, the sister of Astrophel, for her brave mind with its heavenly graces and ''in her sex more wonderful and rare.''

John Donne joined those who valued the literary work of the countess when he wrote his poem ''Upon the Translation of the Psalms by Sir Philip Sidney and the Countess of Pembroke, his Sister.'' He mentioned the poor versions used in churches and in England and the better ones used in private homes and on the Continent. He concluded:

> So though some may, some have some Psalms translate
> We thy Sydnean Psalms shall celebrate.

Perhaps no one was better fitted than John Donne, clergyman and poet, to comment on versions of the Psalms.

It may be safe to conclude that no other woman in Renaissance England was praised as often, as sincerely, and by as many people for qualities she possessed and for both personality and literary work as Mary Herbert, Countess of Pembroke.


Mary Herbert also persuaded her brother Sir Philip to begin his writing — and that was a service to literature. The time was 1580. He felt himself exiled from the court because he had written the defense of his father's work in Ireland, had refused to humble himself to Oxford after the quarrel at the tennis court, and had worded and signed the letter with the objections of important Englishmen to their queen's marriage to Alençon. His plans for the future had failed to interest the queen. She had not rewarded Sir Henry Sidney for his service. Sir Philip must have known of other difficulties that were leading up to the frank letter his father wrote Walsingham in 1583, when the question of Philip's marriage to Walsingham's daughter came up. In that letter Sir Henry explained his lack of money. He spoke of his losses years earlier on his first trip to Ireland—losses of all his "household stuff and utensils," his wife's clothing and jewels, and many horses with "stable stuff." In 1583, he told Walsingham, he was £5,000 in debt and worse off by £30,000 than he had been at the death of Edward VI.

So from about 1578 to 1580, Sir Philip Sidney brooded over his own and his father's problems. In a letter to Hubert Languet, March 1, 1578, he described his attitude, which doubtless had a mixture of melancholy: he accused himself of slothfulness, of avoiding self-examination, of inability to write, and of playing the stoic, adding that he would become a cynic unless Languet reclaimed him. One biographer, M. W. Wallace, said of him at this period, "Always inclined to melancholy, he now felt utterly depressed by Elizabeth's failure to show any adequate appreciation of his father's services or to be really interested in his own plans." Wallace added, "Sidney's inaction and consequent gloom are reflected in all we hear of him."

It seems almost certain that in 1580 Mary Herbert would have known the main facts about the queen's neglect of her father, even if her father and brother tried to conceal the difficulty in paying her portion—as they might well have done. It seems equally certain in 1580 when her brother was spending weeks of time at Wilton House, that she would discover the chief reasons for his melancholy and his absence from court. And it seems safe to conclude that she shared her brother's concern. Few records if any suggest that Mary Herbert, though she was Countess of Pembroke, attended court while Elizabeth was queen. When her husband paid a visit to court in 1595, Rowland Whyte reported to Robert Sidney that the queen treated him very well "at his departure" and sent "my lady your sister a jewel." His report carries a faint suggestion, at least, that the earl's visit was unusual. Perhaps we need no stories from gossips to explain the absence of Mary Herbert from the court of Elizabeth but only need facts about the Sidneys and the queen. It is a matter of record that Mary Herbert and her daughter made appearances at court after James came to the throne.

It also seems evident that in 1580 Mary Herbert would wish to divert her brother from his melancholy. That the *Arcadia* was written or mostly written in those weeks or months at Wilton House is generally accepted as fact, and when Philip Sidney dedicated the work to his sister he explained her influence on its composition:

> But you desired me to do it, and your desire, to my heart, is an absolute commandment. Now it is done, only for you, only to you: if you keep it to yourself or to such friend who will weigh errors in the balance of good will. . . . For indeed, for severer eyes it is not, being but a trifle, and that triflingly handled. Your best self can best witness the manner, being done in loose sheets of paper, most of it in your presence, the rest by sheets sent unto you as fast as they were done. . . . And so you will continue to love the writer, who doth exceedingly love you, and most heartily prays that you may long live to be a principal ornament to the Sidney family.

Eventually Mary Herbert assumed the task of editing and publishing all her brother's literary work after his death. Though her establishment of Wilton House as a center for literature touched many lives, her publication of her brother's prose and poetry gave the world in satisfactory form the work of a greater writer than any she had aided at Wilton House. Recalling that the first edition of *Arcadia* had been unfinished and that the early edition of *Astrophel and Stella,* issued without her help, was filled with errors, one might safely conclude that she did much for his reputation and performed a service for the world. Perhaps her supervision of his work for publication was her greatest service to literature.

The first work by her brother that she guided through the press was *Arcadia.* In 1588, two years after the death of Sir Philip Sidney, it was entered in the Stationers Register for publication. One day Ponsonby, a responsible bookbinder, came to Fulke Greville, who had been an intimate friend of Sidney, to warn him that someone meant to bring out the older version of the work and to ask if this was being done with the consent of Walsingham or other friends. Greville then sent Sidney's widow, at her request, a corrected copy, "fitter to be printed than the first, which is so common," and even it was "to be amended by a direction set down in his own hand." Sidney had started revising the work, but his revision seems not to have progressed beyond the middle of the third book. As a result, Ponsonby published a first edition in 1590, probably with the help of Greville, possibly with some of Greville's editing and his chapter divisions. But the work broke off within Chapter III.

Another edition, called the authorized one, was published in 1593 under the direction of Sidney's sister. The "Address to the Reader" with it was signed H. S., no doubt indicating Henry Sanford, a long-time secretary to the Earl of Pembroke, acting for Mary Herbert. The writer of the address said that "the disfigured face" with which the work had been published earlier had "moved that noble lady to whose honor it was consecrated, to whose protection it was committed, to take in hand the wiping away of those spots wherewith the beauties thereof were unworthily blemished." Readers should also understand "that though they find not here what might be expected, they may find nevertheless as much as was intended, the conclusion, not the perfection of *Arcadia,* and that no further than the author's own writings or known determinations could direct. . . . But . . . it is now by more than one interest the Countess of Pembroke's *Arcadia,* done as it was for her, as it is, by her."

Probably Mary Herbert acted as honestly as she could in issuing the authorized edition. As Sidney's revision had not progressed beyond the middle of the third book, she left unfinished several stories that he had added in the rewriting. She completed the third book and added the fourth and fifth books from the earlier version. If she left out chapter divisions that had appeared in the first edition, she probably believed them to be the work of Fulke Greville.

In 1591, five years after Sidney's death, Mary Herbert came to the rescue of *Astrophel and Stella.* It had been published "from a circulating manuscript by Thomas Newman, who later in the same year printed a second version (altered in some 350 places) based on a manuscript either supplied or approved by the Sidney family." According to Jack Stillinger, Lord Burghley ordered the first edition confiscated, presumably at the request of the family or of Mary Herbert. The earlier version is full of garbled phrases or misprints. In sonnet 31 the moon climbs the sky with a *mean* face instead of a *wan* face; in sonnet 39 sleep is addressed as the *bathing* place, not the *baiting* place of wit; and in sonnet 102 a line reads "How doth the color fade of those vermillion *eyes,*" instead of *dyes.* Though there may be a question about the exact date of the second edition, whether it was also in 1591 or a little later, there is no doubt about its comparative value. Again, for this corrected edition, we are indebted to Mary Herbert.

In 1595 two editions of *The Defense of Poesy* were published. One, issued by Ponsonby, was apparently edited with care and was described as "the first authorized edition." Again the person responsible was undoubtedly Sidney's sister. In 1598 another volume of his work came from the press. It contained *Arcadia,* with Sidney's dedication to his sister and the address to the reader signed by H. S.; certain poems called sonnets that had not been published before; *The Defense of Poesy;* the *Astrophel and Stella* sonnets in their final form; and a minor work *The Lady of the May,* earlier presented to the queen at Wanstead. All these works in a final authorized form we owe to the Countess of Pembroke. It is a large debt.

The literary production of Mary Herbert consisted entirely of translations, one work published with her name, the "Dialogue between Two Shepherds in Praise of *Astrea,*" being a mere trifle. Even her versions of the Psalms, which she made into individual Elizabethan poems, were translations in the strict sense, since she made every effort to express the original thought. Also all her own literary work, so far as we know, was done within a period of fifteen years after the death of her parents and her brother. All of it, excepting some of the Psalms, dealt with death. If Sir Philip Sidney had lived for a normal length of time, would Mary Herbert ever have done any literary work, either editing and publishing or translating from the French and Italian? It is an interesting idea, even if it must remain a speculation.

She signed her translation of Mornay, *A Discourse of Life and Death,* on May 13, 1590, at Wilton. She signed her *Antonius,* a translation of *Marc Antonie* by Robert Garnier, November 26, 1590, at Ramsbury. The two were published in 1592 in one volume with one title page. Though we do not know when she began the work, translations such as these are not usually done in haste. She may have planned and started translating or at least mulling over the work soon after she heard of her brother's death. The Mornay especially may have developed from her personal struggle to adjust to the accidental death of a man so young, gifted, and beloved as her brother had been. Philip Sidney and Mornay had become close friends. They met first on the Continent through Hubert Languet. In 1577 when Mornay came to England to ask help from Queen Elizabeth for the French Protestants, an intimate friendship developed between the two men. When Mornay returned in 1578 for a longer stay, bringing his family, Sidney stood as godfather for his son. It is highly probable that Sidney's sister also became acquainted with the Mornay family. About this time Sidney began to translate another work by Mornay, *De veritate Christiana;* but being busy, he asked a scribe, Arthur Golding, to finish it. In 1587 the scribe published it as *A Work concerning the Trueness of the Christian Religion.* While Mary Herbert was translating *A Discourse of Life and Death,* it was possible for her to recall memories of a time when her brother was alive and to find consolation for her loss in Mornay's ideas, since the essay developed both Stoical and Christian philosophies about the acceptance of death. Her translation began:

> It seems to me strange . . . that the laborer to repose himself hasteneth as it were the course of the sun, that the mariner rows with all force to attain the port . . . and that we in the mean while, tied in this world by a perpetual task, tossed with continual tempest . . . cannot yet see the end of our labour but with grief, nor behold our port but with tears, nor approach our home and quiet abode but with horror and trembling.

Toward the close of her translation she said:

> To end, we ought neither to hate this life for the toils therein, for it is sloth and cowardice, nor love it for the delights, which is folly and vanity, but serve us of it, to serve God in it, who after it shall place us in true quietness. . . . It is enough that we constantly and continually wait for her [death's] coming, that she may never find us unprovided. . . .

Mary Herbert's *Antonius,* signed in the same year and published with the translation of Mornay, was probably not chosen for the same personal reason; it dealt with death, but in a quite different way. It may have grown from an interest in classical drama, and it came early in a series of Senecan dramas translated in the 1590s. Thus it was important in the reaction of intellectuals against romantic drama, a reaction that Philip Sidney had possibly furthered by his discussion in *A Defense of Poesy.* Samuel Daniel, following her in 1594 with his *Cleopatra,* clearly indicated that he was translating it at her suggestion; in 1605 he wrote *Philotas* on the same Senecan principles. By 1594 Thomas Kyd had translated *Cornelia,* another tragedy by Robert Garnier, signing his dedication to the Countess of Sussex as T. K. He had promised to put Garnier's *Portia* into English, it is said, but if so, apparently his death in 1594 prevented him. Though he followed the Senecan tradition in the plays that are mentioned here and perhaps in an early version of *Hamlet,* no available evidence indicates that he came under the personal influence of the Countess of Pembroke.

Mary Herbert also translated the first and second chapters of Petrarch's *Trionfo della Morte* as *The Triumph of Death.* Though she was reproducing the ideas the original author had expressed, at least she chose the material. The only definite date connected with her work is 1599, when Thomas Moffett, dedicating to her *The Silkworms and their Flies,* asked her to "Let Petrarch sleep, give rest to sacred writ." In the first chapter of her English version death appears as a woman in black, ready to destroy youth and beauty, and with innumerable victims in the past—civilized nations, barbarians, people in every period of history; popes, kings, and emperors, forced to leave behind them all the honors they had struggled to gain in this world, with even their names forgotten. Thus the ideas are personal and universal; they resemble those in *A Discourse of Life and Death.* Again, the material may have been chosen by the translator in an effort to temper her own losses. Unlike other early translators of the *Trionfo,* she used the difficult terza rima; and though Frances B. Young admits that her phrases were sometimes obscure, she adds that the countess was faithful to the thought of the original.

Evidence that Mary Herbert had poetic talent depends largely upon her translation or poetic recreating of the Psalms. It is generally agreed that her brother's work included only forty-three Psalms, and that she changed the other hundred and seven into Elizabethan poems. He may have begun his work at any time after 1580; he probably finished by 1585 when he went to the Low Countries. She may have settled to serious work on them about 1587 or 1588 (there is no definite evidence); she must have made real progress by 1594 when Samuel Daniel praised her work, predicting that it would outlast Wilton House. She probably completed them about 1599 or 1600, judging partly from Moffett's mention about 1599 and partly from the statement that she sent the queen a complete manuscript with a dedication in 1599. Also J. C. A. Rathmell, the recent editor of the Psalms, estimates that she had begun her work by 1593 and had completed it before 1600. Though the Psalms were passed about in manuscript, were known to John Donne, and may have influenced George Herbert's *Temple,* they did not appear in print until 1823; the modern edition with the excellent introduction by Rathmell was published in 1963.

During the reign of Elizabeth, Psalms were versified and issued for use in churches because both Anglicans and Puritans approved them. By 1562 *The Whole Book of Psalms* had been published, and one hundred fifty editions eventually appeared. But they were utilitarian versions. The Psalms of the Sidneys, as Rathmell said, were literature; they had "energy, intensity, and emotional piquancy"; they emphasized an allegorical significance and used a variety of forms, adapting the form to the emotion of a particular Psalm. They resulted from an effort to use all the resources of the Elizabethan lyric; and both the Sidneys, Rathmell concluded, tried to create for each one "a unique combination of stanza pattern and rhyme scheme'' adapted to the individual Psalm.

Neither of the Sidneys, according to Rathmell, knew Hebrew; and though Philip knew Greek well enough to read it easily without a translation, neither needed Greek for work on the Psalms. They compared versions in the psalter of the Prayer Book with the two current English versions of the Bible (the Geneva Bible of 1560 and the Bishops' Bible of 1568). They also used the elaborate commentaries on the Psalms; those of Beza had been translated into English by Gilby and those of Calvin by Golding. Mary Herbert especially often expanded an image because the commentaries gave her the right to do so. Of course the *Vulgate* was available, but Rathmell did not mention it; and they would probably not have considered using the version authorized by the Catholic church. However, they may have read Beza in French. In Rathmell's opinion, the work that ''most obviously served as a model to the Sidneys is the French psalter of 1562,'' a collection based on fifty Psalms that Clement Marot composed between 1532 and 1543 and that Beza completed at Geneva in 1562.

Informed critics express the view that the work of Mary Herbert with the Psalms was superior to that of her brother. In the nineteenth century A. B. Grosart had said that the Psalms she created are ''infinitely in advance of her brother's in thought, epithet, and melody.'' Quoting him, Rathmell added that ''they demand to be considered not only in the context of Elizabethan psalmody, but as significant and attractive poems in their own right.'' Again he said, ''The Countess has, in a devotional sense, meditated on the text before her, and the force of her version derives from her sense of personal involvement; she has taken into account Calvin's interpretation of the verse, and it is her capacity to appreciate underlying meaning that vivified her lines.'' Quoting from *The Poetry of Meditation* by Louis L. Martz, Rathmell agreed with his statement that the work of the Sidneys was ''the attempt to bring the art of the Elizabethan lyric into the service of psalmody, and to perform this in such a way that it makes the psalm an intimate, personal cry of the soul to God.'' The comment, he added, ''applies . . . with even greater force to the Psalms of the Countess of Pembroke.''

Mary Sidney Herbert, Countess of Pembroke, one may conclude, should be remembered for her gracious, generous personality, her services to other writers, including her brother, and her own poetic talent. Perhaps she deserved the epitaph written for her by either William Browne or Ben Jonson:

> Underneath this sable hearse
> Lies the subject of all verse,
> Sidney's sister, Pembroke's mother.
> Death, ere thou hast slain another,
> Fair, and learned, and good as she,
> Time shall throw a dart at thee.

# CHAPTER SIX

# *Margaret Beaufort,*
# *Countess of Richmond and Derby*
## 1443-1509

When Margaret Beaufort is judged by her character and her own achievement, she seems one of the most remarkable women of the Tudor Age. Though she did not know Greek and deplored her lack of Latin, she was a literary woman. She became a patron of printers, a translator from the French, a publisher of works she translated, and a reader of religious and secular books. Though she never ruled in her own right, she did much to establish her son Henry VII on the throne, exerted some influence on his rule, and held positions requiring an unusual degree of executive ability. Her many-sided contributions to the public welfare leave no doubt that she was an outstanding woman of her period.

Margaret was the great-granddaughter of John of Gaunt; and like

SOVVENT ME SOVVIENT

Though the identity of this portrait of Margaret Beaufort was long questioned, restoration has convinced experts of its authenticity.    Right: Facsimile of signature as "M Rychmond."

Right: Coat of arms of St. John's College, Cambridge. In founding this college, Margaret Beaufort made her greatest single contribution to liberal education.

Opposite: Torrigiano effigy of Margaret Beaufort in Westminster Abbey.

the other immediate descendants of Catherine Swynford, was called Beaufort from her grandfather's birthplace, Beaufort Castle in France. Catherine had been the caretaker of John of Gaunt's children by his first wife, Blanche of Lancaster; then the mistress who bore him four children outside wedlock; and finally, about 1396, his third and legal wife. She was a woman of dignity, social training, and probably literary interests. After her marriage to John of Gaunt, the pope issued a bull making her four children legitimate, and in 1397 Parliament confirmed their new status.

John of Gaunt's oldest son, John Beaufort, had a son John who became the first Duke of Somerset, but he died in 1444 leaving his infant daughter Margaret as his heiress. She became the ward of William de Pole, Duke of Suffolk; but after his death in 1450, Henry VI granted her wardship to his half-brothers Edmund and Jasper Tudor. They were sons of Catherine of France (widow of Henry V) by Owen Tudor, clerk of the wardrobe. Edmund, who may have been born out of wedlock, had been given a declaration of legitimacy and also the title, Earl of Richmond. Seldom has so much real dignity developed from so much illegitimacy.

Because of Margaret's age at the death of her father and of her first guardian, she apparently remained with her mother in their Bedfordshire home. There she received a good education for that time—reading, writing, keeping accounts, the management of a household, small Latin, and facility in French. When the time for marriage approached, she was left almost entirely to her own decision. Praying to St. Nicholas, the patron saint of maidens, to guide her, she had a dream, sleeping or waking, she did not know which—only that a bishop appeared and advised her to accept Edmund Tudor. She did so. They were married in 1455 when she was about twelve years old, if the accepted date of her birth is correct. In 1456 her husband died of the plague. Henry, a posthumous son, was born in January 1457 in Jasper Tudor's castle of Pembroke, Wales.

When Henry VI died in 1471, Margaret's son Henry automatically became head of the house of Lancaster, when he was fifteen years old. His mother gave the boy into the care of his uncle Jasper Tudor, who promised to guard him as his own son—and kept that promise. But after sieges, captures, and escapes from the ruling Yorkist forces, Margaret encouraged the uncle to take Henry out of the country. Going by boat from Tenby, Pembrokeshire, they were driven by a storm to the coast of Brittany. She did not see her son again for about fourteen years, when he returned to become Henry VII.

Meantime Margaret Beaufort lived her own life and waited. About 1459 she was married again, this time to Henry Stafford, a younger son of the first Duke of Buckingham; he died about 1481. Her third husband was Thomas Stanley, a trusted minister of Edward IV, whom she married about 1482 or 1483. He survived until July 1504. When Richard III took over the throne, he sent Stanley to the Tower; but soon, realizing his need for powerful friends, the king freed him again and appointed him steward of the royal household. Both Stanley and the Lady Margaret were summoned to attend Richard's coronation, and she was to carry the train of the new queen. As the royal robes were made of forty-eight yards of crimson velvet trimmed with miniver, decorated with buttons, silk, and gold tassels, and covered with a mantle of lace, her work was no light duty. But if she had refused to attend, death or imprisonment would have kept her from helping her son become king.

Eventually Margaret Beaufort became a woman of action, risking property and life to put her son on the throne. Her first positive but subtle action seems to have been a talk with the second Duke of Buckingham. The duke had joined Richard and had been great chamberlain at his coronation. But some three months later he quarreled with the king; perhaps he heard that the little princes had been killed in the Tower. According to James Gairdner, he was brooding about trying to claim the throne for himself. On his way back to Wales, he had a chance meeting with Margaret Beaufort. Through talking with her, he "suddenly remembered" that she and her son had a better right to the throne of England than he had. She may have had the tact and the self-effacement (as her biographer Enid M. G. Routh suggested) to persuade Buckingham that he was developing his own thoughts. At least he soon had what he considered a wonderful idea: let Henry Tudor marry Elizabeth, the daughter of Edward IV, and thus unite the rival houses of York and Lancaster.

Buckingham went on to Brecknock Castle after his talk with Margaret Beaufort. There he had a long talk with his prisoner, John Morton, then Bishop of Ely. The two men began to work with Margaret and with Reginald Bray, receiver-general and steward for the Staffords — and the plot was under way. Margaret was to do two things: communicate with Queen Elizabeth (the widow of Edward IV) who did not dare leave her sanctuary in Westminster, and secure secretly from Henry in Brittany his solemn oath to marry her daughter.

For the first task she used Doctor Lewis, a physician in Wales who had his medical training at Padua. As a physician he had access to the queen if she needed him, and having had word that her sons had been murdered in the Tower (it is said) and being frantic with grief, she had great need of help. Thus the consent of both mother and daughter for the marriage was secured. For her second duty Margaret used Chrisopher Urswyck, a priest in her service who made trips to the Continent. She sent a large sum of money to her son and suggested that he land in Wales.

Meantime Buckingham was gathering men to help Henry when he landed. But in 1483 when he tried to enter Milford Haven in Pembrokeshire, storms kept him from any effective action. He retreated. Buckingham's army was made useless by floods along the Wye and the Severn. He was captured and was executed at Salisbury.

Margaret Beaufort was also in trouble. An Act of Parliament declared her guilty of treason. But Richard, remembering again his own need for friends, remitted her attainder, disabled her from holding property, and made her the prisoner of her husband, Lord Stanley. If she outlived him, her property, saving the interests of others, was to come to the king. Her husband was charged with the duty of secluding her at home and preventing her contact with servants or any others who might help her communicate with her son.

After the second entry into England in 1485, when Henry was victorious at Bosworth Field and Richard III lay dead at his feet, it is said that Reginald Bray found in a bush nearby the crown that the king had been wearing on his helmet. Lord Stanley put the crown on the head of his victorious stepson while the soldiers shouted for King Henry. Perhaps Henry's mother had not found her confinement too irksome and had not been unduly hampered in aiding her son on his second venture into England!

Those who helped put Henry on the throne were well rewarded. As both architect and statesman, Sir Reginald Bray became a trusted member of the Council, made improvements in St. George's Chapel at Windsor, and probably designed the beautiful chapel of Henry VII in Westminster Abbey. Christopher Urswyck was sent on diplomatic missions, was dean of York from 1488 to 1494, and dean of Windsor from 1495 till his death in 1522. Lord Stanley was continued in all his offices and also became Earl of Derby.

Margaret, now Countess of Richmond and Derby, received many material rewards as well as the king's gratitude and affection. Parliament repealed the earlier act that had taken away her property. That body passed another act giving her the right to operate "by the name of Margaret, Countess of Richmond," as if she were a feme sole, and to handle all her property herself, although her third husband was living and by law all her property should have been under his complete control as long as the marriage lasted. Queens had been granted the right to operate as feme sole, but no other instance of a king's mother being granted the privilege seems to exist. Later Henry gave his queen the right to manage property as if she were a feme sole, but the grant lacks the detail and the enthusiasm of the one to his mother. The law for his mother provided that she might "sue all manner of actions real and personal . . . plead and be impleaded for all manner of causes in all manner of courts, spiritual and temporal . . . "; that she might take and receive "feoffments, leases, releases," and any number of other things; and that no action was to be "voided or voidable by reason of coverture." To the layman, at least, the details seem to cover everything, as they were doubtless meant to do.

Margaret also received far more than an annulment of her previous disabilities. In March 1487 her son issued letters patent granting her innumerable holdings in Devon, Somerset, Derby, York, Northampton, Rutland, Lancaster, Westmorland, Cambridge, Essex, Hertford, Suffolk, Lincoln, and Dorset as well as a residence in London. The volumes of the *Calendar of the Patent Rolls, Henry VII* (where these property grants are listed) are filled with special licenses or grants of all kinds by the king to his mother—the right to found chantries, to have the custody of lands and the wardship of the little Duke of Buckingham and his younger brother, to hold fairs at a Devonshire manor, to make the next appointment to a canonry or to a prebend, or to hold for life another manor.

One of the many chantries she founded was at Wimborne Minster in Dorset. It provided prayers for her soul and the souls of her parents, other ancestors, and all Christian souls. The chantry was placed at the tomb of her parents, beside the altar. Henry VII issued letters patent for it in March 1497. Henry VIII confirmed the original grant in 1509, with additional funds of six pounds a year, and in 1511 added funds of eleven pounds a year. By the deed of 1511 the chaplain, Richard Hodgekynnes, was to reside within the college, opposite the room of the sacrist and "to teach grammar to all comers after the form and manner used at Eton and Winchester."

Margaret and her son exchanged letters suggesting unusual affection, as an undated one from the king indicates when he wrote to grant her request that she be allowed to use her funds at Cambridge instead of Westminster:

> Madam, my most entirely well-beloved lady and mother, I recommend me to you in the most lowly wise that I can. . . . And, my Dame, not only in this, but in all other things that I may know should be to your honor and pleasure and weal of your soul, I shall be as glad to please you as any heart can desire it, and I know well that I am as much bounden so to do as any creature living, for the great and singular motherly love that it hath pleased you at all times to bear toward me. Wherefore, mine own most loving mother, in my most hearty manner I thank you. . . .

Writing to her son in 1501, Margaret said:

> My dearest and only desired joy in this world, with my most hearty loving blessings and humble commendations, I pray our Lord to thank and reward your grace. . . . I now pray almighty God to give you as long, good, and prosperous life as ever had prince, and as hearty blessings as I can ask of God. At Calais town, this day of Saint Anne, that I did bring into this world my good and gracious prince, king, and only beloved son.

She signed the letter "Margaret R." as she signed other letters also. Some scholars have concluded that she meant "Margaret Regina." A. F. Pollard cited a letter so signed and added a footnote pointing out that she had no right to this royal signature. In a recent note to *Moreana,* E. E. Reynolds made a similar comment. But sometimes, perhaps in more formal letters, she signed as "Margaret Richmond," doing so when she thanked the Earl of Ormonde, who was then chamberlain to the queen, for his gift to her of a pair of gloves. Letters seem to indicate that the Lady Margaret was humble in relation to her son, she was not insensitive to people and situations, and she was capable of grasping legal rights. Enid M. G. Routh stated in her biography that without question the signature meant "Margaret Richmond." Perhaps she was right.

The forceful personality of Margaret has contributed to erroneous conclusions about the meaning of her signature. Foreign observers of the English court often credited her with great influence. Among them were Ayala, the Spanish ambassador to Scotland, and another Spanish gentleman who was writing to Ferdinand and Isabella. Speaking of the Stanleys about 1503 or 1504, Garrett Mattingly remarked that their "real head" was the king's mother; he said also that she exerted an influence against Catherine of Aragon, whom she had never approved as a bride for Prince Henry and whom she treated "with open hostility." But her attitude did not prevent the marriage.

Though no clear evidence indicates that Margaret tried to influence her son's major decisions as king, she had a place of honor when she appeared at court, and she was arbiter of court etiquette. About 1486 she prepared "Ordinances against the deliverance of a queen and also for the christening. . . ." About 1493 the king commanded her to reform the dress of all royalty and of other ladies and gentlemen for a period of mourning. The rules she formulated stated in great detail "the size, form, material, and ornaments of the hoods, trains, surcoats, tippets, mantles . . . of the various ranks of gentlewomen." The details of her own dress were to be like those of the queen.

Usually she attended any great ceremony at court. She was present when Prince Henry became Duke of York in 1494. For the occasion she traveled from Sheen to Westminster with the king and the queen; in the formal procession her husband, the Earl of Derby, carried the cap of estate and she walked next to the queen. She also attended the jousts held to honor the prince and his new title. After the marriage of Prince Arthur and Catherine of Aragon in November 1501 she gave a magnificent dinner party at her London house, Cold Harbor, to honor the high-ranking Spanish nobles. The dining hall was decorated with beautiful tapestries, the service included gold and silver plate, the food and the wines were excellent and abundant, and an English guest was seated beside each Spanish one to act as a personal host or hostess. In January 1502, the Lady Margaret attended the formal betrothal of her older granddaughter Margaret to James IV of Scotland. In July 1503 when the girl was fourteen and was going to her wedding in Scotland, her father took her to Collyweston, Northamptonshire, to say good-by to her grandmother. No doubt the king's mother attended most formal affairs at court as well as christenings or other family affairs.

Margaret Beaufort was an extremely religious woman; it may have been a religious scruple that motivated her opposition to the marriage of her second grandson to Catherine of Aragon, widow of Arthur. In addition to founding many chantries, with prayers for souls, she was admitted into the fraternity of at least five religious houses—Westminster, Crowland, Durham, Wimborne, and the London

Charterhouse—and she had the prayers of others. Her special patronage of religious houses included the Carthusians at Sheen, the Observant Franciscans at Greenwich, and the Bridgettines at Syon House; these houses stressed integrity of life. At Syon House, from the influence of Richard Reynolds and Richard Whitford, learning was equally important.

Since Margaret had extensive holdings of lands, she often found herself involved with ecclesiastical bodies in lawsuits. She sometimes lost in these suits, as she need not have done if she had been willing to bring pressure. Charles H. Cooper cited an example of the suit she carried on against Richard Ashton, Abbot of Peterborough; the abbot recovered many annual payments for manors she held. The management of her household had strong religious connotations. She not only kept twelve poor people in her household—providing them with food, drink, and clothing—but she also talked with them often, giving them evidence of a personal interest. At her own expense she provided learned men to administer justice for many people who had called upon her asking such help. She had said many times, Bishop Fisher reported, that if the Christian princes would only make war on the enemies of the faith, she would follow the armies and help to wash their clothing, all for the love of Jesus. The bishop said of her that she possessed all that is worthy of praise in a woman, "either in body or soul," and that she was noble by manners, by blood, and by nature— the last kind of nobility being a tendency to noble deeds found sometimes even in those of humble parentage.

In her observance of religious rites she tended to be medieval in some attitudes. She not only kept the fasts but she also wore hair shirts and girdles that pierced her skin. While her third husband was still living, she secured from him a promise to let her adopt a chaste life and made a vow of chastity before Bishop Fitzjames. After her husband died in 1504, she renewed her vow before Bishop Fisher, who had first become her chaplain and then her confessor. Mentioning these details in the sermon for her month's mind, the bishop added that she kept her soul ordered to God by much prayer and weeping, by confession as often as every third day, and by receiving communion about a dozen times a year. Her concern for the future life was indicated by other chantries and by her establishment of three priests in Westminster Abbey to pray for her soul perpetually.

Margaret may have exerted a religious and also an artistic influence on her son to complete King's College Chapel, though the evidence is only circumstantial. In 1506 when she and the king were traveling together, they visited Cambridge University. At this time the structure, begun by Henry VI, was about half finished and was not yet covered by a roof. After other formalities the party went in solemn procession to visit the incomplete chapel. With Fisher in charge of the service, they attended Mass there. About three years later when Henry was making plans before his death, he gave £ 5,000 then and directed his executors to advance later, from time to time, funds for the "perfect finishing" of King's College Chapel. It seems a fair inference that his mother exerted a tactful influence, and that without her he might not have provided the money to complete the beautiful building.

Margaret Beaufort was a patron of the arts, the printing of books, and varied educational activities. Like many persons of rank, she had a group of minstrels who traveled under the protection of her name. In 1491 the treasurers of Cambridge in their accounts with the corporation listed fivepence for red wine given to the minstrels of the king's mother. And on February 18, 1494, the expenses of the king's privy purse included ten shillings for her minstrels; in 1497 "the king's mother's poet," whose name is not given, received more than three pounds from the king. According to James Lees-Milne, she was the patroness of a song writer named Farthing—probably the Thomas Farthing who lived from 1475 to 1520 and is listed among the alumni of Cambridge as a composer and singer in her private chapel. Though he went to the chapel royal with Cornish about 1508, she left him an annuity. She was also the patroness of a musician named Aston— probably the Hugh Aston, living from 1480 to 1522, who was an ecclesiastic and a composer for the virginal and who received university degrees in 1505 and 1507. "His position in music is one of considerable importance. . . ." He may be the Sir Hugh Ashton described as a controller of Margaret's household, an executor of her will, and the receiver of an annuity mentioned in her will. In a period when men spelled their own names in several different ways it remains uncertain whether Aston and Ashton were the same man, but it seems likely that they were.

Lady Margaret exerted much influence on the translating and editing of books and was a patron of three printers—Caxton, Wynkyn de Worde, and Pynson. Though most of the books she sponsored were religious, two were secular. *Blanchardine and Eglantine,* printed by Caxton in 1489, was one of the two; but only a fragment of it remains. Through an extract from the dedication, Caxton may tell his own story:

> Unto the right noble . . . puissant princess, my redoubted
> lady . . . mother unto . . . Henry VII . . . I, William Caxton,
> his most indigne [humble] subject and little servant, present
> this little book I late received in French from her . . . and her
> commandment . . . to . . . translate into our . . . English
> tongue, which book I had long to fore sold to my said lady and
> knew well that the story of it was honest and
> joyful. . . . Wherefore at the . . . request of my said lady,
> which I repute as for a commandment, I have reduced this said
> book out of French into English. . . .

The other secular book was *The Great Ship of Fools of this World,*
published in Paris in 1509 by Wynkyn de Worde. In the prologue we
learn that Henry Watson had translated it from French into English at
the request of the printer but "through the enticement and exhortation
of the excellent Princess Margaret. . . . Grandame unto our most
sovereign lord, King Henry the VIII. . . ."

Margaret also owned secular books. Among them were the
second volume of Froissart, described as a great book of vellum covered
with black velvet; a great book of vellum "named John Bokas,
lymed" — perhaps Boccaccio or Lydgate in an illuminated manuscript;
the story of the siege of Troy in English; and another vellum book of the
*Canterbury Tales*. She also received a bequest of books about 1480 from
her mother-in-law, Anne Stafford, Duchess of Buckingham. The gift
included an English book of saints legends, a French book containing
"Lucan" and other classics, a French copy of the epistles and the
gospels, and a prayer book with clasps of silver gilt and a binding of
purple velvet. Among the books she owned, other writers have named a
French book of vellum with a varied collection of stories, an illuminated
book of Genesis, and a printed French copy of the Magna Carta. Thus
her tastes were varied, and compared with other book owners of the
period she owned and read many books.

The religious works published through the influence of the Lady
Margaret included one dedicated to her by Caxton in 1491, beginning *O
Jhesu . . . ,* and *This Treatise concerning the Fruitful Sayings of
David . . . ,* consisting of seven sermons delivered by Bishop Fisher
and published by Wynkyn de Worde in 1508 at the request of the Lady
Margaret. Other books issued by her influence or dedicated to her
include *Brevarium . . . Hereford* in 1505, published at her expense;
*Scala perfectionis* in 1494; *Brevarium . . . Sarum* in 1507; and *Sermon
for Henry VII* in 1509. The *Scala* has a two-stanza l'envoi explaining
that it was printed in the house of Caxton by Wynkyn de Worde and
that the king's mother directed him to publish the book for her. According to Henry R. Plomer, she commissioned Caxton to publish *The
Fifteen Oes* at her expense.

Margaret is credited with two translations from French into English. One, *The Mirror of Gold for the Sinful Soul,* is listed under Dionysius the Carthusian, who probably translated it from Latin into French. The preface states that it was translated into English by Margaret, Countess of Richmond and Derby, and that the work is divided into seven chapters so that the sinner may have a mirror for his soul each day of the week. Pynson issued an undated edition, followed by other editions by various printers. Her other translation was the fourth book of *De imitatione Christi.* William Atkinson had translated the first three books into English at her "special request and commandment," and she commanded also the publication of the fourth book. The latter is a discussion of the sacrament.

Besides her influence on the publication or translation of books Margaret aided education in varied and generous ways. She was a benefactor to university students. When Bishop Fisher preached the sermon for her month's mind, he stated that among those who had cause to lament her death were "students of both the universities, to whom she was as a mother, the learned men to whom she was a patroness, and the priests and clerks to whom she was a true defenderess." The other evidence of her aid to univeristy students is the letter she wrote from Windsor on January 12, 1493, asking the chancellor and the regents of Oxford University to dispense with the services of Maurice Westbury because she was retaining him to instruct certain young gentlemen "at her finding." Since *finding* means supporting, her request implied that she was paying for the education of these young men, making them a part of her household, and employing Westbury as their tutor. In citing the letter, Charles N. Cooper assumes that the students were living in her residence at Collyweston, Northamptonshire.

Working with Bishop Fisher, Margaret established divinity readerships at Cambridge and at Oxford, thus furthering education in religion. After Fisher became chancellor of Cambridge University in 1504 (a position he held till the day he was executed because the university refused to appoint a successor while he was a prisoner in the Tower), she contributed funds for the divinity readerships he established. These were planned to reform preaching and to educate the common people in religion. Often sermons of the day emphasized many-sided interpretations of a text from scripture; logical subtleties; and many quotations from the classics or from the learned doctors, used for their own sake. Fisher and Erasmus (who worked for several years at Cambridge with Fisher) deplored these tendencies. Men who held the new readerships were trained without cost to themselves and were then sent to London and other cities to preach simple, earnest sermons aimed at changing the lives of listeners. Bishop Fisher and Erasmus, in the years the latter spent at Cambridge working with him, each held one of the readerships for a time. In explaining the whole plan, James Bass Mullinger concluded that it was one of the great ecclesiastical reforms of the century.

Also through the influence of Bishop Fisher, Margaret founded two colleges at Cambridge — Christ's College and St. John's. Gradually she accepted the idea of using her money for these educational centers instead of Westminster Abbey; then she secured the king's consent to the change in the arrangements they had made together. Fisher planned Christ's College, directed its building, drew up the statutes for it, and became a supervisor during his life. He made plans to train promising students in theology and in the liberal studies; he established lectures in dialectics, logic, and philosophy and in the orators and poets. Probably the influence of Erasmus led him to include liberal subjects, for his own early training had been narrow. By letters patent dated May 1505 the king gave his mother the right to refound a decayed institution known as God's House and to name it Christ's College. Several other grants between 1505 and 1507 gave her the right to use certain properties to increase the revenue of the new institution.

To provide funds sufficient for St. John's College later, Margaret added a codicil to her will declaring her intention to dissolve the hospital of St. John in Cambridge; to change it into a college of secular persons (a master, fifty scholars, and essential servants); to build and endow it; and to provide it with all the essentials, from a kitchen to a library. She directed her executors to take the profits of her enfeoffed lands in Devonshire, Somersetshire, and Northamptonshire to carry out the plan; but unfortunately her codicil had no seal affixed to make it legal.

As Henry VII died about three months before the death of his mother, her executors confronted Henry VIII over the will. The question was whether the new king would ratify a codicil depriving him of property, even when Margaret's intention was perfectly clear. Bishop Fisher and seven others, including Bishop Fox, Lord Herbert, three knights, and two clerks were the executors. Fox and one of the clerks, Hugh Aston, were more concerned with Oxford; the knights had little interest in any college whatever; and only one clerk, Henry Hornby, supported Fisher with enthusiasm. The necessary bull from the pope finally came. In August 1509 the king licensed the founding of the new college; but though he permitted fifty fellows and scholars, he limited the revenue to fifty pounds above the amount to be gained from the hospital. Fisher waged almost a one-man fight for the amount Margaret had assigned the college in the codicil of her will. When he brought suit in Chancery under Archbishop Warham, he won a decision. But the crown brought another suit, and the executors gave up their claim. So the bequest she had planned was forever lost to St. John's College. Later the new king did give his permission for the suppression of another decayed God's House at Ospringe, Kent, and the transfer of its revenue to the new college, bringing it an income of about eighty pounds.

St. John's College was opened in July 1515, perhaps with formal ceremonies in 1516, as authorities give both dates. Without Bishop Fisher it would not have been planned, but Fisher was able to act only with the financial support of Lady Margaret. Fisher drew up statutes similar to those he had drafted for Christ's College, placing the same emphasis upon liberal arts, including orators and poets. Fisher was a visitor or inspector; and in 1518 he used his opportunity to appoint as its third headmaster Nicholas Metcalfe, his archdeacon at Rochester. Metcalfe served until 1537. Roger Ascham attended the college under his leadership and praised him with enthusiasm for his encouragement of learning, even though he was a "papist."

Under Metcalfe and Fisher, St. John's became the great center of liberal education in England. Sir John Cheke was educated there. Other St. John's men were William Grindal, a tutor of the Princess Elizabeth for a brief period till his death; James Pilkington; William Bill; and William Cecil. It seems ironical that many of these men became leaders of the new religion, though Margaret Beaufort herself held with tenacity to the old faith. In founding St. John's College she made her greatest single contribution to liberal education. Her total support of education, including her help to university students, her establishment of divinity readerships, and her founding of two colleges at Cambridge probably surpassed that of any other woman in the Tudor Age.

Margaret Beaufort and Bishop Fisher had collaborated from about 1495 until her death in 1509. But in 1527 when he published his work on the sacrament and dedicated it to Bishop Fox, Fisher said that Fox had been the cause of his success—that Fox had recommended him to Henry VII for appointment as Bishop of Rochester. As Fisher was a man of unusual veracity, he probably did not make the statement merely to comfort a fellow bishop in his blind old age. When the king wrote his mother in 1504 asking her approval of his making her confessor a bishop, he seemed to imply that it was entirely his own idea. Fisher had wisdom, cunning, virtue, and other desirable qualities; and since he had promoted many men unadvisedly, he was anxious to make recompense by promoting one who was worthy. But though Henry did not mention any recommendation by Fox, it may still be true that he first suggested the appointment.

With her interest in books and education and her magnificent efforts to further learning, Margaret Beaufort seems to have been a practical business woman who managed well the vast properties her son had trusted to her. She also directed her great household well, as Bishop Fisher stated in his sermon for her month's mind. She drew up careful rules for all to observe and had her officers read them aloud four times a year, with the members of the household assembled to listen. Her son trusted her enough to name her one of the executors of his will. After his death, one of her first actions was to draw up a list of the counselors Henry VII had trusted most and to name a few of them to guide the inexperienced young king as he took over the power.

Probably Margaret Beaufort also held for two years the most unusual executive position of High Commissioner of the Council of the North. In suggesting that such an appointment existed, Rachel R. Reid pointed out that there is no formal record of any appointment from 1507 to 1509 and that the lack of a record might mean the appointment was unusual. Meeting resistance at the beginning of his reign, Henry VII had filled the position up to 1507; Thomas Savage, Archbishop of York, had served from 1502 until his death in 1507. Miss Reid also argued that the cautious king would not have left the office unfilled because he knew well that to do so was dangerous. The area had been hard to control for both geographical and political reasons: great unpopulated, wooded uplands separated valleys with a few inhabitants; three noblemen (the Duke of Lancaster, the Earl of Northumberland, and the Earl of Westmorland) held most of the land; and if they united, they could defy the king. When the uninformed Henry VIII came to the throne, he left the position vacant, and before 1525 trouble had grown into active resistance to taxes. He was forced to plan a firm council with his natural son, the Duke of Richmond, as a nominal head. His experience seems to confirm the belief that his more cautious and informed father would not have left the place vacant from 1507 to 1509.

Positive evidence exists, in addition to the circumstances just summed up, for the belief that Margaret Beaufort was High Commissioner of the Council of the North from 1507 to 1509. In 1529 Thomas, Lord Darcy, framed a petition opposing the commission that had been given to the Duke of Richmond. On the outer leaf of his petition, Lord Darcy wrote:

> Mem., how the like commission that my lady the king's grandam had, was tried and approved, greatly to the king's disadvantage, in stopping of many the lawful processes and course of his laws at Westminster Hall . . . and none gain commonly by any such commission but the clerks. . . .

Lord Darcy had a chance to know the facts when he spoke of the "like commission" given to the grandmother of Henry VIII. He was a contemporary (1467-1537), a northern man with the family seat at Templehurst, Yorkshire, and he had held numerous offices in the north of England. In 1508 he was appointed warden-general of "the marches of England toward Scotland," with the special duty of keeping down fighting or riots; in 1509 he was warden of the forests north of Trent; and in 1511 warden of the east and middle marches. So his information may be sound.

Interesting evidence of some unusual appointment for Margaret Beaufort is furnished by the arguments of certain lawyers associated with Henry VII and his mother. They included Thomas Marowe, Humphrey Coningsby, Robert Brudenell, and Edmund Dudley. Marowe argued that a woman could be appointed a justice of the peace by a commission, whether she was a feme covert or a feme sole, or she could be a "gaoleress" or a sheriff. In a Lenten reading at the Inner Temple about 1495, Coningsby supported the proposition that under certain circumstances widows might appoint justices of the peace. Brudenell insisted, apparently in a reading at one of the Inns of Court, that a woman, but not a monk, could be appointed a bailiff. Edmund Dudley argued at Gray's Inn that the king could appoint as "justices in eyre" two men, whether or not they were trained in the law; two aliens; two "villeins"; or even two women, either married or single. In citing these details, Bertha H. Putnam suggested that the arguments were being used to justify some appointment of the king's mother.

Further indirect support for the idea that Margaret Beaufort had held some unusual position was given by outstanding lawyers during their readings at Inns of Court in the seventeenth century. One of them was William Noye, attorney-general from 1631 and author of *A Treatise of the Principal Grounds and Maxims of the Laws of this Kingdom*. In

August 1632, at a reading on forest law at Lincoln's Inn, the question
was raised whether a woman could be a justice of the forest. The
question led Noye to say that Margaret Beaufort had been a justice of
the peace. He had searched without success for the commission appointing her, but he had found many of her arbitraments. Like Rachel
R. Reid, Miss Putnam suggested that the position was not enrolled
because it was an unusual appointment and not merely that of a justice
of the peace.

Robert Callis — serjeant-at-law, commissioner of sewers for Lincolnshire, and author of *The Reading . . . upon the Statute . . . of
Sewers*—also had a comment on Margaret Beaufort. His material was
used in discussion at Gray's Inn in 1622 but not published until 1647.
Defending the right of women to hold various commissions, he cited
God's order to Adam and Eve in the plural, directed to both of them, as
"the first commission ever granted." It was customary, he said, to
appoint women as executors of great estates and as guardians of
children who would inherit great properties. For certain positions
women "have been secluded as unfit, yet they are not in law to be
excluded as uncapable." From precedents he named, he concluded that
it was warrantable by law to name the Countess of Warwick on the
commission of the sewers. "And the wise and renowned lady,
Margaret, Countess of Richmond, was put in the commission," he
asserted. But he never reached the point of telling us *what* commission
she held.

From the comments of Noye and Callis, one might infer that
neither had seen a record of the appointment given the king's mother
and that the affairs she handled may have been greater than either
realized. Thus the statement of Lord Darcy is the best evidence that for
two years, 1507-1509, she was High Commissioner of the Council of the
North.

The Lady Margaret, Countess of Richmond and Derby, mother of
Henry VII, was a versatile woman, we may conclude — a kingmaker with
political ability, the manager of great estates, and probably for two
years the High Commissioner of the Council of the North. If she held
this last-named position, she was almost the ruler of the northern part
of England. Though she was born too soon to have the chance at a
classical education, she made a many-sided contribution to her times by
her patronage of minstrels, a poet, and musicians; perhaps by in-
fluencing her son to provide funds for completing King's College

Chapel; by the help she gave university students in completing their education; and by her own translations from the French and her encouragement of books and publishers. Her money and her vision, guided by suggestions from Bishop Fisher, led to the establishment of divinity readerships at the universities to reform preaching and thus to change people's lives. She also founded two colleges at Cambridge, again with the help of Fisher — Christ's College and the remarkable St. John's College.

She died on June 29, 1509. She was buried in the magnificent chapel of Henry VII. Erasmus wrote an epitaph for her, and Skelton an elegy. Torrigiano the Florentine reproduced her features in marble, creating a memorial that some consider the most beautiful statue in Westminster Abbey.

*Experts consider this picture by an unknown artist the only authentic large-scale portrait of Catherine of Aragon.*

*Facsimile of the signature "Katherina the Qwene" as appended to a letter written to her daughter Mary about 1525.*

*Below and Right: Catherine enjoyed field sports and often rode to activities such as hawking.*

*Right: Catherine and Henry honeymooned at Greenwich Palace. This view, after a drawing by A. van den Wyngaerde, is from the north.*

# CHAPTER SEVEN

# *Catherine of Aragon*
## 1485-1536

Catherine of Aragon would be judged an unusual woman by anyone willing to grant her the right to follow her own religious beliefs and her own conscience. She belonged to the new breed of women influenced by the Renaissance: she was a classical scholar, and she encouraged scholarship in others. Although she was not a ruler in her own right, she aided in the rule of England as an unofficial advisor to the young Henry VIII and as regent while he was in France. In these political situations and in defense of her position as queen later, she worked with vigorous intelligence. When she could not control outer circumstances because of the king's royal power, she maintained her integrity in spite of imprisonment, privations, bribes, and threats against her life and possibly the life of her daughter.

Catherine was the last child of Ferdinand, the king of Aragon, and his wife Isabella, ruler of Castile. A basis for understanding Catherine lies in an estimate of her mother—vigorous, ambitious, and fanatical in her religious zeal. She won her rule of Castile by force, driving out her niece, who was heir to the throne. She spent ten years (about 1481-1491) expelling the last of the Moors from Spain, often riding at the head of her troops with her personal standard flying, inspiring in them her passionate desire to drive out the infidels. With that work completed, she turned her religious devotion against her Jewish population for what she considered the glory of God. On March 30, 1492, she gave them four months to accept Christian baptism or leave Spain. About two hundred thousand scholars, patrons of arts, engineers, scientists, lawyers, physicians, and bankers went into exile, leaving most of their wealth and a country where their ancestors had lived a thousand years and more. Without their wealth and their loyalty Isabella would never have conquered the last of the Moors.

Both Ferdinand and Isabella had lied, schemed, and fought their way to power; but in joint action the driving force was usually Isabella, "the only reigning queen in the first century of the Renaissance." Probably she dominated the plans for their sons and daughters—plans to give them a liberal education, to train them for future rule, and to arrange gains in power through their marriages. Catherine was no doubt indebted to her mother, by heredity and environment, for the dominant traits of her life—a capacity for cool thinking and decisive action, a deep devotion to religion and her church, and a grim persistence in a course of conduct when she considered it a matter of conscience and the will of God. But the intrigues and lies of her father and mother, by which they enlarged their power, seem to have left her untouched as if she had been protected from their existence. She had to learn the hard way during her early years as queen in England that her father was duping Henry VIII and using him as his political tool.

Catherine was indebted to her mother also for an excellent Renaissance education—a sound classical training and orthodox Christianity, with the full participation of women. Two women lectured on the poets, one at Salamanca and one at Alcala. Isabella secured the best available humanists as teachers; her efforts brought chairs of Hebrew and Greek to Salamanca before they were established at Paris or Oxford.

Catherine and her sisters were trained to be future queens, but they also learned all the humble household tasks—spinning, weaving, baking, cooking, and managing a great household. They were taught to sew, embroider, draw, dance, perform as musicians, ride horseback, handle falcons, and hunt wild game. Since they were to marry into other royal families, they learned heraldry and so-called history. Catherine's classical education included the Christian poets (Prudentius and Iuvencus), the fathers of the church (Augustine, Ambrose, Gregory, and Jerome), the classical philosophers with emphasis on Seneca, the Latin historians, and some civil and canon law. As Hebrew and Greek were being taught at Salamanca, she may have had Greek. Later, both Erasmus and Vives expressed amazement at her classical learning, and on that subject neither man was given to idle compliments. As a result of the education Isabella arranged, Catherine and her sisters were able to answer ambassadors extempore, in correct classical Latin.

Catherine's connection with England began early—so early that her ancestry was partly English through John of Gaunt. As his second wife he married Constance, a daughter of Pedro I of Castile. Their daughter, called Catherine of Lancaster, married Enrique III; their son, Juan II, was the father of Queen Isabella. When Catherine, the daughter of Isabella, was three years old, English ambassadors came to arrange for a marriage between her and Prince Arthur, older son of Henry VII. As Garrett Mattingly has suggested, perhaps she could hardly remember a time when she was not called Princess of Wales. When Catherine was about fifteen and a half, on May 21, 1501, she began the long journey to England. On August 17 she and her huge escort took ship at Corunna. After being beaten back to the Spanish coast by storms, they finally landed at Plymouth Hoe on October 2, 1501.

Henry VII and Prince Arthur met the Spanish party at Dogmersfield, Hampshire, where a state reception and a formal betrothal were held. According to Garrett Mattingly, the king was pleased: "He saw a well-grown girl with a beautifully poised head and sturdy supple body, light step and erect carriage, small hands and feet, clear, untroubled grey eyes, a mass of russet-gold hair, half-framing in the Spanish fashion an oval face as freshly pink and white as any English lady's." After supper that evening Catherine invited the king and the prince to her rooms: "minstrels had been summoned, and after low bows to the king, Catherine and two of her ladies danced one of the stately dances of Spain. Next she and a partner danced a rapid dance, as gay and furious as the other was langorous and slow. . . ." It seemed a good beginning.

They were married in St. Paul's Cathedral, Catherine and the slight fifteen-year-old Arthur, who looked less mature than his sixteen-year-old bride. When the indoor festivities and the tournaments ended, they traveled to Ludlow Castle, where Arthur resumed his nominal position as head of the Council of the West. Soon he became ill, perhaps with tuberculosis and then the sweating sickness. He died April 2, 1502. Catherine was stricken also but recovered after weeks of illness. In the warm weather of summer, attendants took her in a litter to the queen at Richmond.

The seven years from 1502 to 1509 were difficult. Catherine either had a will of iron or she developed one. She was a political pawn between two tightfisted kings. Her parents told her she must get along with whatever funds Henry VII chose to provide. She had been persuaded to renounce her claim for the return of the money already paid on her dowry and for her widow's jointure—one-third of the revenues of Wales, Cornwall, and Chester. For a time Henry paid her £100 a month—hardly half the amount she would have received from her jointure. She was formally betrothed to Prince Henry on June 15, 1503, after he had become Prince of Wales; and later Pope Julius had granted a dispensation for the marriage. When Henry had completed his fourteenth year, they were to marry—if the other half of the dowry was in London ready to be paid. The half was to be 65,000 crowns in gold coins, 15,000 in Catherine's gold and silver plate, and 20,000 in her jewels. Since Catherine had brought her plate and jewels with her to England and had to pawn part of them later to buy food when Henry cut off her allowance, the details of the dowry caused endless bickering. In June 1505 the prince appeared before the Bishop of Winchester and other members of the Council (perhaps at the instigation of his father) and repudiated the contract of marriage—as he had a legal right to do at fourteen. Though Catherine did not know of the repudiation for nearly two years, after she learned of it, she still waited with stubborn persistence. She had come to be queen of England.

Another problem was the difficulty of communicating with her parents in an age when letters were carried by personal messengers. In 1504 Isabella died, and on the day of her death Catherine was writing that she had not had a letter from her father in more than a year. With the death of Isabella, the kingdoms of Castile and Aragon fell apart. Philip the Handsome (through his marriage to Catherine's sister Joanna, now called Joanna the Mad) had inherited the rule of Castile.

Even if communication had been easy, Ferdinand would probably have put his own political desires above the welfare of his daughter.

A constant problem was the bickering between the witty, aristocratic Don Pedro de Ayala, Spanish ambassador to Scotland (who found life in London more desirable) and the blunt, loyal, competent Dr. Roderigo De Puebla, Spanish ambassador to England. Ayala was constantly interfering and complaining to Spain about De Puebla.

A thorny problem for a time was the high-handed control of Catherine's entire household by the duenna Doña Elvira Manuel. But when the duenna plotted to bring about a meeting between Philip the Handsome and Henry VII to the detriment of Ferdinand, De Puebla discovered the facts and revealed them to Catherine. A stormy interview followed between Catherine and the duenna, and the latter left for the Continent. But the king, saying that it was improper for Catherine to live alone, ordered her to join the court, and thus she lost her independence.

Catherine's outstanding problem from 1502 to 1509 was the lack of money. Even when she had her own household at Durham House and was receiving the allowance of £100 a month from the king, that sum barely covered the cost of food, with nothing left to buy new dresses for herself and attendants, new uniforms for the servants, or other necessities. After the death of Isabella, commercial agreements between England and Castile lapsed in August 1505. Hundreds of English returned home bankrupt. Ferdinand refused to intervene because he would not risk his small authority in Castile. In retaliation, Henry cut off his allowance to Catherine entirely; she was forced to pawn her plate and jewels. At times he lodged Catherine's household in outbuildings, over the stable at Greenwich, or in a decayed manor house at Fulham. When Fuensilada, Ferdinand's special ambassador, came in 1508, he reported that he had seen on Catherine's table ''stinking fish such as he would not give his horse boy.'' And because she had no money, Catherine could not provide properly for her Spanish maids of honor, who should either return to Spain or have dowries assigned them for marriages in England. Inez de Venegas, who married Lord Mountjoy later, and Maria de Salinas, who became the wife of Lord Willoughby, remained loyal. Others intrigued, quarrels broke out, living conditions were impossible, and the future seemed hopeless.

What effect these seven years of insecurity and privation had on Catherine of Aragon we can never know fully. But apparently they did not rob her of the ability to enjoy pleasure and deeper happiness later; they probably matured her for her real work as queen and deepened her fortitude for the troubles in the distant future.

From 1509 to about 1527 Catherine was queen of England with no doubt about her status. When Henry VII died on April 21, 1509, the payment of the dowry and the value of Catherine's plate and jewels became unimportant. Henry VIII and Catherine were married about six weeks after the burial of the late king, and they were crowned together June 24, Midsummer Day. Henry was eighteen, and she was midway between twenty-three and twenty-four.

Catherine was slender and graceful, moving with the rhythm of a dancer. Sir John Russell remembered her as beautiful, so beautiful that it would not be easy to find her equal. As Londoners saw her first after the marriage, she was carried to the coronation in a litter of cloth of gold between two white riding horses; her dress was white satin, her long shining hair was hanging down her back — the costume of a virgin bride. She was "beautiful and goodly to behold."

Henry was handsome, with a huge, athletic body. "The face above it," said Mattingly, "was the face of an angelic adolescent, round apple-blossom cheeks just touched with golden down, a crown of ruddy gold hair above features engagingly immature, reminding observers of a cherub in an Italian church." At that time, there is every reason to believe, he was an amiable idealist.

Henry was devoted to Catherine and continued to show his devotion for an almost unbelievable time. He wore her favors in tournaments, he invented allegorical devices to proclaim his worship, he was her "knight of the loyal heart," and he accepted his prizes in the lists only at her hands. At this time she enjoyed fine dresses, jewels, rich colors, splendid furnishings, and elaborate entertainments. She loved music, dancing, hawking, and riding in the chase, as her husband did. He sought her out to share a new book, a newly discovered musician, or the report of a returning ambassador, whom he preferred to receive in her rooms. At that time they shared an interest in literature — theological and devotional books and the classics. Her early education, as well as her reading in the idle years from 1502 to 1509, had given her an excellent background. She was a listener the king could trust; she gave him confidence in himself; she heard with interest his ideas on the kingship. This almost idyllic relationship of Henry and Catherine lasted, perhaps, until 1514 — though it is hard to pinpoint the instant when a prolonged diminuendo dies into silence.

In the years 1509 to 1518, the first half of her life as an acting queen, Catherine was a political advisor to Henry, she acted as regent while he was making war in France, and she was trying to give her husband a male heir to the throne. When she married Henry, she was her father's accredited ambassador to England and had her husband's complete confidence; hence she slipped easily into the position of his political advisor. "For five years after her marriage," Mattingly says, "Catherine continued to be the real ambassador of Spain in England. . . ." But she used her influence so unobtrusively that few realized how great it really was. She acted on the principle that Spain and England were natural allies against France (a principle that may have been sound if applied with caution); and she had an innocent trust in a father whom she had not seen since 1501 and whose political trickery she had never had a chance to realize.

Henry was just as naive as Catherine. His father had sheltered him almost as if he had been an adolescent girl. He was not permitted to go outside the palace except to exercise in the park surrounding it. No woman and no ambassador was permitted to talk to him. He ate many of his meals alone and spent most of his time in his own room, with only one entrance, through his father's bedroom, and the king selected the tutors and the companions who were allowed to approach him. His tutors included Bernard André, historian and poet; Giles D'Ewes, author of a French grammar; and perhaps for a brief time, John Skelton, who said that he taught the prince his letters. William Blount, Lord Mountjoy, was a companion for his studies in history and introduced him to the works of Erasmus. Summing up his education, H. A. L. Fisher said, "Henry became proficient in Latin, he spoke French with ease, he could understand Italian; he applied an energetic intellect to the problems of philosophy and theology . . . he made himself expert on the lute, the organ, and the harpsichord." But in spite of this excellent formal education, one might conclude that when he became king at eighteen he did not understand the rulers and the intrigues of Europe any better than he would have understood them if he had just arrived from another planet.

As a result of his political innocence, Henry had a burning desire to conquer France—a desire nourished by youthful confidence and love of action and also by his reading about Crécy and Agincourt. Perhaps he did not realize the might of France: it had a population sometimes estimated at 15,000,000, while England had about 3,000,000 in 1500, rising to about 3,500,000 by the middle of the century; the French king had unlimited power of taxation and controlled an experienced

professional army. These differences are emphasized by Garrett
Mattingly.

In these early years the English were losers three times against
experienced politicians on the Continent. The first situation developed
between 1510 and 1512. At the suggestion of Ferdinand, England
signed a treaty with France in 1510. The purposes were to disarm
French suspicions, please the pro-French members of the Council in
England, secure certain trade advantages, insure the next payment on
the sum France paid England for keeping the peace, and give England
and Spain a chance to attack France. In 1511 Spain and England signed
a treaty for a joint invasion of Gascony. Henry sent troops to San
Sebastian believing that he was to take Guienne with help from Ferdinand. But the promised help never arrived. The English forces spent
the summer of 1512 in a mere holding action while Ferdinand grabbed
Navarre. After a long hot summer with too much unfamiliar red wine,
idleness, and dysentery, the English troops mutinied: they were going
home. The officers decided to go with them. Henry was humiliated and
furious. The spoils had gone to the experienced poker player Ferdinand. This time Catherine found excuses for her father—excuses she
believed.

The English were losers again in 1513. England and Spain signed a
new treaty: Ferdinand was to invade Guienne and to keep the seas to
Finisterre; an English force would control the Channel while an English
army issued from Calais and repeated the glory of Agincourt. But the
English soon learned that Ferdinand had signed a treaty with France
agreeing to a truce for a whole year. This time the Spanish ambassador
Caroz became the scapegoat: he had misunderstood his instructions.
The English decided to invade France anyway, but Emperor
Maximilian found it impossible to furnish the troops he had promised
England. However, he offered to serve under the banner of the king of
England and to give his experienced advice if the English would pay his
expenses and those of his household troops. Henry did take Tournai
and Therouanne, he was proud of having an emperor serve under him,
and he enjoyed action; he was not unhappy. But since the fortified
towns Henry had taken jutted awkwardly into Hapsburg territory, their
capture profited Maximilian. So England paid the expenses and did
most of the fighting, while another experienced poker player,
Maximilian this time, took the spoils.

In 1514 and 1515 Henry and Catherine suffered the desertion of
both their allies. Ferdinand and Maximilian had signed the treaty of
Lille on October 17, 1513, binding both of them to join Henry in another
invasion of France. But the English learned (about April 1514) that

Ferdinand had later extended for a year his truce with France. Shortly after they discovered this treachery, they found that Maximilian was changing his mind about the marriage of Charles of Ghent to Mary, younger sister of Henry VIII. This time Catherine made no effort to smooth over the desertion they had suffered at the hands of their pretended allies. She informed the Spanish ambassador that she did not wish to see him and had nothing to discuss with him.

However she did lend her support in 1515 when Wolsey and De Mesa, the Spanish ambassador, were drafting a new treaty for trade between Spain and England. She wrote her father that it was a good treaty with limited and definite commitments on both sides, it had commercial advantages for both nations, and it did not include any plans for war or conquest. After that she left Spanish and English relations to Wolsey and De Mesa.

In these years of work as Henry's informal political adviser, Catherine had demonstrated a capacity for vigorous action, ability to analyze and evaluate ideas, and skill in persuasion. Apparently she was also self-effacing, so that neither Henry nor the new Spanish ambassador realized the extent of her influence. But her Achilles heel was her ignorance of her father's character and of the undercurrents in European diplomacy. Unfortunately Henry lacked the same essentials for winning the political game, and to know the essentials was his responsibility.

During the same years, Catherine acted as regent when Henry went to France in 1513. At Dover just before he embarked, Henry issued a proclamation leaving the country in her charge. She had traveled to Dover with him when he and his army, in all their extravagant splendor, entered their 400 ships. Henry took along for his own use fourteen fine horses with trappings of velvet, gold, and expensive silver bells; the total forces included the singers of his chapel and many priests. Earlier, Catherine had been helping in the preparations, checking muster rolls and lists of army equipment, and interviewing the Venetian ambassador about hiring galleys to add to the fleet in the Channel. Thus she had already proved her ability.

Catherine's work as regent indicated that she had unusual executive skill. As H. A. L. Fisher commented, "no Englishwoman could have met the crisis in a prouder or more buoyant spirit." She ordered part of the Council—headed by Archbishop Warham, old Sir Thomas Lovell, and the seventy-year-old Earl of Surrey—to guard the north. As soon as Henry crossed the Channel, the Scots began to move in spite of the treaty he had made with James IV, the husband of his sister Margaret. "While Catherine summoned 40,000 men from the southern counties to meet in London, Sir Francis Lovell collected 15,000 at Nottingham, and Surrey 26,000 at York," said Fisher. Having hurried the first of her forces north to support Surrey, Catherine collected troops from Wales, Buckinghamshire, and all the western and southern counties. She planned a reserve army of 60,000 men, which she herself would lead to York. By the end of August, couriers were bringing word that King James, with a well-equipped army estimated at 40,000 to 100,000 men, had already crossed the Tweed.

In early September Catherine rode out of London with her forces and with cannon from the Tower. She had reached Buckingham by September 14, ready to support Surrey at need or to place a strong force between him and London. But the battle of Flodden Field—one of the bloodiest battles of Henry's reign—had begun on September 9; and soon, as Mattingly said, "the last stubborn ring of spearmen had fallen around the dead body of their king." About 11,000 to 13,000 Scots were killed, one historian says, and fewer than 1,500 Englishmen. Another estimates that 10,000 Scots died.

Catherine wrote Henry the letter of a loyal wife, not a conquering general. She had the plaid of King James sent to Henry at Therouanne, a natural act for one who had been trained in heraldry with the customs of the medieval period. She had hoped to send the king of Scotland himself as a prisoner of war, but the valor of the English did not allow him to survive. The victory was Henry's, she told him, given him by the bravery of his subjects and the grace of God; it was a greater honor to him and his realm than a conquest of France could be, but *his* victory, as if he had been there in person. She added, "I make an end, praying God to send you home shortly, for without that, no joy here can be accomplished . . . and now go to our Lady at Walsingham that I promised so long ago to see." Henry had gone to that shrine in 1511 to give thanks for the son who lived about two months; her words would tell him that she meant to give him a son. Thus the letter combined in an unusual manner the loyal wife and the woman guiding the nation.

Catherine turned her efforts toward peace as soon as the battle of Flodden was over. Knowing the great financial drain of two wars, she began at once to disband her own reserve army and to reduce the forces under the command of Surrey. She sent her sister-in-law, Queen Margaret of Scotland, a message of comfort and assurance that Henry would support her as regent while she kept the peace with England. She also took measures toward a permanent peace between the two countries. As Garrett Mattingly said, both her preparations to meet the war and her firm steps to end it "showed her complete fitness for the hard task Henry had left in her hands."

While Catherine was meeting the challenge of an invasion from Scotland, she was also carrying on well (with the help of the Council) the other part of her work as regent: getting supplies to the king and his army on the Continent. She saw to it that commissions of array functioned, that musters were held, and that assessments for special taxes were arranged. And she did not neglect her duties as a wife: to contribute to Henry's peace and comfort in France. She wrote him at least once a week, and every messenger she sent with a letter was to bring back another letter, from the king if possible, but if he were involved, one from Wolsey. Repeatedly she asked Wolsey about her husband's health. She begged Margaret of Austria (once her sister-in-law as the wife of her brother Juan) to find the best physician she could and to send him to Henry. She feared that Henry was too rash in battle, that he would become overheated and thus take cold! She rejoiced when the Emperor Maximilian joined him, thinking that Henry might risk himself less in battle. She even managed to send him supplies of fresh linen. And she never overlooked a chance to praise his victories. Again she seemed to combine well the concerned wife and the director of national affairs.

Meantime Catherine had not been neglecting her chief duty: to give Henry VIII a male heir to the throne. In 1510 her first child, a girl, was born dead. On the first of January 1511 she gave birth to a boy who seemed healthy; but after fifty-two days, during the elaborate tournaments in his honor, he died. In September 1513 she had a miscarriage — perhaps the result of her work as regent. In December 1514 another child was born, perhaps the boy who "lived not long after." Princess Mary, the only child who lived more than a few weeks, was born February 18, 1516. In 1517 or 1518 Catherine was pregnant for the last time, but no child survived.

Whatever the cause, Catherine should not be blamed for her failure to bear healthy children. Catherine's mother had borne five children who lived to be married, though her only son Juan had died shortly after marriage, and his child was born dead. Syphilis, the "pox," was spreading in Europe. It has been suggested that Henry's illness in 1513 after his campaign in France may have been syphilis and not smallpox. Most students of the period assume that Henry had

syphilis in his later years. A recent biographer, J. J. Scarisbrick (after
calling a medical expert to his aid) states that Henry's symptoms in his
later years might have come from an aggravated varicose ulcer or from
osteomyelitis. Mortality among children was high in the period; among
royal Tudors few sons were born and often they died early. Margaret
Beaufort, from three marriages, had one child. Henry VII and his
queen, from seven children, had lost four (two sons and two daughters)
by 1503 when the queen died; after Arthur's death the male line
depended on the son who became Henry VIII. Margaret, older daughter
of Henry VII, had one son by her first husband, James IV of Scotland;
and the younger daughter Mary, wife of Charles Brandon, besides two
daughters, had one son who died in adolescence. Henry VIII did not
fare better with sons from other marriages; Anne Boleyn lost a son by
miscarriage shortly before her arrest and execution. Edward VI and
Henry Fitzroy (the natural son he acknowledged and brought to court)
died at sixteen and seventeen.

By 1518 at the latest, and probably earlier, both Henry and
Catherine must have recognized the fact that she would bear no more
children. By this time she had suffered many losses. Her links with
Spain were gone—her maids of honor; her Spanish confessor; and her
parents, her mother having died in 1504 and her father in 1516. Her
religious attitudes had deepened: she attended more Masses; visited
more shrines; and under rich dresses and jewels, she had begun
wearing the coarse garment of the third order of St. Francis. On state
occasions she appeared with queenly dignity, but she sometimes withdrew early from merrymaking at court. With six or more pregnancies,
her figure had thickened and her appearance had changed in other
ways. She had lost her exalted place in Henry's affections, but if she
had been able to give him sons who reached maturity, Henry and
Catherine would probably have remained man and wife officially while
they both lived.

For nine more years (1518-1527) Catherine was queen without
public question, though the years of political activity and child-bearing
were over. She managed the royal household as she had done since her
marriage, including the care and embroidering of her husband's linens
and other small comforts he now took for granted. She supervised all
those who did the work in any palace where they were living, and she
looked after everything when they moved the huge household from one
palace to another. She continued to manage her personal properties

that were scattered over England, presiding over her council for the management of these estates, looking into prices, presenting a worthy candidate to a clerical living, investigating the character of a woman who wished to be an abbess, and deciding other economic problems. Her life was orderly and filled with many duties.

During these years one major crisis came in Catherine's serene life. About 1525 Charles V, her nephew (king of Spain since 1516 and emperor since 1519), began negotiations with the aim of breaking his marriage treaty to the Princess Mary, the daughter of Henry and Catherine. Being sixteen years older than the nine-year-old girl, he had decided that he could not wait for her to grow up. Though Henry had broken his part of the treaty by failing to make war on the French (at the time he did not dare ask more money for war), he was resentful and bitter—more so because mismanagement and a series of accidents had left him to learn through his own ambassadors in Spain that Charles meant to arrange terms with the French and to marry a Portuguese princess. The situation was a crisis within Henry and a crisis in his relations with Catherine.

A major result of the king's resentment was his advancement of his natural son Henry Fitzroy. In a ceremony of many steps the boy became a knight, Earl of Nottingham, and Duke of Richmond and Somerset; he was proclaimed Lord Admiral of England and other territories, Knight of the Garter, Keeper of the City and Castle of Carlisle, and first peer of England. Though the king had not made him Prince of Wales, it seemed clear that if he could manage it, Fitzroy would become king of England. Catherine protested the boy's status as an insult to her and to her daughter; and apparently as a result of her protest, Henry ordered Wolsey to reorganize her household. Wolsey removed all the women he did not consider to be his own tools. When Catherine objected, Wolsey told the king that the women he removed had caused the queen to complain about the advancement of Fitzroy. Then Henry curtly rejected her pleas to keep her friends as members of her household.

Another result of the king's resentment was his order for Mary to take up her duties at Ludlow Castle as Princess of Wales and nominal head of the Council of the West. It was common for royal children to live apart from their parents, or for other children to be sent to strange households. But Catherine's affection for her only surviving child was stronger than usual. She had taught her daughter to read and to write, had corrected her Latin exercises, and probably had hoped to continue the direct supervision of her education. Henry softened the blow when he allowed the Countess of Salisbury, a friend of both Catherine and Mary, to go with the girl to Ludlow as governess of her household.

From 1527 to 1536, the last nine years of Catherine's life, her dominant qualities were devotion to religious principles and a firm persistence in obeying her conscience and her view of God's will. In June 1527 Henry told Catherine that his conscience was troubling him because she had been the wife of his brother Arthur and for eighteen years they had been living in sin. (Somehow this conscience, always remarkably pliant, failed to remind him that Anne Boleyn's sister Mary had been his mistress, and according to canon law, a marriage to Anne would be the same sin.) The queen burst into sobs, and unnerved by her tears, Henry rushed from the room. Later when she was calm, she told Henry that her first marriage had never been consummated; that she had married him by the advice of wise men in two kingdoms and by the dispensation of the pope; that she had been publicly crowned; and that as long as they both lived, she would be the true queen of England and his wife. It was still her duty, she believed, to obey the man who was both her king and her husband unless he commanded her to violate her conscience and the divine will. She would obey him as her husband by going wherever he ordered. No threat and no bribe could make her forsake these principles.

In June 1529 Wolsey and Campeggio, after interviews with Catherine to find out her views, opened a legatine court at Blackfriars. They planned to determine the validity of the marriage. Though she had lodged complaint about this court and was appealing to Rome, she came for one dramatic appeal, with faith in Henry's essential goodness. He would not deny what he knew to be the truth. When her name was called, she knelt at her husband's feet, reminded him of her loyalty and obedience through twenty years of marriage, and said: "And when ye had me at the first, I take God to be my judge, I was a true maid, without touch of man. And whether this be true or not, I put it to your conscience." She waited for his answer. He did not deny—he merely sat motionless and said nothing. Finally she rose, left the court, and though called back officially, refused to return.

From time to time Catherine was subjected to interviews that were efforts to break her will. She was asked to throw herself on the king's mercy. She refused. When news came that the pope had summoned the case to Rome, Campeggio convened his court only to announce that it was a Roman court, and as the holidays had begun there, he would recess until the first of October. In September 1529 Eustace Chapuys came as ambassador from Spain; and in spite of his determination to keep an objective detachment, he found himself becoming Catherine's champion. On May 31, 1531, some thirty counselors visited her and tried to persuade her to accept a trial at Cambrai. Answering their arguments with clarity and courage, she refused.

On July 11, 1531, the king left Catherine at Windsor (riding off with a hunting party that included Anne Boleyn) without saying good-by. They never saw each other again. A few weeks later the Council asked her to move from Windsor to the More (an old house once the property of Wolsey) because the king wished to return to Windsor. In another message they asked her to choose a nunnery or a small royal manor as a permanent residence, to accept a reduced suite, and to avoid seeing her daughter Mary again. From 1531 to her death she was moved from one obscure residence to another—from the More to Easthampstead (a royal hunting lodge), back to the More, to Ampthill (a manor in Bedfordshire), and in July 1533 to Buckden, Yorkshire. When the Duke of Suffolk came in December 1533 with orders to move her by force if necessary and to exact an oath from her attendants to call her the Princess Dowager, he offered the usual bribe of better living if she would agree that her marriage to Henry had always been null and void. Again she refused. But when Suffolk mentioned Fotheringhay and Somersham, places she considered dangerous because of their damp-ness, she said that to consent would be suicide—a sin her husband had no right to ask. Finally she left Suffolk to argue with her locked door. Partly because groups of common people hostile to him were gathering and partly because he had no heart for his errand, he retreated. In May 1534 Catherine was taken to Kimbolton, Huntingdonshire, a fortified manor house, where she remained until her death. Henry was afraid to lodge her near London or to imprison her in the Tower because many Londoners loved her, and he probably feared she might make war against him for the sake of her daughter.

Often deputations brought offers of a better residence and a generous income if she would admit that the marriage had been invalid and thus bastardize her daughter. Although her allowance was so small that she could not make her usual gifts to the poor, pay her servants who remained loyal, or buy anything but bare necessities, she refused. When a messenger demanded her jewels for Anne to wear, she refused at first because she could not believe that Henry had completely lost his sense of fitting conduct: she demanded a request in his own hand-writing. It came—and she surrendered the jewels.

Events were moving swiftly. In May 1532 Henry secured the Submission of the Clergy, giving him the right to pass judgment on all laws, past or future, adopted by the Convocation. In August 1532 Arch-bishop Warham died; and Anne, sure now that she would be queen, surrendered physically to Henry. In 1533 Chapuys had ready his plan to move Catherine and Mary to a place of safety on the Continent. But Catherine refused to escape or to give encouragement to any act of war for herself or her daughter. In May 1533 Cranmer (who had been confirmed as archbishop) held court at Dunstable and declared the marriage of Henry and Catherine null and void. Later, on May 28, he declared that Henry had married Anne, but he did not say when, and that the marriage was valid. Anne was crowned June first. About three months later, in September, she gave birth to the Princess Elizabeth. In March 1534 the pope announced that the marriage of Henry and Catherine had been valid. His decision was too late.

After the Act of Succession was passed in 1534, a commission came to exact from Catherine and her attendants an oath to support it — and thus to admit the queen's life of sin and to bastardize her daughter. Catherine based her refusal on the pope's announcement. About two weeks later another group, headed by Lee and Tunstall, came to exact the same oath. Again she refused. Reminded that refusal was treason, she replied that she was ready to die — in the sight of the people. As she knew, that was the right by law of any person convicted of treason. Lee and Tunstall finally concluded their work by arresting some members of her household, accepting modified oaths from some and securing no oaths at all from others. Apparently the members of the commission and Henry himself believed that they could not risk making Catherine a martyr.

In February 1535 when the Princess Mary was ill, Catherine asked the king, through Chapuys, to send their daughter to her, so that she might nurse her with the advice of her own and other doctors. Though rumors of poisoning were abroad, Mary's symptoms may have come from fear and tension. Finally the king did send his doctor to confer with Catherine's doctor, Miguel De la Sá, and permitted Mary to lodge near enough so that De la Sá could make regular visits — after he extorted a promise from Catherine that she would not try to see her daughter. She had perhaps seen the girl only once since 1525, a brief stolen visit in 1531 when Anne and the king were away. Catherine did not see her daughter again.

Catherine of Aragon died early in 1536. On December 29, 1535, Chapuys had word from De la Sá that she was dying, and through an interview with the king he was granted permission to visit her. In the few days he spent at Kimbolton, she talked to him of her concern for the king and for England. Because of her decisions bad men had gone to eternal punishment, good men had suffered, the kingdom was full of heresy and sedition, the bonds that united England to Christendom had been broken — and yet she could not commit the sin of denying that she was Henry's wife or the sin of leading an army against her husband and her king. She was debating the eternal problem of the conscientious person forced to choose, not between good and evil, but between evil and evil. Chapuys reassured her before he left, so that she was able to eat and sleep again.

Maria de Salinas, Lady Willoughby, who remained loyal to her former mistress, also returned when she heard that Catherine was dying. One dark stormy night Sir Edmund Bedingfield, the guard, heard a woman's voice calling across the moat, demanding that he let her come in. At first he refused. He had his orders not to admit anyone. The voice insisted: the night was cold, the roads were muddy and slippery, she had fallen from her horse, and she was not going one mile farther. He yielded. Once inside, Maria disappeared into the queen's rooms.

On January 7, 1536, Catherine received the sacrament and wrote two letters, one to Charles V and one to Henry. Among other details, she said to Henry: "For my part, I pardon you everything, and I wish and devoutly pray God that he will pardon you also. . . . . I commend unto you our daughter Mary, beseeching you to be a good father unto her, as I have heretofore desired." She asked him to give marriage portions to three maids who were still with her and to pay her servants their wages with an extra year's money, so that they might not be left without a means of living. After receiving extreme unction, she prayed aloud for the souls of the English people, for her daughter, and for her husband. She died that afternoon in the arms of Maria de Salinas. By command of the king she was buried in Peterborough Abbey with the ceremonies for a princess dowager.

In the thirty-five years that Catherine of Aragon had lived in her new country and had slowly changed into an Englishwoman, what had she contributed to England? Though her work of four or five years as Henry's political advisor was not an unqualified success because she trusted her father and because Henry had limitations of romanticism and inexperience, she gave him confidence in himself and she used some sound principles of statesmanship. Perhaps one may conjecture that Henry, with his abysmal ignorance of political realities and his temporary idealism, would have done worse without her help. During the same years her work as regent seems to have been highly successful. She met the invasion by the Scots, channeled supplies to France, provided for Henry's personal comfort, and gave him approval and praise. But in her desire to give Henry a male heir, she was frustrated by circumstances beyond her control.

In her refusal to accept the status of a princess dowager and to bastardize her daughter—a refusal she continued with unwavering firmness from 1527 to her death in 1536—she waged a war like that of Bishop Fisher and Sir Thomas More. She too assumed that the individual conscience must sometimes assert itself against the power of the state. That principle (discussed for centuries before the Tudor Age) will emerge as long as human beings try to act on religious or ethical bases. Her resistance never faltered, either for threats or for bribes. Fisher and More were heroes; she was a heroine who deserves equal honor. Thomas Cromwell, who had an unusual ability to judge situations and people objectively (without letting that judgment interfere with his immediate actions), once said to Chapuys after Catherine had resisted the demands of a delegation: "Nature wronged the Queen in not making her a man. But for her sex, she would have surpassed all the heroes of history."

Catherine of Aragon did many other things for England. One was to further a sound classical education in an age when it was extremely useful. Because of her education in Spain she was prepared to exert an influence, partly through her plans for the education of her daughter and partly through her aid to English scholars. Though it is difficult to separate her influence from that of More, the ideas for the education of the Princess Mary seem to be largely hers. Linacre and Vives turned her ideas into books. Linacre's revised grammar *Rudimenta grammatices,* dedicated to the Princess Mary, was undated but was published about 1523. It is said to have been more thorough than the work he had prepared for Colet's school some years earlier, and Colet had rejected that early version because it was too difficult for the tender minds of the young. Linacre's reputation as a grammarian apparently rests upon this later work. Perhaps he also tutored the Princess Mary for a brief time.

Catherine probably commissioned Vives to write *De institutione Christianae foeminae,* a work he completed in 1523. Certainly he dedicated the work to her, and in the opening sentences of the dedication he suggested that he had written it because of her life and character: because of "the favour, love, and zeal that your Grace beareth toward holy study and learning. . . ." In the same year Vives published *De ratione studii puerilis,* directed to the education of girls;

he had written this work for the Princess Mary at the request of her mother. In 1524 he published *Satellitium animi sive symbola,* with a dedicatory epistle to Mary, whom he saluted as *Princeps Cambriae,* Prince of Wales. It had been customary, he said, to provide a satellitium or guard for the physical safety of princes: "But I . . . often requested by your mother, an illustrious and most holy woman, will set around thy soul a guard, which will preserve thee more securely and safely than any spearmen or bowmen whatever." So he provided her with 239 mottoes, each having not more than five words and each being "a satellite in the guard." Thus Catherine had requested or inspired a considerable amount of Vives' literary work.

Catherine formed around Mary "a school for the daughters of noblemen on the pattern of that for noblemen's sons once formed around her brother Juan," Mattingly said, "and she even persuaded a number of the older ladies of the court, notably her sister-in-law the Duchess of Suffolk, to resume the study of Latin and take up a course of serious reading." But he gave no source and did not mention the More school, which was nearer Catherine both in place and time. More was also the admirer and friend of Catherine from 1501 (when he praised her beauty and charm as she entered London) to the moments after his condemnation when he told his accusers they sought his blood because he "would not condescend to the marriage." It seems reasonable to assume that the queen had followed More's school with interest, that it had some influence on the school she established for Mary, and that her school in turn exerted influence on other women.

As a result of these plans Mary had a sound education, though scholars later seldom gave her the highest praise. Her education had begun when both parents were creating a world of affection about her — when her mother taught her letters and penmanship or corrected her Latin exercises and when her father often beat time for her practice on the virginals or guided her fingers on the lute. It continued at Ludlow Castle, with the Countess of Salisbury at the head of her household and Richard Fetherston as her tutor. Even then her mother longed to see some of her Latin exercises and to rejoice in her progress.

Mary learned Latin, Greek, and French; she knew a little Italian but never spoke it well; she understood but did not speak Spanish. She learned "to ride, dance, sing, and play upon lute and virginals," said H. F. M. Prescott; "for music she had her father's natural bent."

Catherine encouraged education in other ways. She contributed to lectureships at both universities, Mattingly says, "maintained a number of poor scholars at both universities, and kept herself informed of their progress." Even when she and Wolsey were at odds about other ideas, she continued to inquire with interest about the colleges he was founding; unlike many conservatives, she never opposed his plans to suppress decayed religious foundations and to use the money for education. In 1518 she combined a visit to the shrine of St. Frideswide with a tour of Oxford colleges, dining at Merton and being received everywhere with signs of affection. On March 29 of that year More wrote his famous letter to the same university, rebuking the Trojans, who "always learn too late," and pleading for the study of Greek and other humane letters. We do not know, unless further evidence appears, whether More's letter and the queen's visit occurred about the same time by accident or by design. But we do know that the king, who was at Abingdon nearby, continued his hunting and did not come to Oxford.

Queen Catherine encouraged many learned men. William Blount, Lord Mountjoy, became her chamberlain at the time of her coronation. At the beginning of the century he was one of the few noblemen with a classical education; he was the pupil and friend of Erasmus. He married Inez de Venegas, one of Catherine's Spanish attendants, and was long an intimate friend. Thomas Linacre (who had been at Ludlow Castle as tutor and physician to Prince Arthur) probably became the court physician in 1509 through the influence of Catherine. Her physician, Dr. Fernando Vittorio, who had humanistic interests, was the associate of Linacre in founding the Royal College of Physicians. Without Catherine to recall Linacre from obscurity, perhaps he would not have had the chance to perform this service and his other remarkable services to England. Catherine tried to keep Erasmus in England and, when he left, to lure him back. She read and valued his books; in the early days of her marriage to Henry, she and the king enjoyed them together. Erasmus praised her learning and often acknowledged his indebtedness to her. Vives worked in England about five years, receiving a pension from the queen and also one from the king, until his support of Catherine and persecutions from Wolsey drove him from the country. John Leland, the antiquary, had access to the queen's library both at Greenwich and at Richmond. Catherine was a frequent visitor at Syon House, largely from her interest in the piety and the scholarship of Richard Whitford. Her influence on the careers of More and Pace seems uncertain; the king might have appointed them to the same positions even without her friendship.

Through her charities Catherine did much for the common people of England, working both as queen and as a member of the third order of St. Francis. Though the period seemed prosperous in some ways, great landlords were enclosing land because they could double their profits by raising sheep. Even if one landlord deprived only five families from a hundred of their means of living and their homes, the impact on the whole country might be evident. Also, no provision was made for maimed soldiers; they were forced to beg on the streets. Though Catherine read *Utopia* and is said to have held conversations with More about its ideas, probably she did little for the poor except to relieve them with alms. She increased the funds for the official called the queen's almoner and also made efforts to see that the money she gave was wisely spent. She supported a number of aged poor people. At some of her manors, funds were regularly set aside for charity, but in the early part of the century the poor were fed at the gates of most great houses. An early biographer (probably William Forrest, *A History of Grisild the Second*) states that she had the habit of inquiring into the needs of the poor in any area where she was living and that she visited them without revealing her own status, perhaps by wearing the garments of a lay sister of her order. When Vives, in his book *De subventione pauperum,* made one of the first attempts to analyze the problems of poverty in a scientific way, we can detect in his pages, Mattingly has said, the echoes of questions from Catherine. Perhaps she was beginning to think beyond the mere use of alms.

Other traditions about the work of Catherine for England may be repeated as traditions, even though they cannot be verified. She furthered lace-making in the Midlands, providing people with a means of making a living and thus going beyond mere alms; and she brought in fruit trees as well as new materials for salads from the Low Countries.

An interesting tradition is concerned with her part in saving the apprentices who had rioted on Evil May Day, May 1, 1517. These young Englishmen resented the aliens who were busy with fine fabrics, leather, and metals and who ate well and dressed well, while the English were unemployed. Aided by vagabonds, beggars, and sanctuary men, the apprentices had opened jails, ransacked shops, and set fire to houses. When the rioting was finally stopped, thirteen leaders had been hanged, and about four hundred young men with ropes around their necks were led before the king. An official version of the incident reported that Wolsey's advice and the resulting clemency of the king saved the lives of the rioters. A tradition used in the old play *Sir Thomas More* credited More with a number of eloquent speeches on respect for authority; thus he calmed the rioters and persuaded them to use reason. But a foreign eyewitness, Francesco Chieragato, papal nuncio, reporting to Venice, emphasized the part of Catherine. When the four hundred prisoners were waiting, he said, "our most serene and most compassionate queen, with tears in her eyes, and on her bended knees, obtained their pardon from his majesty, the act being performed with great ceremony.'' Wolsey spoke later, and then the king spoke at some length. The official record and the account by Chieragato are alike except for the addition of Catherine in the Venetian report, and it is hardly reasonable to suppose that Chieragato's details were pure imagination. The queen's action may not have been considered seemly or important enough for the official record.

A ballad that remained popular for a half-century described Catherine as a suppliant for the apprentices. Having loosed her hair and exchanged her rich garments for mean attire, in the best tradition of the role she came to kneel before the king and beg for their lives. As a result the king pardoned them:

> For which kind queen, with joyful heart
> She heard their mothers' thanks and praise
> . . . . . . . . . . . . . . . . . . . . . . . .
> And lived beloved all her days.

Catherine's greatest service to England was her refusal to lead or to consent to others leading a civil war for her or for her daughter. Her refusal was based on her conviction that she had no right to disobey the man who was her husband and her king unless obedience to him would force her to violate her own conscience and the law of God. She would not leave England nor aid any plan for removing her daughter from the country, even when she may have believed that the girl's life was in danger. As she had grown older, she had developed an aversion to all bloodshed and war — partly through the influence of Erasmus, More, and Vives and partly through her own maturity. Adherence to these principles for nine years (1527-1536) took all the determination she had inherited and all that she had developed as a widow after the death of Arthur. Before her death she was torn by doubts as she thought of the evils that had followed, but she knew she could not have done anything else.

Henry VIII saw the danger if she decided to make war. ''The Lady Catherine is a proud, stubborn woman of very high courage,'' he told his Council in 1535. ''If she took it into her head to take her daughter's part, she could quite easily . . . muster a great array, and wage against me a war as fierce as any her mother Isabella ever waged in Spain.'' He may have been remembering also what he did not put into words — that Isabella's early war had ousted another ruler and had made her ruler of Castile.

Chapuys tried to trigger such a war almost as soon as he found himself becoming Catherine's champion. He could manage everything, he thought, but the leader; Catherine herself was the logical choice for that. She had proved her iron will in resisting Henry's demands and her organizing ability in meeting the threat at Flodden Field years earlier. Many English people loved her. Many of the nobility would follow her — some because they hoped for power through her rule, some from personal friendship, some because she was an aristocrat like themselves, and others because they shared her ideas. Another possible leader was James V of Scotland, the son of Henry's older sister Margaret; he was about three years older than the Princess Mary and a possible husband for her. He was a spirited young man, with the best claim on the throne of England of any living male. But the English might not have been willing to follow him unless Catherine had also raised her standard. Reginald Pole, with some right to the throne through his mother, had spent years on the Continent; thus he had no knowledge of English political life at that time and no practical experience in war. He also could have done little without the active aid of Catherine. Mary would have accepted either James V or Reginald Pole as her husband. At this time she was young, loved life, and wished to be queen.

Support for Catherine existed in all parts of England, ready to join a national leader. In the north there were John, Lord Hussey; Thomas, Lord Darcy, of Templehurst in Yorkshire; Thomas Stanley, Earl of Derby; Lord Dacre of the North; William, Lord Sandys; and perhaps even Henry Percy. In the west Sir James Griffith ap Howell was ready to lead half of Wales in support of Catherine. Lord Abergavenny, a son-in-law of the unfortunate Duke of Buckingham, was a leader of many men and was inclined to take revenge for his wife's family. George Talbot, Earl of Shrewsbury, would either join or refuse to help the king. South of them, another leader was Henry Courtenay, Marquess of Exeter, with claims on the throne; he was urged on by his wife, the daughter of Lord Mountjoy, who was Catherine's chamberlain and her friend. In his group were Henry, Lord Montague; his brother Geoffrey Pole; Sir George Carew; Henry Parker; and Sir Thomas Arundel. In the south and east near London, Edmund, Lord Bray, reported that twenty peers and a hundred knights were ready to fight for the queen. They included Sir Thomas Elyot; Sir Thomas Kingston, Constable of the Tower; Thomas Manners, Earl of Rutland; and Sir Thomas Burgoyne (who was also a son-in-law of the Duke of Buckingham).

What would have happened if Catherine had led a rising is a question for speculation. Perhaps not all these men would have responded, or perhaps more would have hurried to her support. If the

English had risen, the pope would probably have published the brief he had drawn up deposing Henry. Then Emperor Charles V would have given support for the sake of his own prestige and his political future. If the rising had come at the best possible psychological moment, with Catherine leading, Henry might have been toppled from his throne. Or the rebellion might have failed. In either case, reprisals and executions would have followed—even a prolonged civil war. Looking back at the period without the intense religious concerns of Catherine herself, one remembers her comment that if she had not brought good to England, she would be all the more unwilling to bring it harm. And it seems that Catherine of Aragon should be remembered and honored for her greatest service to England—her refusal to plunge the country into civil war.

*Portrait of Catherine Parr, attributed to William Scrots, is now considered to be her only authentic likeness.*

*Below: Facsimile signature, "Kathryn the Queen Regente."*

*Bottom: Coat of arms of Trinity College, Cambridge. Presumably as a result of Catherine's persuasion, a few weeks before his death Henry set aside a generous sum for a "college of literature, sciences, philosophy . . . ."*

KATHARINE PARR

*The family of Henry VIII. The picture, now at Hampton Court, is by an unknown artist, possibly a follower of Hans Holbein. The three seated figures are Henry, with Prince Edward at his right and a queen at his left; Elizabeth stands at the right and Mary at the left. The identity of the queen is disputed. Some insist she is Jane Seymour, that a wax effigy was used as a model, and that the king meant to honor the mother of Prince Edward. Others hold that the queen is Catherine Parr, who had united the king's children as a family. Judging from the ages of the children, the picture dates from about 1546-1547.*

# CHAPTER EIGHT

# *Catherine Parr*
## 1512-1548

Of the six women Henry VIII married, only two had the character and the definite aims that enabled them to hold an exalted position and also to make a contribution to English life. They were the first and the last—Catherine of Aragon and Catherine Parr. Certainly Anne Boleyn, Jane Seymour, Catherine Howard, and Anne of Cleves accomplished little, though some credit Anne Boleyn with an influence on religion and she had the rare luck to give birth to the Princess Elizabeth. But the last of his queens worked to spread her religious views, had reasonable success in her efforts, used her limited power to promote harmony between England and other nations, and acted as regent for the king; as

the wife of Henry VIII and stepmother to his three children, she influenced the development of England. Considered as a woman of her period, perhaps she was more influential than Lady Anne Bacon and Catherine, Duchess of Suffolk, and was clearly surpassed by the many-sided Margaret Beaufort and by Queen Elizabeth.

Historians have differed greatly in their estimates of Catherine Parr. Protestant writers of religious history often overestimate; others, repelled by exaggeration, underestimate. Of recent historians, G. R. Elton said, ''She was a mild and moderately sensible woman, much given to matrimony, but she scarcely merits the somewhat sanctimonious praise bestowed on her by the reformers and often echoed since.'' She exerted influence because she was mild; if many marriages be sin, Tudor England was full of unrepentant sinners who married whenever bereaved; and due praise is realistic. H. A. L. Fisher quoted Eustace Chapuys, once ambassador from Spain to England, who said that she was not as beautiful as Anne of Cleves; Fisher added that she had something better than beauty: ''gentleness, discretion, and culture. Watchful of the king's abrupt and angry humours, she was prompt to employ such influence as she possessed on the side of clemency, and in that fierce and licentious court, the mild Queen Catherine, with her books, her devotions, her seemly reverence for the Lady Mary, her strict sense of discipline, is a refreshing figure.'' When Conyers Read named the two objectives of Henry's religious settlement (''to establish the royal supremacy over the English church'' and ''to maintain an orthodox position within the church on all matters of creed and ritual''), he added: ''The Protestant position had been definitely strengthened by the sympathy and covert support of Catherine Parr. . . .'' J. J. Scarisbrick, in *Henry VIII*, emphasized the danger of her position and described her as ''an elevated, purposeful queen . . . who, riding above those who jockeyed for position as the old king neared his end and would have liked to undo her, did much to take away some of the bleakness of his last days.'' These varied estimates suggest her achievements to be discussed here.

To sum up the life of Catherine Parr is difficult because we lack definite dates, other facts, and the letters we might expect to find written by a woman who was queen of England about three and a half years. More than a hundred years ago Agnes Strickland made two suggestions about the lack of information. First, after Catherine's death, Thomas Seymour, her fourth husband, brought suit to recover jewels she had worn as queen, claiming that they had been her personal property. His servant made a thorough search of Hanworth, Catherine's former royal residence. (Apparently Hanworth and Chelsea manor, listed in *Letters and Papers* in 1544 under "Life Grants," had been part of her jointure on her marriage to the king.) This servant may have destroyed records of her early life or her life as queen either carelessly or intentionally. Second, she presumably wrote personal letters to her sister Anne, wife of William Herbert, Earl of Pembroke, and during that marriage the mistress of Wilton House. A great fire at Wilton House in 1647 "destroyed all but the center of the east front and most of the contents."

Judging from the facts that remain, her early life was not unusual. Her parents were Sir Thomas Parr and his wife Maud Green Parr. She was born in 1512, presumably in Kendal Castle, Westmorland. Her father, a master of wards and a controller in the king's household, died about 1517, leaving his wife with three small children — Catherine, William, and Anne. It is generally believed that Catherine was the oldest child. In his will the father provided eight hundred pounds for his daughters' marriage portions, the sum to be divided between them. In the early sixteenth century these sums were generous. William had as a special gift a great chain of gold worth a hundred forty pounds; it had been a gift to his father from the king. Sir Thomas named his brother Sir William Parr and Cuthbert Tunstall as executors; his wife was either another executor or an overseer of the will, but missing words leave her function uncertain.

Unlike the typical sixteenth-century widow, Maud Parr did not marry again; apparently she gave her time and attention to her children. Since all of them were praised later for their education, perhaps she had the help of Cuthbert Tunstall in providing tutors for them. Later William attended Cambridge. Though Catherine gave no evidence of being a Greek scholar, no doubt all three were well grounded in Latin. Later Roger Ascham wrote to Anne in Latin and she lent him a Latin volume of Cicero; she also wrote him at one time that the education in her family had been modeled on that of the More household. It would be something of a feat to use the More household as a model and to leave out Latin! Prince Edward's congratulations to Catherine in a letter of June 1546, offered by G. Fenno Hoffman, Jr., as evidence that she had learned no Latin early, do not seem overwhelming support for that idea! She was involved then in the English edition of the *Paraphrase* of Erasmus; and when nine-year-old Edward

wrote of her progress ''in Latina lingua et bonis literis,'' it is possible
that he did not understand her project in the least and tended to equate
her need for Latin with his own childish struggles. And she may have
been trying to motivate him by mentioning her use of Latin. Additional
evidence of Catherine's skill comes from the fact that manuscript copies
of her letter to the Princess Mary urging her to publish her translation
of the Gospel of St. John and to permit the use of her name with it are in
Latin. Catherine knew also French and presumably Italian. She wrote a
devotional poem in French, she received a letter in Italian from the
young Princess Elizabeth, and she owned an Italian volume of Petrarch
published in Venice in 1534. This volume, bound in velvet with
Catherine's arms and quarterings on the cover, was found in the library
of Edward VI.

Catherine Parr may have had some education at court along with
the king's daughter Mary. Her father was a controller for the royal
household, but that did not necessarily mean that his wife and three
small children lived all the time at court. However, Garrett Mattingly
said that Catherine of Aragon organized a royal school for her daughter,
bringing in outsiders, even older women, including the king's sister
Mary. But he gave no evidence. A recent biographer of Catherine Parr,
Anthony Martienssen, assured us that she and the Princess Mary
(daughter of the king) were fellow pupils with Vives as their teacher. He
also gave no evidence. It is true that Vives came to England about
1523, that he prepared books to help Catherine of Aragon educate her
daughter, that he was paid sums for several years by the king and by
the queen, and that he was an excellent scholar and a teacher of Latin.
As the king sent his daughter to Ludlow Castle in 1525 to join the
Council of Wales and the Marches as Princess of Wales, she and
Catherine Parr might have had two years together with Vives. If we
assume good early tutoring arranged for Catherine with the help of
Cuthbert Tunstall, two years could have given her a sound training in
Latin with some Greek. But where is the evidence?

The first marriage of Catherine Parr occurred about 1529 when she
was seventeen, according to the *Complete Peerage*. Her husband was
Sir Edward Burgh of Borough, Gainsborough. He was not a lord when
she married him and never became one, for he died without issue
before April 1533, while his father was still living. His younger brother
William succeeded to the title, becoming Lord Burgh in 1550. Apparently Catherine's husband has been confused with an Edward

Burgh, who was older by some years and died about 1528, and who was not summoned to Parliament because of his insanity. Earlier writers, without the help of the *Complete Peerage,* made the error, and recent writers have followed them.

As her second husband, Catherine married John Neville, Lord Latimer, who lived at Snape Hall, Yorkshire. He had been involved in the Pilgrimage of Grace, but he profited by the general pardon of December 1536; when a fresh outbreak in support of the old religion came in 1537, he did not become involved. Lord Latimer had two children, John and Margaret, by a previous marriage; they gave Catherine her first experience as a stepmother. Though Lord Latimer has been described as senile, he was born about 1490; and when he died in 1542 or early 1543, he was only about fifty-two. Catherine received property from him, in addition to an unencumbered jointure, it is said, from her first husband.

If Catherine won a victory over Thomas Cromwell that led to his downfall, the event would have occurred while she was the wife of Lord Latimer. Citing vaguely a document in the Throckmorton family, Agnes Strickland stated that Catherine was interceding for her aunt, the wife of Sir George Throckmorton. For two years Sir George had been kept in the Tower without a trial through the influence of Cromwell. By accusing Throckmorton of denying the king's supremacy, Cromwell had hoped to seize some of his land; and since Throckmorton's brother was in the service of Reginald Pole, the accusation was more dangerous. Sir George's son related the incident in a rhyming history of the family; and the family papers are said to contain a prose statement that ''Sir George was released through the influence of his kinswoman, the Lady Katherine Parr, and advised with by the King, at her suggestion, about Cromwell, immediately before the arrest of that minister.'' According to Martienssen, Catherine, with help from Cuthbert Tunstall, secured an interview with the king without Cromwell's knowledge. At that time she presented facts to exonerate Throckmorton and told the king of bribes Cromwell had accepted from Lord Latimer and Sir Richard Rich to secure her uncle's release. Catherine had another motive in going to the king, Martienssen said: she and her husband Lord Latimer had felt themselves under the threat of Cromwell's displeasure ever since the Pilgrimage of Grace. After Catherine had left the king, he sent for Rich and probed that surprised and frightened man thoroughly. Rich finally said that Cromwell boasted he would bring not only the realm but the king himself to his own opinion. That was the final blow—the king ordered the arrest of Cromwell. Though Martienssen does not give his sources, other biographers of Rich say that he testified against

Cromwell. The details about Rich make the action of Catherine a little less important but more plausible.

Catherine had plans after the death of Lord Latimer and was only waiting for a decent interval to pass before she married Thomas Seymour, but she felt compelled to postpone that marriage. Henry VIII wished to marry her, his fifth wife, Catherine Howard, having been executed on February 13, 1542. Apparently she considered his wish a command; and her letter to her brother (*Letters and Papers,* 1543) describing the request as "the greatest joy and comfort that could happen" to her may have risen from duty, not complete truth. Cranmer issued a license on July 10, 1543, permitting the ceremony to be performed at any church, chapel, or oratory in the kingdom without the asking of banns. Two days later the king and Catherine Parr were married at Hampton Court. Among the wedding guests were Henry's daughters Mary and Elizabeth; Lady Mary Douglas, daughter of Henry's sister Margaret by her second husband; Catherine, Duchess of Suffolk; the bride's sister, Anne Herbert, Countess of Pembroke; Lady Anne Dudley; and Anne, Countess of Hertford. The king's daughter Mary was the bridesmaid; she received two gold bracelets set with rubies and twenty-five pounds as her gift from the bride. Catherine had no children by her first two marriages; but when she married Henry VIII, she became a stepmother for a second time—to a daughter of Catherine of Aragon, age twenty-seven; a daughter of Anne Boleyn, age ten; and a son of Jane Seymour, age six.

When Henry VIII died on January 28, 1547, and Catherine became a widow for the third time, she was married secretly within a short time to Thomas Seymour, Baron Seymour of Sudeley, younger brother of Edward Seymour. Both men were brothers of Queen Jane, the third wife of Henry VIII. After the death of Henry VIII, Edward had become the Protector in March 1547; he was Earl of Hertford and then Duke of Somerset; in the early years of the reign of Edward VI he was the most powerful man in England. After her secret marriage Catherine began trying to secure, through the Protector, the permission of Edward VI for her to marry Thomas Seymour. Bickering developed, the Protector became angry enough to withhold jewels that Catherine considered hers, and a struggle for precedence went on between his wife and the dowager queen. At last Catherine and Thomas Seymour were publicly married.

On August 30, 1548, Catherine gave birth to a daughter who was named Mary, but soon the mother developed child-bed fever. On

September 5 she made a nuncupative or oral will, giving all her property to her husband and wishing that its value were a thousand times greater. About two days later she died. After her death Thomas Seymour, who had been engaged in traitorous activities including a plan to marry the Princess Elizabeth, was arrested, convicted of treason, and beheaded on March 20, 1549.

Before analyzing the serious contributions that Catherine Parr made to English life, it may be well to admit that she lacked judgment in situations involving Thomas Seymour. Her secret marriage to him shortly after the death of Henry VIII was a serious error in judgment. She ran the risk of bearing a child with an uncertain paternity and an equally uncertain claim on the throne. Her tendency to condone Seymour's freedom of behavior toward the Princess Elizabeth (who remained a member of her household by the order of the Privy Council) as if it were mere harmless romping, when she was present herself, was another error that might have had serious consequences. When she finally realized that a dangerous emotional situation could develop, she sent the girl to a household of her own under the care of Sir Anthony Denny and, instead of blaming her, remained on friendly terms.

Catherine's nuncupative will, leaving everything to her husband and ignoring her newborn child, was perhaps another error in judgment, if not an empty gesture made in ignorance of the law. Some legal experts, including William Noye, said that lands "pass not but by writing," and only chattels may be willed orally. In 1549-1550 Parliament passed a statute making it possible for Mary to inherit, but not the lands her father forfeited to the king when convicted of treason. The child Mary was sent first to her uncle, Edward Seymour the Protector; then by the dying request of her father to Catherine, Duchess of Suffolk, but without the furnishings and the funds that had been promised with her. Apparently she went next to her uncle William Parr. Then she disappeared from available records. Two traditions about her have been reported: that she died early and that she lived to marry and to have a child or children, with people named Lawson claiming descent from her. If Catherine Parr had any real concern about her child's future, it does not appear in the accounts of her death.

Perhaps some basis for a partial understanding of her attitude to Thomas Seymour lies in the probability that the first marriages of Catherine were conventional arrangements, but she had chosen Thomas Seymour for himself — handsome, unprincipled scoundrel though he was. Then it became necessary to marry the king and, before he died, to nurse an ulcerated obesity. When she was free to marry Seymour, her emotions were stronger than her judgment. Her letters, published by Samuel Haynes, confirm her attachment to Seymour; so does her letter Ballard transcribed from manuscripts in Elias Ashmole's study: "My lord, ye charge me with a promise written with my own hand, to change the two years into two months; I think ye have no such plain sentence written with my hand. . . ." After teasing Seymour about being a paraphraser, she continued: "When it shall be your pleasure to repair hither, ye must take some pain to come early in the morning that ye may be gone again by seven o'clock . . . without suspect. I pray you let me have knowledge over night at what hour ye will come, that your porteress may wait at the gate to the fields for you." This letter must have been written about the time of the secret marriage of Thomas Seymour and the Dowager Queen Catherine Parr.


Catherine Parr's important achievements are of two kinds: those intended to further the religion of the reformers, but chiefly outside her actions as queen, and those performed because she was queen and the wife of Henry VIII. Of course they overlap in time and in motivation, but they will be separated somewhat for purposes of discussion.

In her religious efforts she operated with the zeal common in the convert, for like her friend the Duchess of Suffolk she was presumably baptized in the older faith held by her parents and by her first and second husbands. She made a mature choice of the reformed religion for herself. When and exactly why she made the change seems uncertain. Though James K. McConica said that, while she was Lord Latimer's wife, her household "had become the resort of Coverdale, Latimer, and Parkhurst," his statement is refuted by William P. Haugaard. The latter said "no evidence has been brought forward to suggest that Katherine knew any of the three men before she married Henry, nor that she knew Coverdale or Hugh Latimer while Henry lived, nor that she ever knew Latimer personally at all." Her recorded efforts to further the reformed religion came after the death of Lord Latimer, but though we are left uncertain about the time of her change, no doubt exists about its reality.

Perhaps Catherine, Duchess of Suffolk, had influenced Catherine Parr's change of religion; the duchess was one of the guests when Henry married his sixth wife, and in mentioning her presence, Evelyn Read spoke of the two Catherines as old friends at this time. Soon after Catherine Parr became queen, she appointed John Parkhurst as her private chaplain; Parkhurst proved himself a sincere reformer by going into exile at the accession of Queen Mary. Probably he remained in Catherine's service till her death in 1548, for he stated in 1571 that he had been her chaplain until twenty-three years ago. At some time Miles Coverdale was the almoner of Catherine Parr, but since he was on the Continent from 1540 to March 1548, he must have served in the last few months before her death. He also conducted her funeral service.

When Catherine Parr published *Lamentation of a Sinner* on November 5, 1547, she left no doubt about a change. She had once worshipped images made by man, she said, and had sought "for such rifraf as the bishop of Rome hath planted in his tyranny and kingdom. . . ." A personal reading of the New Testament in English, she implied, had been the cause of her change. So she began making it possible for others to read the English Bible.

The major reasons for the influence of Catherine Parr were that she was mild in temperament and that she supported the moderate religious ideas that became known as Erasmianism. In broad general terms Erasmianism meant the subordination of form, ceremony, and complex theology; the approach of the individual to religion by reading the Bible for himself; and an inner change expressing itself in worthy action. Its early development in the attitudes of Margaret Beaufort, Richard Whitford, Catherine of Aragon, the Blunt and Pole families, and others, was analyzed by McConica in *English Humanists and Reformation Politics*.

In the early 1500s similar ideas were developed by More and Colet as well as Erasmus. Before Erasmus came to England, his early contacts with the Brethren of the Common Life and their ideas known as the *devotio moderna* had influenced him. Though the Brethren were orthodox, they did not emphasize theology and ritual, but cultivated simplicity and "a constant ardour of religious emotion and thought." In *The Sir Thomas More Circle* (1959) this writer attempted to summarize the ideas of these men in England. The essentials of the Christian religion, they believed, were inner attitudes, a love of God and of human beings, and a resulting worthy action. They wished to ignore most comments of the Schoolmen, to return to scripture and the early fathers of the Christian church, and to find and publish the true text of these sources. With these ideas Catherine Parr apparently would have agreed; but while they remained loyal to the universal church, she renounced the papacy.

Catherine Parr did much to further her views on religion, but it is doubtful whether she was able to exert much influence on the Windsor persecutions, at least in the large and general way described by some Protestant historians. As a basis for understanding those presecutions it is necessary to recall that Henry VIII had two aims in his break with the universal church: first, to make himself the supreme power over the church in England; and second, to maintain complete orthodoxy in ritual and doctrine for himself and, as soon as he could safely do so, for England. He needed and used the support of religious reformers to accomplish his first objective; he had achieved it by 1534 or 1535. A few years later he felt that he might secure uniform orthodoxy. With the help of Stephen Gardiner, Bishop of Winchester, and other orthodox bishops and with his own intervention to stop the efforts of the reforming bishops, he secured the passage of the Six Articles by Parliament in 1539.

The first of these articles supported the doctrine of transubstantiation, the belief that the bread and wine, when consecrated by the priest, were changed into the real body and blood of Christ. Second, communion in both kinds was not necessary; that is, laymen did not need to take both the bread and the wine at communion. Third, priests were forbidden to marry. Fourth, vows of chastity were perpetual, even when monks and nuns were turned out of their religious houses. Fifth, private Masses were both fitting and necessary. Sixth, auricular confession, or confession to a priest, was not only desirable but necessary. For denying the first article, burning at the stake was the penalty; for denying any one of the other articles twice, the penalty was the same as for a felony. This statute, sometimes called the "whip with six strings," gave firm legal support for the burning of Anne Askew in 1546; it encouraged Gardiner and Sir Thomas Wriothesley, who became chancellor in 1544, to watch Catherine Parr and the ladies of title who were her friends at court. It was also the basis for the Windsor persecutions.

The leader or the chief accuser in making charges of heresy was John London, who attached himself to Stephen Gardiner and became a canon at Windsor about 1540. Soon after that date he began to accuse people of disagreeing with the Six Articles. Since the king and Catherine Parr were married on July 12, 1543, she was apparently not in a position to exert much influence before that date. Many accusations had been made and the guilt or innocence of those accused had been decided much earlier.

Among the accused were Philip Hoby, Thomas Cawarden, Edmund Harman, William Snowball, and their wives; Thomas Starnald of the king's chamber; and Simon Haynes, Dean of Exeter. According to *The Acts of the Privy Council,* Hoby was sent to prison in the Fleet on

March 18, 1543, but was released only six days later. Archbishop
Cranmer learned at least by early April that he had been accused, but
the king at that time made him head of a commission to try his own
case. Simon Haynes was called before the Council on March 23; it was
decided on April 22 to refer the charges against him to a commission.
Four bishops to examine him were named on May 4; he was called
before the Council July 4, exhorted about his future behavior, and then
set free. While it is true that a formal pardon was issued in September
1543 for Philip Hoby, the decision to exonerate him had been made
several months earlier. Robert Testwood, Henry Filmer, and Anthony
Parsons (two of them at least had been accused in March) were burned
to death at Windsor on July 26 or 28, and though Catherine had then
been queen about two weeks, she did not save them from death.

It seems doubtful whether Catherine had any part in convicting
John London when he was indicted for perjury in making his accusations, though his indictment came much later than her marriage.
He was convicted and sent to prison in the Fleet, where he died before
the end of 1543. Some Protestant historians credit her with his
downfall; Gilbert Burnet, in *The History of the Reformation,* stated that
''one of the queen's servants'' was sent to his trial to reveal his villainy.
Back of that vague, unconvincing statement is the question of who
accused him and why and how he was brought to trial. In his biography,
*Thomas Cranmer,* Jasper Ridley assigns the credit for revealing the
plot that London had masterminded to Thomas Legh, Sir William Butts,
Sir Anthony Denny, and Ralph Morice. Accounts of these men in the
*Dictionary of National Biography* indicate that they had the right at-
titudes and also the chances to get information that might well bring
London to justice. If the opportunity had presented itself, no doubt
Catherine Parr would have been glad to help. But there seems to be no
definite evidence that she could or did contribute to the conviction of
John London.

Catherine Parr's work as author and editor furthered her religious
principles. Her first venture was *Prayers or Meditations,* published
twice in 1545 and eight or nine times through 1559. A subtitle described
the aim of the work as ''stirring the mind unto heavenly meditations'';
the prayers were ''collected out of holy works by . . . Catherine, Queen
of England, France, and Ireland.'' Her material was reprinted also with
*The King's Psalms* as *The Queen's Prayers. . . .* This volume was
issued five times from 1568 to 1608. Though some professed to see

Catholic theology in the work, it probably was universal, with nothing to offend a follower of either religion. The publication of editions from 1545 to 1608 under five rulers seems evidence for this conclusion. The sixty-four page *Meditations,* according to G. Fenno Hoffman, Jr., is from Richard Whitford's version of the *Imitation of Christ,* Book III, but shortened by "judicious skipping," with pronoun changes and other small alterations. Since Thomas à Kempis, author of the *Imitation,* was the greatest writer connected with the *devotio moderna,* this fact gives additional support to Catherine Parr's connection with Erasmianism.

Catherine was the author of another book, *The Lamentations of a Sinner,* published November 5, 1547, about nine months after the death of Henry VIII, though she may have written it while the king was living. She denounced the pope and all vain superstition; asserted that Christ is the only savior; approved justification by faith but pleaded for continuing good works; and denounced extremes, including the idea that a knowledge of God's word is harmful because it causes dissension. Though the book was published again in 1548, no other edition appeared until 1563. Of course it would not be reprinted under Queen Mary. William Cecil wrote and signed a preface for Catherine. He praised her by name and emphasized her change in religion, saying that she had "forsaken ignorance wherein she was blind, to come to knowledge whereby she may see, removing superstition wherein she was smothered, to embrace true religion."

Catherine Parr's most ambitious project in publishing appeared early in 1548 as *The First Tome . . . of the Paraphrase of Erasmus,* though it was under way much earlier. Nicholas Udall, her general editor, explained her plan in his prefatory dedication. She had distributed the whole New Testament "by portions to sundry translators, to the entent that it might all at once be finished, ne the devout English readers any long time defrauded of so fruitful and profitable a work. . . ." She had done this, he added, without expecting any reward except being commended to God in prayer.

In a longer dedication to Catherine, placed before the Gospel of St. John, Udall summed up the religious work being carried on by women of all classes:

> When I consider, most gracious Queen Catherine, Dowager, the
> great number of noble women in . . . England, not only given to
> the study of humane sciences and of strange tongues, but also
> so thoroughly expert in holy scriptures that they are able to
> compare with the best writers as well as indicting and penning
> of godly and fruitful treatises to the instruction and edifying
> whole realms in the knowledge of God, as also in translating

good books out of Latin or Greek into English for the use . . . of such as are rude and ignorant of the said tongues, I cannot but think . . . the famous learned antiquity so far behind these times that there cannot justly be made any comparison between them.

After naming famous women of the past and noting their small number, Udall continued:

It is now no news in England to see young damsels in noble houses and in the courts of princes, instead of cards and other instruments of idle trifling, to have continually in their hands either Psalms, homilies, and other devout meditations, or else Paul's Epistles . . . and as familiarly both to read or reason thereof in Greek, Latin, French, or Italian as in English.

Every good person is doing his best to harvest the Lord's corn, Udall said, ''some by instructing the youth, some by teaching schools, some by preaching to their simple flocks, some by godly inducing of their families, some by writing . . . goodly treatises for . . . such as are willing to read, and some by translating good books out of strange tongues. . . . Noble women and those of the lowest class join in this work. . . .'' So England can never thank Queen Catherine enough for setting forth diverse meditations and for causing these works to be published.'' And England will never be able to praise enough ''the most noble, the most virtuous, the most witty, and the most studious Lady Mary's Grace . . . for . . . translating this paraphrase of the said Erasmus upon the gospel of John. . . .'' When the Princess Mary developed a long and grievous illness, Udall added, she turned the work over to Master Francis Mallett, that it might be finished quickly. In a letter of September 20, 1544, from Hanworth, Catherine urged Mary to publish and to use her name as the translator. This version was translated from the Latin by Sir F. Madden:

I beseech you to send me this beautiful and *useful* work, when corrected by Mallet, or some other of your household; and at the same time let me know whether it shall be published under your own name or anonymously. In my own opinion, you will not do justice to a work in which you have taken such infinite pains for the public (and would have still continued to do so . . . had your health permitted it) if you refuse to let it descend to posterity under the sanction of your name. For since everybody is aware what fatigue you have undergone in its accomplishment, I do not see why you should refuse the praise that all will deservedly offer you in return.

Udall, who translated Luke, sent her his manuscript in September 1545, according to E. J. Devereux; and Thomas Key, at the suggestion of George Owen, a physician to the king, became the translator of Mark. Though Matthew and the Acts were prepared about the same time, no one seems to know who did the work. One may wonder whether Catherine Parr translated them herself, though no one else, so far as this writer knows, has made that suggestion. But she may have been doing so when an innocent little Prince Edward was congratulating her on her progress in Latin. Most of the material used in the first part of the *Paraphrase* was perhaps in the hands of the queen by the end of 1545, though there was no plan to publish it while Henry VIII was living.

After the death of Henry VIII on January 28, 1547, Richard Grafton, who had become king's printer to Edward VI, issued *Injunctions* under the date of July 31, 1547. These ordered all parishes within three months to provide a complete Bible in English, and within twelve months a copy of the *Paraphrase* of Erasmus upon the gospels and to place it where parishioners might conveniently read it. In three months more, every parson, vicar, curate, priest, and stipendiary under the degree of bachelor of divinity was to provide himself with the New Testament, in Latin and in English, and the *Paraphrase* and "shall study and compare the texts." Within twelve months each was to secure a copy of the first part of the *Paraphrase* and to place it where parishioners might conveniently read it. As this first volume of the English *Paraphrase* carried the publication date of January 31, 1548, the terms of the *Injunctions* were adjusted to it. It is apparent also that Catherine Parr lived long enough to see in print the work she had sponsored.

Authorities seem to disagree about the influence of the English translation of the *Paraphrase,* though the disagreement may depend upon a lack of clarity in statements and may be more apparent than real. William P. Haugaard described Catherine Parr as one who "read Latin easily and had some knowledge of Greek," and who "patronized the vernacular version of the book which was, next to the New Testament, the most influential single contribution of Renaissance Christianity to the English Reformation. . . ." If Haugaard meant that the original work of Erasmus was influential, his statement may be completely sound. However E. J. Devereux noted that the English version sponsored by Catherine and promoted by the *Injunctions* of Edward probably had small influence: it was not printed later than 1552, after the first few years of Elizabeth's reign it was seldom mentioned in articles of visitation, and in 1583 the printer gave up the copyright; hence he concludes that it had little influence on the development of Anglican thought. One who understands human inertia is likely to be skeptical about the number of parishioners who read the *Paraphrase* and the number of the clergy who provided themselves with the proper texts and compared them as the *Injunctions* ordered. But Catherine Parr, who could not foresee the short reign of Edward VI and the return of the papal power with Queen Mary, had demonstrated her zeal, her willingness to work for the religion she professed, and her ability to carry through a large plan with some success.

When Catherine Parr died in September 1548, her place as a sponsor for the *Paraphrase* was taken by Anne Stanhope, the second wife of Edward Seymour the Protector. (As he became the Earl of Hertford in 1537 and the Duke of Somerset after the death of Henry VIII in 1547, she appears under many different names.) A second volume of the *Paraphrase,* dated in 1549, is available at the Folger Shakespeare Library, catalogued as *STC* 2854.3. Between the Epistle to the Hebrews and the First Epistle of St. Peter, the editor John Old placed his dedication to Anne Stanhope, the Duchess of Somerset, praising her also for pursuing Christian studies and spreading God's word. Since the two women had struggled for precedence at court after the death of Henry VIII, it seems ironic that Anne Syemour succeeded Catherine Parr as sponsor of the second volume of the *Paraphrase* by Erasmus.

Catherine's efforts to further her own knowledge of scripture and in turn to help others were appreciated by those who shared her opinions. John Foxe reported that she employed "divers well learned and godly persons to instruct her thoroughly in the same," and that she was persuading the king to finish his work by clearing the church of superstition. About 1545 Francis Goldsmith wrote to thank her for admitting him to her household, adding that God had formed her mind for pious studies and that her rare goodness made every day seem like Sunday—"a thing not heard of before, especially in a royal palace."

Only a few books were dedicated to Catherine, but the few were religious works with serious tributes related to her values. In addition to the comments made by Nicholas Udall in the first part of the *Paraphrase* of Erasmus, Sir Anthony Cope addressed her in the preface

of *A Godly Meditation upon Twenty Select and Chosen Psalms* in 1547.
Cope had been her vice-chamberlain and then her chamberlain. He had
considered what gift to her would best help him "declare my loyal and
obedient heart toward you, of whose heaped goodness I have so much
tasted that I can never be able to deserve the thousandth part, but only
with my prayer and hearty service." Finally he had decided, he said, to
make an exposition of the Psalms, because their harmony is sweet and
because they give the Christian all that he needs to do, think, or say.
Catherine Parr is not credited with other dedications. Considering her
concern with religion and her position as queen, that fact seems strange
unless she knew all the methods of discouraging those who wished a
reward for flattery.

        After Catherine became queen, she used another method of
furthering religious opinions. As she was reading scripture daily with
persons who were both learned and godly helping her, she began including the ladies and gentlemen who were her attendants. She and the
others gave an hour to these studies every afternoon, with greater
emphasis during Lent. Sometimes her group also listened to sermons
on abuses in the church. Though she held these meetings with the
approval of the king and even discussed them with him, they may have
roused the fears of such conservatives as Thomas Wriothesley and
Stephen Gardiner.
        Reports about the heresy of Catherine Parr were discussed
elsewhere while she was queen — at the very time when the king, after
the adoption of the Six Articles in 1539, was trying to maintain orthodoxy in ritual and theology. When Chapuys was writing to Mary of
Hungary early in 1547, he linked her and Catherine, Duchess of Suffolk,
together as heretics with influence on the king. The racking of Anne
Askew after she had been condemned (an event verified by others in
addition to John Foxe) was based on a desire to get evidence against
other ladies at the court. Among the suspects were Catherine, Duchess
of Suffolk, the Countess of Sussex, the Countess of Hertford (then Anne
Stanhope Seymour), Lady Denny, and Lady Fitzwilliam. Three other
women with possible heretical opinions who were in the confidence of
the queen were Lady Herbert (Anne Parr, the queen's sister), Lady
Tyrwhitt, and Lady Lane.
        Such details help make credible the story of Stephen Gardiner's
attempt to arrest Catherine Parr for heresy. The incident was related by

John Foxe; and though we justly ignore his invectives and diatribes, he spent both time and money in checking facts.

One day, according to Foxe, the king and queen with Stephen Gardiner present were discussing the fact that the king had licensed an English translation of the Bible and then had suppressed it. (The king's change of mind is a matter of record.) As the three talked, Henry became irritated by something the queen said; after she left the room he expressed his anger and Gardiner saw his chance. Filling the king's mind with fears, he suggested a search of the rooms used by the queen and her ladies for evidence and the arrest of the queen. Through a faithful servant or through a paper dropped by accident, the plan reached the ears of the queen. She became ill, partly feigned and partly real, in an attack of hysterical agony. Finally her outbursts became so loud that the king heard them. He ordered himself carried to her bedside and saw her suffering.

By the next day she had recovered enough to visit the king. She apologized for seeming to disagree with him on any religious opinion, for of course he was always right. She had only meant to divert his mind from his suffering and to find out the truth for herself. Perhaps, as others have suggested, the king had not been alarmed by her deviation from orthodoxy but by her independence of mind.

When Chancellor Wriothesley came with a group of men to arrest Catherine, Henry called him "beast, fool, knave," and ordered him to leave. It is said that Catherine interceded for Gardiner, but that Henry never forgave him. Certainly he did strike Gardiner's name from the Council, and he did not list him among his executors. Another reason for the king's reaction against Gardiner has been suggested by J. R. Elton: Gardiner's refusal to exchange some lands with the king. Both motives, of course, may have operated together. Others suggest that the king was testing Gardiner and never meant to allow the arrest of Catherine.

A biographer of Gardiner, James A. Muller, supports the story told by Foxe. Admitting small inconsistencies rising from the dislike of Foxe for Gardiner and from his desire to present Henry as a loving husband, Muller concluded that much of the account "has the appearance of truth." Catherine and the king often discussed theological problems, he added, the king's temper flared easily when he was seized by physical pain, and the arguments of Gardiner after Catherine left the room are authentic. Muller concluded, "there is nothing inherently improbable in the story."

Catherine Parr's actions as queen when she was not trying to support her religious views were characterized by judgment and initiative. She sometimes included the Princess Mary in her informal interviews with foreign visitors. In 1544 the two made a favorable impression on the Duke of Nàjera from Spain. The duke reported that Catherine was a virtuous woman — pleasing, lively, and magnificently dressed, wearing rich jewels. The Princess Mary, also pleasing and richly dressed, had goodness, discretion, and modesty. Mary was beloved, almost adored, he added, throughout the kingdom.

The report of Chapuys was also favorable, in spite of the fact that in a later letter to Mary of Hungary he branded Catherine as a heretic. On January 3, 1545, he and Van der Delft reported to Emperor Charles V about their talk with Catherine. The two met Henry VIII as he came out to go to Mass and gave him letters with the emperor's greetings. After the king entered his oratory, the two were taken to the oratory of the queen, though they had not asked to see her. She soon entered. The two envoys gave her the emperor's greetings and thanked her for what she had done to preserve friendship between the English king and the emperor and for "the favour she showed to the Lady Mary." Her answer was gracious, including the statement that "what she did for the Lady Mary was less than she would like to do and was only her duty in every respect." She promised to do nothing that might prevent the growth of friendship between the two countries and she hoped there would be no dissension. Thus she tried to further peace while acting with discretion and initiative.

Again, when Chapuys paid his farewell visit to the king on May 9, 1545, Catherine Parr acted with queenly dignity. As Chapuys approached the king's apartments an hour earlier than the time of his appointment, he was told by his attendants that the queen and the Princess Mary were following quickly behind him. As they exchanged greetings, Catherine again spoke of her desire for future amity, asked him to carry back all that he had learned about the king's sincere good will, and hoped that his report in person would accomplish more than any exchange of letters. She inquired about the emperor's health, adding many expressions of courtesy and kindness.

When Chapuys asked to salute the Princess Mary, Catherine agreed at once and withdrew far enough so they might speak privately. His talk with Mary was brief. She thanked him for the emperor's good wishes and promised to continue her prayers for his health and prosperity. When the queen saw that they had finished, she returned, asked about the health of the queen dowager of Hungary, sent her affectionate greetings, and praised her prudence and virtue. Then, without permitting Chapuys to stir from his chair since he suffered from gout, she returned to her lodgings. Perhaps no other queen of Henry VIII except Catherine of Aragon, who had been trained from infancy to be a queen, would have managed these situations with the same good taste and initiative.

Catherine Parr seems to have been a good executive while she was regent from July 7 to October 1, 1544, when Henry was in France. Instead of proclaiming her himself, as he had done with Catherine of Aragon, he had his Council confirm her appointment. Five men were given her as a special Council, one of them being Archbishop Cranmer; and in case of need the Earl of Hertford was to be chief captain of her armies. Though she met no problem as serious as the one Catherine of Aragon confronted when she organized forces for the battle of Flodden, she had to handle many different situations. Through July several letters dealt with the threat of an invasion from Scotland in spite of the punitive expedition Hertford had led across the border in May as a warning. A number of Scots were taken prisoner: the question was whether to send them home or to let the king continue paying for their keep. On July 22 Catherine wrote to Sir Ralph Evers, thanking him for his victory over the king's enemies; and on July 25 when she wrote to Henry, she praised the diligence of the members of her Council. Later she reported on a Scottish ship that had been captured. While these were not earth-shaking problems, she was meeting them without apparent strain. Perhaps she managed without the Earl of Hertford, for he seems to have been at Boulogne when it was captured. But Cranmer was in constant attendance on her, according to Jasper Ridley; he traveled with her on her progress through Surrey and Kent, and he was her guest at his own manor house in Otford, a place he held as Archbishop of Canterbury. She closed her work as regent tactfully by proclaiming a public thanksgiving for Henry's safe return to England.

Another service of Catherine Parr as queen, this time to education, was her plea to the king for Cambridge University about 1545 or 1546. Parliament had met the king's need for money by putting at his disposal "the revenues of all the hospitals and colleges in England." Cambridge University made an appeal to the queen, she used all her influence with the king, and then she reported that he had listened to her prayers, "his Highness being such a patron to good learning, doth tender you so much that he will rather advance learning and erect new occasion thereof than to confound those your ancient and godly institutions. . . ." Describing herself as a studious person, she asked those she addressed to further learning as the Greeks had done but to give a secure place to Christian learning.

Catherine may have stretched the truth when she called the king "a patron to good learning," but this time her promise for the future was exceeded by his gift. A commission was appointed to examine the finances of the colleges, and when the examination was complete, this group reported that the colleges had scarcely enough to pay essential expenses. When they took their findings to the king and he had examined the details, "in a certain admiration he said to . . . his lords that stood by that he thought he had not in his realm so many persons so honestly maintained in living by so little land and rent. . . ." He told the colleges to hold their own—he would not force them further. He did more. On December 19, 1546, only a few weeks before his death, he issued letters patent for a "college of literature, sciences, philosophy, good arts, and sacred theology." His generous foundation became Trinity College. As he had never before given any great sum to education, it seems reasonable to suppose that he would not have done so this time without the persuasions of Catherine Parr.

The contributions Catherine made to the welfare of her three royal stepchildren—that strange brood of varied ages and different mothers—was an outstanding service to them as human beings and probably to England. Prince Edward had never known his own mother, who died a few days after his birth. Princess Elizabeth was not yet three years old when her mother was executed, though she may have been unconscious of the facts at the time, for she was living in her own household at Hunsdon, in charge of Lady Bryan. The Princess Mary had been separated from her mother in 1525 when she was about nine years old and was sent to Ludlow Castle as Princess of Wales. Except for a stolen visit in 1531 she did not see her mother again. After she made a bitter submission to her father in 1536, she and Elizabeth were sometimes at the court together for special occasions, one of them being the christening of Prince Edward; but no other queen united them as a family. Now the three were often at court together, and the king began thinking of them all as his "dearest children."

About six months after Henry VIII and Catherine Parr were married, Parliament passed an act in January 1544 settling the crown on Edward, Mary, and Elizabeth, in the order named, and giving the king some additional right to change the succession by his last will and testament. So far as his own children were concerned, Henry accepted the terms of Parliament (if he did not actually request them to take action); but if they failed to leave heirs, he excluded the Stuart line (from his older sister Margaret) and asserted the right of the Suffolk line (from his younger sister Mary). No evidence appears so far to prove that Catherine influenced the king to recognize the right of all his children to the crown; but her kindness to them and the time when the action was taken create a strong probability that she was partly responsible.

Catherine exerted a great influence on the education of Edward (and on the education of Elizabeth as well) when she moved the household to Hampton Court and reorganized both the household and the royal school. Earlier, Thomas Cromwell, with the help of Archbishop Cranmer, had established Sir William Sidney as chamberlain for the prince's household, with Sir Richard Page as second in rank, Lady Bryan as mistress, and Doctor Richard Cox as a tutor; but when Catherine was reorganizing, Sidney wished to retire. It was Catherine, according to J. K. McConica, who brought in John Cheke. He had made a brilliant reputation at St. John's College, had published a translation of the homilies of St. Chrysostom, and had been appointed in 1540 as the first regius professor of Greek. He also had connections with Doctor Butts, physician to the king. Cox was made dean, though he was hardly the "venerable dean" that some have called him, being only forty-four years old at the time. Cheke was to assist him in teaching.

Those who write on the education of Prince Edward usually assume that Sir Anthony Cooke was one of his teachers, but the question of who appointed him and when is elusive. Strangely enough, the prince did not mention Cooke when he wrote in his *Journal* about his education. He said of himself:

> At the sixth year of his age, he was brought up in learning by
> Mr. Doctor Cox, who was after his almoner, and John Cheke,
> master of art, two well learned men, who sought to bring him up
> in the learning of tongues, of the scripture, of philosophy, and

> all liberal sciences. Also John Belmaine, Frenchman, did teach
> him the French language.

The first person to mention Cooke as a teacher of Prince Edward may have been Roger Ascham in December 1550, when he was praising Mildred Cooke Cecil to his friend Sturm. Naming her as one who spoke Greek as well as she spoke English, he did not know whether she was to be envied more for her knowledge, "for having the noble Anthony Cook for her father and teacher, the associate of John Cheke in instructing our young king, or . . . for having married William Cecil. . . . " Ascham clearly meant to describe Cooke as the associate of Cheke in teaching Prince Edward, and with his connections he should have known the facts.

A number of other boys, mainly from titled families, were selected to be in the school with Prince Edward. They included Henry Brandon (who became Duke of Suffolk in 1545); Thomas, Lord Howard; John, Lord Lumley; Barnaby Fitzpatrick; and Henry Hastings, later Earl of Huntingdon. Perhaps the king encouraged these additions to the school more readily because he remembered his own solitary childhood, but it was a plan that many noblemen in England and elsewhere tended to follow in educating their children. William Parr (it is said) had shared the studies of Henry Fitzroy, natural son of the king, with John Palsgrave and Richard Croke as teachers, though Parr was about six years older than Fitzroy. Henry Howard, Earl of Surrey, commenting on his own life, said that he had spent his childhood from about 1530 to 1532 at Windsor with a king's son, who must have been the same Henry Fitzroy.

If Catherine Parr chose the teachers and planned the enlargement of the school for Prince Edward, she deserves the comment of Mc-Conica that she was "clearly the creative force behind the augmented school." As a result she exerted a great influence on the little prince, who was six years old when she married the king and who began his education at that age. Through her choice of great scholars who were Protestant sympathizers, she also influenced religious thought in England to a degree that is beyond calculation.

The letters of Prince Edward when he was six to ten years old seem adequate evidence that Catherine gave him four years of training and affection. In one, written in May 1546, he addressed her as "Illustrious queen and beloved mother" and gave her "hearty thanks for your loving kindness to me and my sister." But since the only real love, he said, is directed toward God, he added this request:

Preserve, therefore, I pray you, my dear sister Mary from all the wiles and enchantments of the evil one, and beseech her to attend no longer to foreign dances and merriments which do not become a most Christian princess. And so, putting my trust in God for you to take this exhortation in good part, I commend you to his most gracious keeping.

The concern of the nine-year-old prince about the conduct of his thirty-year-old sister must have been his own idea, though he may have had help with his Latin in composing the letter.

In January 1546 Prince Edward wrote Catherine explaining that he had not written lately because he wished to improve in correctness first and that her desire for his improvement was "a token of your signal and lasting love toward me." He continued:

And this love you have manifested to me by many kindnesses, and especially by this New-year's gift, which you have lately sent me, wherein the king's majesty's image and your own is contained, expressed to the life. For it delighteth me much to gaze upon your likenesses, though absent, whom, with the greatest pleasure, I would see present; and to whom I am bound by nature as well as duty.

Since the Princess Mary was twenty-seven years old at the time of her father's last marriage, Catherine had no chance to influence Mary's development, but perhaps she made life a little more pleasant for her. Of course Catherine gave Mary the chance to develop the affection that grew up between her and the small Edward when she brought them to court together. Since Catherine was only four years older than Mary, the two exchanged gifts as adults. At one time when Mary gave her stepmother a purse, Catherine sent a letter of thanks by a messenger who would be welcome to Mary, she said, because of his skill in music. As a gift one New Year's, Mary prepared for her stepmother "an embroidered manuscript volume of prayers translated into various languages." A letter quoted earlier indicated that Catherine persuaded Mary to translate the Gospel of St. John and to publish it with her name, in the first *Paraphrase* of Erasmus. Through the later 1530s and the early 1540s, McConica said, "a conservative humanist and pietist group continued to meet and write in the private court" of Mary, and Catherine brought this group back to the center of affairs. Though the difference in the religious views of Catherine and Mary was based on divergent attitudes to form and ritual and to the papal power, both were controlled somewhat by the laws and the will of Henry VIII, but even more by the queen's gift of tolerance.

 

To the Princess Elizabeth, Catherine Parr was an affectionate mother, from the time of her marriage to the king until his death. The young girl remained in Catherine's household after her father's death because the Privy Council committed her to Catherine's care. The earliest extant letter of Elizabeth—written in Italian and dated in July 1544—was addressed to the queen. While the king was in France, the young Elizabeth for some reason was out of favor with him. She was told that her stepmother mentioned her to the king in every letter she wrote, so Elizabeth wrote a letter of thanks and begged the queen to ask a father's blessing for her. By the end of that year Elizabeth had a New Year's gift ready for the queen—her own translation from the French of a poem by Margaret of Navarre. Translating from Margaret of Navarre, *Le miroir de l'âme pécheresse,* she used the title *The Mirror of the Sinful Soul.* She enclosed her manuscript in an elaborate embroidered cover, also her own work, with pansies in the four corners and with the queen's initials in the cénter. The formal prose of her translation did not improve the original; but the work, as she said in her preface, was a labor of love addressed to "the most noble and virtuous queen by her humble daughter." As McConica said, the work was "a classic of the French Erasmian movement, emanating from its greatest patroness, and now offered to her present English counterpart." But even if Catherine was aware that her role in England was like that of Margaret of Navarre in France, the eleven-year-old Elizabeth probably had no such thought: she gave no indication that she even knew the name of the author whose poem she translated.

The influence of Catherine Parr led Elizabeth to compose "an elaborate version in Latin, French, and Italian, of Catherine Parr's *Prayers* dedicated to the king and dated 3 December, 1545." W. P. Haugaard added to this statement of McConica by saying that Elizabeth gave Catherine at the next New Year an embroidered manuscript volume of these prayers. It remains among the Royal Manuscripts. About the same time the young princess translated the *Dialogus fidei* by Erasmus from Latin into French, intending it for her father. Though the manuscript has disappeared, the comments of various foreign visitors who saw it at some time in the Whitehall Library prove that it once existed.

Catherine Parr also seems to have been responsible about 1544 for the selection of William Grindal as a tutor for Elizabeth. He held the position until his death of the plague at the beginning of 1548. He was a fellow of St. John's, Cambridge, a favorite pupil of Ascham's, and was called "the greatest Grecian of them all." Perhaps no better appointment could have been made. After Grindal's death Elizabeth was determined to have Roger Ascham, and though Thomas Seymour and Catherine both preferred another candidate for the position, Catherine yielded to the girl's wishes. When Elizabeth was sent away to her own household, Ascham continued as her tutor to the end of 1549. Then, because of a conflict with someone else in her household, he withdrew; but the identity of his opponent and the nature of the conflict are unknown. Thus Catherine Parr seems to have given Elizabeth both affection and intellectual stimulus. When she chose Grindal and permitted the girl to choose Ascham, she furthered the girl's development and thus helped prepare her to be queen of England.

Catherine Parr's care and management of Henry VIII in the most difficult period of his life was humane, and it was also a service to England. In estimating what she did, it makes small difference whether he had syphilis (as many assume) or whether the symptoms might have come from osteomyelitis or from an aggravated varicose ulcer (as Scarisbrick suggests). Catherine spent hours on her knees changing his dressings, trying every method she knew to ease his physical suffering, and talking to him in an effort to take his mind away from his ailments. His body, always huge, had become mountainous from an enormous appetite for food and drink. Four men found it difficult to lift him. Apparently he had occasional moments of intense pain, and it seems safe to conclude that his disposition did not become sweeter as he suffered. The ministrations of Catherine sometimes kept him from impulsive and disastrous decisions about government—decisions triggered only by pain and frustration. Thus her care of him was an indirect service to England.

When Catherine Parr died at thirty-six years of age, her contributions to the public welfare had been personal, educational, political, and governmental as well as religious, Her initiative and her effective mildness in furthering her religious views remain worthy of respect, whether she is being estimated by atheists, agnostics, Mohammedans, Jews, Catholics, or Protestants.

Her funeral service was consistent with her life. It was conducted by Miles Coverdale, with Lady Jane Grey as the chief mourner. At that time Lady Jane was a member of Catherine's household; her parents had sold her wardship to Thomas Seymour, who promised them that he would bring about a marriage between her and the young king, Edward VI. (After the death of Catherine she continued in the household for some weeks.) The funeral was the first royal one with Protestant rites. Psalms and biblical lessons in English were a part of the service, and a Te Deum replaced the penitential requiem Mass. Catherine Parr, dowager queen, was buried in the chapel of Sudeley Castle, Gloucestershire, then held by her husband Thomas Seymour, Baron Sudeley.

*Portrait of Princess Elizabeth at about thirteen by an unknown artist now hangs at Windsor Castle*

*Below: Facsimile signature, ''Elizabeth R''*

*The great bed of Ware is typical of the type of bed that was moved with Elizabeth on her journeys.*

# CHAPTER NINE

# *Queen Elizabeth*
## 1533-1603

Queen Elizabeth began her personal rule with the courtship of the people, it might be said, on January 14, 1559, though she had been ruling since November. Having spent the night at the Tower according to custom, she stepped outside about two o'clock that January afternoon, entered her litter, and began her coronation procession to Westminster. She was crowned next day.

Her subjects, who had gathered by the thousands, saw a confident young woman of twenty-five at the center of a magnificent pageant in gold and crimson. Her large flat litter was covered with gold brocade. The two handsome mules who drew it were draped with the same rich

*Portrait of Queen Elizabeth, attributed to John Bettes II.*

209

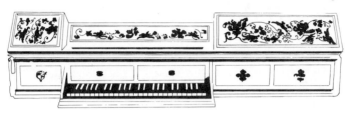

*Elizabeth was reputed to*
*be a skillful performer on the virginal.*

fabric. The queen wore a beautiful robe of cloth of gold and the crown of a princess, without any symbols of sovereignty.

Gentlemen pensioners, marching at each side of the queen and carrying gilt battle-axes, wore garments of crimson damask. Footmen in crimson velvet jerkins, their uniforms decorated with massive gilt-silver ornaments, red and white roses, and the letters E. R., surrounded her.

In front of the queen were her household staff, minor officers of state, bishops, temporal peers, foreign ambassadors, and the king-of-arms. Also at the front were the Earl of Arundel, newly appointed as high steward, the Duke of Norfolk as earl marshal, and the Earl of Oxford as high constable. Immediately back of her rode Robert Dudley, now master of horse to the queen and the future Earl of Leicester. He was leading a spare horse. Back of him were thirty-nine ladies — duchesses, countesses, and other wives and daughters belonging to families of peers. Most of them were riding horses with velvet

*A procession of Queen Elizabeth. Though once called*
*"Procession to Blackfriars," on the assumption that*
*she was going to the wedding of a niece of Mildred*
*Cecil and Anne Bacon, that theory and others about*
*a specific journey have been discarded. Instead, we*
*may assume it presents her normal progress*
*whenever she went abroad in later years. The Lord*
*Chamberlain led, followed by all the nobility and*
*Knights of the Order who happened to be at court.*
*Next came six heralds who carried maces before*
*the queen. After her came fifty gentlemen of the*
*guard, each with a halberd, and the ladies and maids*
*of honor who were at the court. The painting, on*
*canvas, is attributed to Robert Peake the Elder*
*and hangs at Sherborne Castle.*

sidesaddles; about fifteen were in three litters. Henchmen on "stirring horses" and royal guards traveled at the rear.

The streets from Fenchurch to Cheapside were lined with wooden rails and draped with tapestries, velvet, damask, and other rich cloths. Back of the rails stood members of the City Companies dressed in their liveries. As the queen entered the city, she was greeted with "prayers, wishes, welcomings, cries, tender words, and all other signs which argue a most wonderful love of most obedient subjects toward their sovereign." The queen expressed her thanks to distant people by waving and smiling, and to people near by speaking gentle words of appreciation. When a common person moved toward her, she stopped her litter, listened to a request or a petition, or accepted with thanks a simple bouquet of flowers. Near Fenchurch, a child in rich apparel on a beautifully furnished platform with a band of musicians, waited to utter a speech of welcome. The queen ordered her litter to stop and the music to cease while she listened to the child's greeting. And all the people with a great shout echoed the welcome. So the young queen made her way through the city, stopping for every speech, listening with full attention, and thanking the speakers.

Pageants presented ideas on government to the new queen. The

first one stressed the unity of York and Lancaster through figures representing the marriage of Henry VII to the Yorkist Elizabeth, that of Henry VIII to Anne Boleyn, and their daughter Elizabeth. Another presented the four virtues of good government: pure religion (treading on superstition and ignorance), love of subjects, wisdom, and justice. In another, eight children applied to Elizabeth the beatitudes in the fifth chapter of Matthew. At the upper end of Cheapside the recorder of the city gave the queen "a purse of crimson satin richly wrought with gold," containing a thousand marks. Another pageant presented two hills, one green and flourishing, the other withered and dead. From a cave between the hills Time emerged, leading his daughter Truth, who presented the queen with an English Bible. She received it with thanks and placed it against her breast. A last pageant represented Deborah, "judge and restorer of Israel," consulting with her nobility, clergy, and commons for the good government of Israel. Thus Londoners made clear to their new queen what they expected of her, and their noisy welcome left no doubt about their approval.

In her coronation procession Elizabeth had established the tone of her whole reign: magnificence (as much as a thrifty queen burdened with the debts of other rulers could manage), informality, and a personal touch that included the courtship of the common people. She was a successful queen, probably one of the two best of the Tudors, the other being her grandfather Henry VII. Measure her against any other ruler for a hundred years before or after, and she might not clearly come off second best.

Elizabeth was not perfect, of course—she was a human being. Occasionally a hot temper sparked her into a hasty, deplorable action— for example, when John Stubbs wrote *The Discovery of a Gaping Gulf* as a protest against the proposed marriage of the queen to the Duke of Anjou. A court condemned author, publisher, and printer to lose their right hands and to be imprisoned. The queen pardoned the printer but permitted the other two men to suffer. Each made a speech of loyalty before the sentence was carried out. After the hand of Stubbs had been cut off, he used his left hand to remove his hat as he shouted, "God save the queen!" Then he swooned. It was an age when statutes and courts imposed cruel punishments; men sentenced to hanging were commonly cut down and disemboweled while they were still alive. And the queen had neither made the law nor set the penalty. However, in reporting the incident, Sir John Neale commented that for once the queen's good sense had deserted her. But for one incident of this kind, dozens of others reveal her kindness.

She was not perfect. Some think that she should have reformed conditions for her common soldiers and her seamen. She tried, and more will be said later of her efforts, but she was battling against an entrenched system of graft and corruption that even the strongest ruler could not overcome.

She was not perfect, or she would have prevented or terminated sooner the struggle of Essex to gain power. Perhaps for once, when she expected to make him into a useful servant of the state, she misjudged her man — in contrast to the many times she chose men wisely.

She was not perfect. She never gave Sir Henry Sidney any adequate reward for years of loyal, efficient service. Once she offered him a title — without the essential funds to support the honor. Perhaps Sir Henry was not a skilled courtier but only a statesman!

Since Queen Elizabeth was a successful ruler — even a great ruler — what were the elements of her success? One was certainly her ability to continue the personal rule she had begun with her coronation procession and to combine informality with magnificence. For many years her progresses were occasions when she courted the people and they responded with enthusiasm — progresses from one of her own residences to another or to the homes of the gentry and the nobility. She owned about fourteen places that she used, and her movements in the late summer and fall of 1599 seem typical. Early in August she left Greenwich for Eltham, where she stayed three days; she went on to Nonsuch in Surrey for six days; and with a rest stop at Richmond, she moved to Hampton Court, staying there till the end of October, then returning to Whitehall in London. At that time the court was not fixed; it was always with the queen. The work of moving seems formidable. A chaplain of the queen took along his portable altar, and a clerk of the market transported his weights and measures. Sometimes the royal bed was taken along. Minstrels, jesters, and palace pets traveled with the queen; and sometimes a herd of goats was taken for their milk. As many palaces were on or near a river, barges transported equipment and people; the queen rode horseback occasionally, but usually traveled by litter.

Elizabeth spent days and weeks visiting her officials as well as higher and lesser nobility. As William Harrison said in *The Description of England,* ''all is hers, and when it pleaseth her in the summer season to recreate herself abroad and view the estate of the country, and hear the complaints of her poor commons injured by her unjust officers or their substitutes, every nobleman's house is her palace, where she continueth during pleasure and till she return again to some of her own. . . ." Many such visits have been mentioned in earlier chapters.

Physical and tangible reasons for the progresses also existed. Members of the court escaped the plague areas, found fresh food supplies or new hunting grounds, and welcomed better sanitation to supplement the regular work of the "gong-farmers" or "night-soil men" during a residence. But Elizabeth also traveled to win the loyalty of her people and thus to improve her government.

When she stopped in towns, she was usually given a cup with money, the amount varying from twenty to a hundred pounds. At Coventry on one visit, receiving twenty pounds, she commented that the sum was a good gift. The mayor said, "If it please your Grace, there is a great deal more in it." Of course she asked what else; the mayor answered, "The hearts of all your loyal subjects." She answered promptly, "We thank you, Mr. Mayor; it is a great deal more indeed." At Norwich, where a nervous schoolmaster welcomed her in a Latin speech, she gave him her hand and lied royally, saying, "It is the best speech that ever I heard. . . ." At Sandwich, where the wives of officials offered her a banquet of 160 dishes, she ate without the preliminary tasting to guard against poisoning, and then had certain dishes reserved and sent to her lodging. The women whose dishes were thus complimented must have boasted for the rest of their lives about the queen's appreciation of their cooking.

Part of the queen's personal rule was her expression of sympathy to those who had lost members of the family or had other troubles. When the Earl of Huntingdon died in northern England while his countess was in the London area, the queen moved immediately to Whitehall; she sent the lord keeper to tell Huntingdon's wife that he was ill, and a second time to say that he was worse. Thus Elizabeth prepared her for the death that had already occurred. After the countess had been told of her husband's death, the queen went by litter to visit her. As she continued her visits, the friendship between them grew stronger, even intimate, refuting somewhat the charge that Elizabeth seldom made friends with women. Again, when Sir Christopher Hatton (who had served the queen well in offices over many years, becoming her lord chancellor in 1587 and holding the position till his death in 1591) was in his last illness, she paid him a visit and spent the night at his house — not a state visit but a personal call of sympathy.

When Lord Burghley's wife died in 1589, he fell into a deep, lasting melancholy and some two years later asked to give up his office. The queen answered with a half-serious, half-jesting letter that kept him in her service almost to the end of his life. She sent Burghley word at one time that, though he had brought up his son to be as near like himself as he could, he was in all things her Alpha and her Omega. At another time she told him that she did not wish to outlive him — a comment that brought tears to his eyes. In his final illness she visited him and fed him with her own hand. A month before his death he wrote his son Robert, wishing him to thank the queen for her kindness: "Though she will not be a mother, yet she showeth herself by feeding me with her own princely hand, as a careful nurse; and if I may be weaned to feed myself, I shall be more ready to serve her on earth; if not, I hope to be in heaven a servitor for her and God's church." Many other condolences made her rule personal and sympathetic.

Her letters of thanks and congratulations often had a warm, personal tone — for example, a letter to her relative Henry Carey, Lord Hunsdon. During the rebellion of 1569 he had been sent north to bring in Leonard Dacres but he was surprised by Dacres and his son when he had only half the number of their troops. After he won a decisive victory the queen wrote him thus:

> I doubt much, my Harry, whether that the victory were given me more joyed me, or that you were by God appointed the instrument of my glory; and I assure you that for my country's good the first might suffice, but for my heart's contentation the second more pleased me. . . . And that you may not think that you have done nothing for your profit, though . . . much for honor, I intend to make this journey somewhat to increase your livelihood. . . . Your loving kinswoman, Elizabeth, R.

When Peregrine Bertie, by this time Lord Willoughby, achieved a military success, she wrote him (as she had done on earlier occasions), "My good Peregrine, I bless God that your old prosperous success followeth your valiant acts, and joy not a little that safety accompanieth your luck. Your loving sovereign, Elizabeth, R." When Lord Mountjoy was carrying on a campaign in Ireland, ending with his brilliant victory over Tyrone, she wrote him a number of bantering, inspiring, and grateful letters.

Another element in the successful rule of Elizabeth was her many-sided education and the use she made of it as queen. She had been trained in the lighter accomplishments of the Renaissance lady, she had learned much in the hard school of experience, and she had an excellent education by the classical standards of the time.

She played both cards and chess well, doing so in the privy chamber where counselors and other privileged people came. She was a skillful performer on the virginals and the lute. She was fond of walking and of riding horseback, and she took one of these exercises every day when the weather was favorable. She enjoyed hunting and sending her trophies as gifts, having once ordered Leicester to send Archbishop Parker a fat stag she had killed. When she was fifty-six (a courtier reported) six or seven galliards a morning, with music and sometimes other dancing, made up her exercise. When she was sixty-nine, she rode horseback ten miles and did some hunting. In November 1602 she was dancing a coranto, and at her last Christmas that year the gaiety was as usual. Though these details also indicate that she had physical vigor, they are related to her education in hunting, riding, music, and dancing. If they contributed to her mental and physical health, they made at least a small contribution to her success as a queen.

Before she came to the throne, Elizabeth had an informal education in experiences that developed her caution and her native sagacity. After Thomas Seymour, widower of Catherine Parr, had been arrested and members of his household had admitted his plans to marry Elizabeth, Sir Robert Tyrwhitt was sent to examine and, if possible, to incriminate her. His efforts brought small result; damage to her reputation was temporary, and she had learned to cope with subtle minds. When the death of Edward VI was imminent and Northumberland summoned Mary and Elizabeth to court, hoping to get them in the Tower before Edward's death became known, Elizabeth waited instead of moving toward London. Thus she was free of any part in the efforts to put Lady Jane Grey on the throne. After that plot had failed, she rode to the city and then went back to meet her sister. When Mary made her ceremonial entry into London, Elizabeth was next to her as an escort to the new queen. It was a masterly success at being in the right place at the right time, and excellent practice for the future.

After Mary had established Mass at court, Elizabeth had a serious problem when her absence became noticeable. She asked the queen for books and teachers, so that she might learn her errors in doctrine. Soon she began attending Mary's service, but her presence was erratic enough to tell her friends that she followed policy only. When she received permission to leave the court, after traveling ten miles of the journey she sent back to ask for copes, chasubles, and other essentials for the Mass. Apparently she had won in the conflict.

Elizabeth came under grave suspicion from Wyatt's rebellion, since it was a protest against the queen's marriage to Philip of Spain, with the intention of putting Elizabeth on the throne. Though Elizabeth was sent to the Tower for a time and then to honorable captivity, she handled herself so well that she disarmed suspicion; and also Wyatt cleared her of blame in a speech just before his execution. In 1556 she managed to survive another plot, even though a conspirator admitted that the group meant to kill Queen Mary and to place Elizabeth on the throne with Edward Courtenay as her husband. Her own adroitness helped her to survive, with some help from Philip, who was thinking of a possible future. This time she had three months of pleasant guardianship in the care of Sir Thomas Pope.

As a princess-in-waiting, Elizabeth also had the problem of avoiding marriage from 1553 to 1558. The popular choice for her was Edward Courtenay, who had some claim on the throne as a descendant of Edward IV, but he was weak both morally and politically. His death at Padua in September 1556 freed Elizabeth of that problem. Philip wished Elizabeth to marry his own ally, the Duke of Savoy, and finally persuaded Mary to help put pressure on her for his purpose; but when Elizabeth was summoned to court and told of the plan, she flatly refused. Though she went back to Hatfield in disgrace, she was still mistress of herself and her future.

Events like these developed in Elizabeth a wisdom earned by hard experience, as she escaped marriage, prison, and death. She was getting an education in practical English politics and people—the kind that her grandfather had partly lacked when he came to the throne in 1485 after years of exile on the Continent, and the kind that her father lacked because he was sheltered in adolescence. Both men learned, of course, but in learning, her father suffered bitter disillusion that lessened him as human being and king.

The formal education of Elizabeth was extremely useful when she became queen, though we know little about its beginning. A recent biographer, Neville Williams, credits her governess, Kate Astley, with laying the excellent foundation, but the facts we have about Kate scarcely support the idea. Also it seems that a king's child would have had both governess and tutor. Elizabeth may have been taught briefly by John Cheke in 1544, when Catherine Parr was reorganizing the household school for Edward VI; she worked with William Grindal from some time in 1544 until his death of the plague in January 1548, and with Roger Ascham to the end of 1549. Certainly Elizabeth was informally encouraged by Catherine Parr from July 1543 until the death of her stepmother in September 1548; and though Catherine had another tutor in mind after the death of Grindal, she yielded to the insistence of Elizabeth that she have Ascham.

When Ascham ceased to be a tutor in the household of Elizabeth in 1549, the two found occasional opportunities to read Greek and Latin together through the 1550s, as Lawrence V. Ryan tells us in *Roger Ascham*. Elizabeth came to court for about two months in August and September 1555, and at that time they compared the orations of Aeschines and Demosthenes. In a letter to Sturm, Ascham said that she was quicker than he in grasping the text and that she understood the intentions of each orator and the issues they were debating. When she came to London in the summer of 1557, they worked together for a short time; and occasionally the queen permitted Ascham to travel to Hatfield, where Elizabeth was living. When she was just sixteen, Ascham wrote his friend Sturm that her mind had "no womanly weakness, her perseverance is equal to that of a man, and her memory long keeps what it has quickly picked up. She talks French and Italian as well as she does English, and has often talked to me readily and well in Latin, moderately in Greek." Perhaps these comments in private letters approached the truth.

When Elizabeth became queen, Ascham entered her service again as her Latin secretary, and they continued their Greek and Latin readings together. In *The Schoolmaster,* with his public comments, he added Spanish to the languages in which she had a "perfect readiness," said that she was reading more Greek in one day than some prebendaries of the church read Latin in a week, and mentioned her use of the method of double translation daily every forenoon for a year or two. Thus she had gained "a perfect understanding of both the tongues and . . . a ready utterance of the Latin. . . ." As Ryan suggested, her later life "does confirm what Ascham observed about her in her youth, and there is no reason to doubt his sincerity and his reasonable accuracy in describing her accomplishments."

When Elizabeth became queen, she used her linguistic and classical background in the service of the state. English at that time was not the language of diplomacy, and with her training she could speak directly to representatives of foreign governments instead of using an interpreter. Ascham was once present at court, he said, when on the same day Elizabeth replied to ambassadors from the emperor, from France, and from Sweden. She answered one in Italian, one in French, and one in Latin, "not haltingly, promptly, without discomposure, to various matters, as they uttered them in their discourse." The skill of the queen in languages is supported by other kinds of evidence in addition to the comments of Ascham.

Her most famous reply to an ambassador was made to a Polish diplomat in 1597. Because she had been on friendly terms with his father and had been told that he came to seek peace, she received him publicly in the presence chamber. He came dressed in velvet and jewels, and he began by kissing the queen's hand. Then he retired some ten yards and began an attack. England was preventing Poland from trading with Spain and was guilty of other injustices; if Elizabeth would not right these wrongs, the king of Poland would do so. "Rising lionlike from her throne, Elizabeth trounced him in extempore Latin for his insolence and audacity." If a king had directed his manner of speaking, she said, that king must be young and lacking in royal blood; and though he seemed to have read many books, he had not found the chapter on the forms appropriate for use between rulers. Her audience was delighted. Having concluded the interview with the offensive ambassador, she turned to her court: "God's death, my lords, I have been forced this day to scour up my old Latin that hath been long a-rusting."

When she paid visits to universities, Elizabeth found her knowledge of Latin and Greek essential. On a visit to Cambridge in 1564 she was asked at a late hour, after a long series of disputations, to conclude the program with a short talk in Latin. She considered using English, but Cecil told her she must not do so. So she spoke in Latin, emphasizing her high regard for learning, her regret that she had nothing to give a university that had received many gifts from her ancestors, and her hope that she might do something before the end of her life. In 1566 she visited Oxford, finding the streets lined with scholars for her entry. When the Greek reader welcomed her in a Greek oration, she thanked him in Greek and commended his performance. She stayed at the university several days. On the evening before her departure she delivered a Latin speech praising the university and apologizing for her own barbarisms in the use of that langauge. In 1592 she came to Oxford again. As she arrived, she was saluted by the Greek reader in a Greek oration; again she thanked him in Greek. Before she left she gave a Latin address to faculty and students, stressing the need to obey law, both human and divine. Again she apologized for her lack of skill in speaking Latin, saying "I scarcely remember to have used it thirty times in three years."

The translations of the queen indicate continued practice in using Latin, if not speaking it. She had translated the thirteenth Psalm early; it was published in 1548 "as an end piece to her translation of Margaret of Navarre's *Godly Meditation of the Soul.*" If she translated the chorus from *Hercules Cataeus,* the time when she did so is uncertain. Later in her life her translations included Boethius, *Consolation of Philosophy,* 1593. Often she left estimates of the brief time she spent in making these translations. About 1592 she made a verse version in English of Plutarch's essay on curiosity from the *Moralia* and put into English verse part of Horace's *Art of Poetry.* She was certainly working from the originals, Lester Bradner commented, and her translations are quite literal.

The skill of Elizabeth as an orator played a real part in her success as a ruler because she addressed her people on ceremonial occasions and in times of crisis. If her oratory was a by-product of her classical education — and she had read orations with Ascham, appreciating both style and ideas — she had the good sense and good taste to avoid quotations from scripture or from the Greeks and the Romans and to use a simple style. When she came to the throne, she struck the keynote of her reign when she said to the lord mayor and the other officials of London: "I will be as good unto you as ever queen was to her people. . . . And . . . for the safety and quiet of you all, I will not spare, if need be, to shed my blood."

Even in longer speeches she could be simple and concise. In 1566 she delivered a deliberative speech on marriage and the succession to thirty members of the House of Lords and the same number from the Commons. No reader readily forgets this passage:

> As for mine own part, I care not for death, for all men are mortal, and though I be a woman I have as good a courage answerable to my place as ever my father had. I am your anointed queen. I will never be by violence constrained to do anything. I thank God I am endued with such qualities that if I were turned out of the realm in my petticoat I were able to live in any place in Christendom.

Her exhortation to her troops at Tilbury, Essex, in August 1588, shortly after the defeat of the Armada, was one of her most inspiring brief speeches. Because England still feared an invasion by the Duke of Parma, two armies were gathered—one at Tilbury to resist the enemy if he landed, and one at St. James to guard the queen. In spite of the fears of others for her safety, she visited the troops at Tilbury. She began her address to them by saying that some were unwilling to have her come to an armed multitude for fear of treachery. She continued:

> But I assure you, I do not desire to live to distrust my faithful and loving people. . . . And therefore I am come amongst you . . . being resolved in the midst and heat of battle to live or die amongst you all; to lay down for my God and for my kingdom and for my people my honor and my blood even in the dust. I know I have the body but of a weak and feeble woman; but I have the heart and stomach of a king, and of a king in England, too, and think foul scorn that Parma or Spain or any other prince of Europe should dare to invade the borders of my realm; to which, rather than any dishonor should grow by me, I myself will take up arms, I myself will be your general, judge, and rewarder of every one of your virtues in the field.

Another effective speech of Elizabeth was the one she addressed to the Commons on November 30, 1601. The members had attacked monopolies, and the queen had promised them immediate relief for the evil by issuing a royal proclamation. Overjoyed, the members asked to come to Whitehall to convey their thanks to her. When she had the proclamation in their hands, she said, she would receive a deputation. But all wished to come. She replied that space was limited but all would be welcome. She addressed one hundred forty members and their speaker. Among other things, she said:

> And though God hath raised me high, yet this I account the glory of my crown, that I have reigned with your loves. This makes me that I do not so much rejoice that God hath made me to be a queen, as to be a queen over so thankful a people, and to be the means under God to conserve you in safety and to preserve you from danger. . . . It is not my desire to live or reign longer than my life and reign shall be for your good. And though you have had, and may have, many mightier and wiser princes sitting in this seat, yet you never had, nor shall have any that will love you better.

Probably both the queen and her listeners realized that this speech, called her "Golden Speech," might be the last she addressed to the Commons. At its close she asked that all these gentlemen be brought to kiss her hand before they left for their homes. As these events happened less than a year after the execution of Essex, they indicate that the queen still held the affection and loyalty of many people.

The queen's great orations have simple wording and simple sentences; they are brief; their organization is emotional and psychological. Without need of support from the Bible or from the classics, the ideas she presented may have been somewhat indebted to orations by Greek statesmen; but if so, they had become "mere English." They were effective because they stirred emotions that Elizabeth and her people held in common.

Elizabeth could not have become a great queen if she had not been able to solve some unusual problems about the management of her court. In the past, government had usually been a masculine business, with a court centering around a king. But Elizabeth—a healthy, attractive, unmarried young woman of twenty-five—found herself the center of some fifteen hundred people, mostly men, many of them unmarried and uninhibited. As Neale suggested, she was in the position of managing a men's club. She could reduce the number of gentlemen ushers and add perhaps twenty maids of honor, girls of good families who wished to finish their education at court. But large problems remained. Men brought quarrels with them from home; and the struggle for royal favor, offices, and patronage created new and bitter rivalries. Also, her court must have enough splendor to attract courtiers, but she did not have money to waste. With her gift for finances, she handled the problem of a glittering court.

A social problem remained because the queen was entirely responsible for the conduct of the girls who became maids of honor, as if she were a parent to all of them. They came to court with the hope of making good or even brilliant marriages, and those marriages became the queen's responsibility. Thus the marriage of one of them without her permission was a breach of discipline and an affront to her. As she had no intention of allowing them to get into trouble if she could help it, she did not condone sexual laxity at court. She was as strict, said Neale, as ever Queen Victoria could have been. Some offended. The Earl of Oxford had a son by Anne Vavasour, with no intention of marrying her; his imprisonment in the Tower and banishment from the court were probably caused by this offense. It became evident that Elizabeth Throckmorton was pregnant; and though Sir Walter Raleigh admitted his responsibility, married her, and remained loyal to her, both were sent to the Tower and he was absent from court for a time after their release.

Though Elizabeth could not rule by fear alone and fear did not fit with her personality, the problem partly solved itself: men began addressing her with the flattery they would have used in speaking to a king, and they tended to add the admiration and coquetry they would have used with other attractive young women. As a result, according to Neale, they turned the reign into an artificial comedy of young men and older men in love with the queen of England—a game that secured service tinged with emotion. Though Elizabeth had not invented the game, she had the wit to continue it and to keep it "artificial enough for safety." By the time it became absurd, when Elizabeth was an old woman, the older men accepted it as habit; but some younger men rejected it and wished to have a king on the throne. This game of addressing the queen as Gloriana, Belphoebe, Diana, or some other romantic figment is illustrated by an appeal of Raleigh to the sixty-year-old queen when she was leaving court for a progress:

> I that was wont to behold her riding like Alexander, hunting like Diana, walking like Venus, the gentle wind blowing her fair hair about her cheeks like a nymph, sometime sitting in the shade like a goddess, sometime singing like an angel, sometime playing like Orpheus; behold the sorrow of this world once amiss hath bereaved me of all.

Elizabeth was effective in managing her court if it had even half the decency mentioned by William Harrison in his *Description of England*. Though many courts elsewhere were vicious, he said, such "enormities are either utterly expelled out of the court of England, or else so qualified by the diligent endeavor of the chief officers of Her Grace's household, that seldom are any of these things apparently seen there without . . . such severe correction as belongeth to those trespasses." Harrison may have had in mind the penalty as it was described by a statute of the thirty-third year of Henry VIII for any men guilty of striking others while they were within a royal palace: "without all hope of mercy, benefit of clergy, or sanctuary, they are sure to lose their right hands at a stroke, and that in very solemn manner. . . ." Using the vivid details from the statute itself, Harrison described the equipment, the officers, the bandaging of the stump after the amputation, and even the cup of red wine and the bread that were given to the victim. No record indicates that Elizabeth ever imposed the penalty on a courtier, and even Henry VIII is said to have pardoned the first man convicted because he pleaded for his left hand to be substituted that he might keep his right hand to use in serving his king. But courts of law took some action when men threatened to attack others; offenders were not reappointed on commissions and also discovered that they could no longer secure royal favors. Perhaps also the mere existence of the law on the statute books was a restraint.

The queen's encouragement of the learned languages, useful occupations, and intellectual pursuits also helped her to keep an orderly court, judging from the comments of Harrison. A great number of men and women, he said, have a sound knowledge of Greek and Latin and are equally skillful in Spanish, Italian, or French. Instead of being idle, many older women do embroidery, caulwork, or silk spinning; some read the scriptures, English history, or the history of other countries; some are writing books of their own or translating the books of others into English or Latin. Many older women are skillful in surgery or in distilling waters or in other practices connected with the ornament or the "commendation" of the body, and all of them can cook delicious dishes "of their own devising" but usually based on Portuguese recipes. Finally solid reading is furnished to prevent idleness, every office having a Bible, a copy of *The Acts and Monuments of the Church of England,* or histories and chronicles. Younger women often spend their spare time in some kind of music. Thus Elizabeth solved the problem of an orderly court, partly by feminine and unorthodox means, partly by discipline, and partly by encouraging activities and in- tellectual pursuits.

An essential principle in the reign of Elizabeth was clemency, except in an occasional situation where a hot temper overcame her judgment. When she came to the throne, she prayed that God might give her "the grace to govern with clemency and without bloodshed." When discontented counselors were plotting against Cecil, Leicester appointed himself to tell her that many thought Cecil must lose his head or the state would suffer. The queen gave him a sound scolding for his views. She had no idea of treating a chief official as her father had treated Wolsey and Thomas Cromwell. "It was impossible to intimidate her; she was clement and she was astonishingly loyal to her ministers." She was clement with Norfolk when she first learned that he was becoming involved with Mary Queen of Scots, trying to warn him in an audience she had planned for that purpose. After he was convicted of treason, she delayed signing the warrant for his execution; at last she signed and then recalled until Parliament was ready to act for her, before she finally took action. Her clemency to the Queen of Scots lasted from 1568 to 1587—about nineteen years—though delay meant danger to her throne and her life. With the Babington conspirators, again, she had mercy; after six other principal conspirators and Babington himself had been executed with the full harshness of the law and the usual practice of Henry VIII, she ordered that the others should be hanged until they were dead before they were mutilated. She was clement about Essex after he had been guilty of other acts of disobedience, apparently hoping to make him useful to the state. After his final conviction by a jury of his peers, she still hesitated to order his execution. When Henry IV heard that finally the order had been carried out, he exclaimed in admiration, ''She only is a king. She only knows how to rule.'' She permitted only five others to die, sparing the Earl of Southampton because he was humble and contrite.

Another source of strength in the work of Elizabeth as queen was the fact that she had a mind ready to make a pragmatic approach to problems, instead of a philosophic mind grappling only with absolutes. She asked herself whether an action would be effective in a given situation and what the practical results would be — not whether it was right by logic, philosophy, and religious teachings. At the beginning of her reign she waited before making many changes in her Council, she postponed actions that would reveal her religious views, and she finally established a compromise, avoiding the papal power and the Mass but keeping the episcopal system and some formal ceremonies and vestments. Hence she has been called an ''adroit opportunist'' — and with some justice.

Perhaps her pragmatic approach enabled her to be moderate on all questions of religion. It has been said that she had a secular mind. If the phrase means that she considered religious problems with some objectivity, asking herself what course of action would bring results and what might be best for England, then her mind was secular. Her preference for some form and ceremony but not for the Mass, for a centralized control through her bishops, and for a middle way need no repetition here. Her attitude may be shown best by her treatment of loyal Catholics. Even after the pope issued his bull of excommunication in February 1570, releasing Catholic subjects from obedience to her and her laws, Elizabeth used moderation. The effect of the pope's edict was to cast doubt on those Catholics who remained loyal to the queen and the government. It also aroused Protestant hostility, as the sending of missionary priests into England had done, no matter how sincere and dedicated some of them may have been. This hostility led to more severe laws against Catholics, though even the laws of 1581 recognized differences between laymen and priests and "between being and becoming a Catholic." The queen applied the new laws with moderation and took pride in Catholics she considered loyal to her. She had no desire "to make windows into men's souls."


Elizabeth's skill in a game of dissimulation was essential to her success as queen. She was especially adept at using suitors. When Philip of Spain was ready to marry her "as a service to God," if she would profess and maintain his religion and secure absolution from the pope, she told him that if she married, she would prefer him. Philip was useful: he could keep the pope quiet, or even postpone the time when the Catholic opposition in England would become active. As long as Philip was a suitor, she was in a better position to bargain with France. And even after she refused him, Philip must continue to give her some support; as the ruler of the Low Countries, he needed commerce with England for those countries. Finally she told the Spanish ambassador that she could not marry Philip because she was a heretic. That ended the comedy—for on both sides it was comedy, based on a desire for political gain. Later, when she heard that Philip had married the daughter of the French king, "she accepted the news with an easy air, now and then giving little sighs that bordered on laughter."

Elizabeth continued to use suitors like pawns on a chessboard— exactly as the suitors were trying to use her. They included Eric, oldest son of the king of Sweden; the Archduke Ferdinand; and the Archduke Charles. The last two were sons of Emperor Charles V. Ferdinand was soon withdrawn, though Elizabeth kept Charles dangling, reviving his hopes now and then by her attentions to the ambassador from his court. The Scots hoped for a marriage between Elizabeth and the Earl of Arran, but she did not encourage this idea. Perhaps she saw nothing to be gained by prolonging the game. In 1570 Catherine de Medici offered her son, the Duke of Anjou, but he annoyed his mother by refusing to give up his religion. She next offered another son, the Duke of Alençon, three years younger than Anjou and twenty years younger than Elizabeth. Discussions of this marriage were postponed by the massacre of St. Bartholomew; but in 1579 Alençon sent a favorite courtier, Simier, to woo for him. In 1581 he came in person. Consultations, apparently serious, took place as well as wooing scenes and exchanges of presents. Perhaps Elizabeth was enjoying a diversion. Perhaps her biological urges were stronger than usual, making the situation more than a political game. But Elizabeth was about forty-eight, with small chance of bearing a child to inherit the throne, and the English people were hotly opposed to the marriage. If Elizabeth had ever taken the situation seriously, she made a final decision on the basis of her intelligence.

Elizabeth, abetted by Cecil, found dissimulation extremely useful in handling relations with Scotland about 1559 and 1560. Frances II and Mary Queen of Scots were on the throne of France; her Guise uncles were powerful; and her mother, Mary of Guise, was regent in Scotland. Danger existed that these Catholic forces would unite Scotland and France against England. But in Scotland, Protestant rebels and nationalism were also at work; and the "Congregation," as the rebel nobility and the Protestant preachers called themselves, expected help from England. They received the help, although it was a violation of the treaty of Cateau-Cambrésis, signed in 1559. When the rebels started paying their men in Flemish and English money, and when the enemy intercepted a considerable sum, denial became harder. Elizabeth continued to deny the help but with smiles, "as though she was thoroughly enjoying the joke." Laughing, she charged the envoy to repeat her words: the regent of Scotland was hearing nothing but malicious rumors. Reporting on his conference with her, the envoy said, "she is the best hand at the game living." It was a game that neither Mary Tudor nor Mary Queen of Scots could play with the same success, and it frustrated enemies.

Elizabeth's political dissimulation also centered about the execution of Mary. Parliament had tried and condemned her and Elizabeth had signed a warrant without clear directions about the time of its execution. Finally William Davison, Burghley, and the Council executed the warrant. Mary was beheaded. Elizabeth the human being was so grief-stricken that she could neither eat nor sleep—and the grief was probably not all play-acting. Elizabeth the queen declared that she had never meant to send the warrant: her officials had acted improperly. When she wrote these details to James VI of Scotland, one of his chief ministers answered for him: "If the queen follow forth this course to excuse herself, and give some proof of it, without doubt the king shall love and honor her above all other princes." The words that followed implied the need for a scapegoat. Elizabeth complied. For several months Burghley seemed to be under her displeasure; Davison was tried in Star Chamber and sentenced to imprisonment during the queen's pleasure, with a heavy fine. Though he remained in the Tower about eighteen months, he probably had every comfort and some freedom. His fine was remitted, and he continued to draw his pay. Thus dissimulation was effective—with the tacit consent of Henry III of

France and of James VI of Scotland. The latter, of course, found himself a step nearer to the English throne. And each of the two rulers was relieved of the need to take action he had no desire to take.

In spite of her dissimulation Francis Bacon praised her hate of vices and her morality when he wrote "In Felicem Memoriam Elizabethae." The incident he used as an illustration concerned a secretary who was drafting a message for an ambassador to give Catherine de Medici. The secretary inserted an idea of his own, saying that "they [Elizabeth and Catherine de Medici] were two queens from whom, though women, no less was expected in administration of affairs and in the virtue and arts of government than from the greatest men." The secretary was told to delete his comparison. Though Bacon used the incident to illustrate morality, it lends itself to many interpretations. Perhaps the English queen did not like to be compared with other rulers, especially women, or she merely preferred to compose her own letters, or she did believe that her own moral principles were superior to those of the Queen Mother of the Valois; and if she had the last of these ideas in mind, she may have been right.

The ability of Elizabeth to make a decision, even a highly personal one, on the basis of her intelligence, not her emotions, was an invaluable asset to her as queen. She had a chance to learn that lesson as a girl of fifteen in the Seymour affair. If she had married Seymour or if she had been guilty of misconduct she would never have become queen. In her later life, each problem of marriage was resolved by her grasp of political facts. To marry a Catholic would bring her some of the problems that had plagued her sister Mary; to marry outside the kingdom would limit her political decisions or alliances; to marry a subject might fan civil factions into flames. If her emotions were really stirred by the courtship of Alençon her decision was again based on intelligence. But perhaps her hardest personal decision had been made earlier and had concerned the Earl of Leicester. To marry him after the strange death of his wife Amy Robsart in 1560, she knew would cost her the good will of her people. By the summer of 1561, Neale suggested, the romance had not ended, but she had passed the crisis of her attraction to him. "But while not unfeminine or sexless, Elizabeth was a less emotional type than her sister. Experience had added caution to a quick and active mind, and she was consumed with ambition to be a great popular ruler. . . . But in the long run it was the weal of the kingdom and the limits of practical politics that directed her judgment."

Elizabeth could not have succeeded as a queen without her financial prudence, a quality she inherited from her grandfather, it seems, not her father. Henry VII left in the treasury £1,800,000, according to A. F. Pollard; or as he estimated in 1900, about £30,000,000 in "our money." Henry VIII was extravagant in personal expenses and squandered money in foreign wars; thus he exhausted his great inheritance. Several times during his reign gold and silver were debased, and by 1546 silver coins were made with two-thirds alloy, at a time when large quantities of silver "beginning to be imported from Mexico and Peru were producing an inevitable depreciation in its natural value." Henry VIII left "a crippled revenue and a debased coinage," and also a debt of £100,000. Neither the men who ruled for Edward VI nor Queen Mary made much improvement in the situation. Elizabeth inherited a total debt of about £200,000.

As soon as she became queen, Elizabeth hastened the business of establishing sound finances. The French ambassador, as cited by A. F. Pollard, wrote at the end of 1559: "As for money, the queen has been scraping it together from all sides, paying nothing and giving nothing to her people, and spending very little. She . . . has paid off large debts which Mary contracted in Antwerp." She stopped at once the issue of base coins; in September 1560 she called in the inferior coins that had been made after 1543, using first a proclamation to bring the nominal value down nearer to the real value. She actually made a small profit, Pollard added, from "the substitution of a sound for an unsound currency." She sent Sir Thomas Gresham to improve England's position on the Bourse at Antwerp; and some sixteen months after she became queen, he reported "that her honor and credit were so augmented that no prince had the like." As a result she could borrow money at 10 percent instead of 14 percent.

In addition to her inherited debt Elizabeth faced the cost of driving the French from Scotland in 1559-1560 and had to finance an expedition to France in 1562. For the first twelve years of her reign her ordinary revenue from crown lands, customs, and other sources was only about £200,000 a year, and for the last ten years, about £300,000 a year. With this sum she had to pay her personal expenses, keep an attractive court, meet all the normal expenses of the government, just as a nobleman had to finance his own household, and occasionally give sums to encourage friendly Protestant governments.

The queen could call on Parliament for unusual expenses such as fortifications and the cost of essential wars, but the members of that body were more inclined to call the tune than to pay the piper. For the first thirty years of her reign the grants from Parliament averaged about £50,000 a year and were less than £80,000 a year for the whole reign. She could not meet the problem by a national debt. She could only raise short-term loans at Antwerp; pay heavy interest; and if she defaulted, endanger English merchants whose goods might be seized at sea for the debt. Her success with finances was a personal achievement, Sir John Neale estimated, in spite of her ministers.

William Camden praised the queen especially for beginning "by little and little to take away the brass money, and restore good money of clean silver, for the repairing of the glory of the kingdom," and also for lowering prices. She did this "without commotion" by forbidding any man to melt either good or brass money or to take it out of the country. She reduced brass money to its real value and she bought it from the owners with good money (sometimes at loss to herself, Camden added). Thus she deserved the credit for the fact that there was "better and purer money in England than was seen in two hundred years before, or hath been elsewhere in use throughout all Europe." Camden added that Henry VIII had first mixed brass with money, and that his action was "a notable example of riot and prodigality," especially since his father had left him "more wealth than any other king of England had ever left to his successour. . . ."

The queen's financing included heroic efforts to pay her common soldiers, but she did not always succeed in stopping corrupt and established practices. When she sent Leicester to the Netherlands in 1585 and he exceeded his instructions, she paid every penny of the sum she had promised. "And yet, to her alarm and flaming disgust, she found that her soldiers were unpaid and considerable sums still owing from her." When she discovered that troops had been disbanded without pay, though their captains had all that was due them, "she set up a committee of appeal and award for the men, in every county." No doubt her motives were financial prudence and compassion. Old, entrenched corruption was at work also when a local justice of the peace and his helpers chose men for military service; sometimes they acted from malice or they pocketed the money from those who could buy out their services. Doubtless some men thought that a woman queen simply did not understand how these things were done!

In 1593 when Parliament was asked to grant funds for the defense of England and for aid to other countries, the members of that body were reluctant. Three subsidies were granted, but resistance developed to collection of the tax in four years; six were suggested. Francis Bacon led the opposition to payment in four years, and thus he may have contributed to his loss of the post of attorney-general, which had just become vacant—though Edward Coke had better claims by age and experience. Elizabeth was hurt by the opposition. Parliament kept demanding war: "she had performed wonders with inadequate means;

she had practiced eternal vigilance over her own expenses, to the disgust of the greedy cormorants about her . . . she had kept faith with her creditors; she had eaten into her capital rather than pass more than a fraction of her war expenses on to her people.'' The time had come for the people of England to bear more of the burden. She addressed both houses herself:

> The subsidy you give me I accept thankfully, if you give me your good will with it, but if the necessity of the time and your preservations did not require it, I would refuse it. But let me tell you the sum is not so much but that it is needful for a prince to have so much always lying in her coffers for your defense in time of need and not be driven to get it when she should use it.

What England would have been like in 1603 if Elizabeth had been as extravagant as her father, in spite of the growing prosperity, may be left to the imagination.

Elizabeth was prudent in other ways besides in the handling of finances. Impulsive as she sometimes was in dealing with individuals, when she dealt with political problems and foreign governments, she seldom acted with haste or without exploring the views of her counselors and their reasons. Especially with Burghley, she would know all his mind before she acted. Sometimes she waited further to see if circumstances might change. She wished to be prudent in awarding honors. They should flow from the crown. Hence she resented the action of Essex in his 1591 expedition to France: after other unwise escapades and a failure to accomplish his mission he knighted twenty-four followers. Later in Ireland, after his strange parley with Tyrone and after the queen had written him in her own hand forbidding him to knight a single follower, he made thirty-eight knights. Perhaps he was acting this time with his later treason in mind. And for once, perhaps the queen misjudged a man when she thought that she could make Essex into a useful servant of the state — a man who had all the qualities for a brilliant career "save judgment, an equable temper, and discretion.''

Elizabeth's ability to choose and to keep good counselors and to listen but to make up her own mind in the end was a fundamental quality. Sir Francis Walsingham was outstanding. Sir Christopher Hatton, though appointed without great previous evidence of ability, was an excellent lord chancellor. Leicester was sometimes dependable but not superior. She never decided to trust Anthony or Francis Bacon, though their father Sir Nicholas had been loyal and competent. Essex has been well compared to a wild colt that refused to be broken into a useful statesman. William Cecil trained his son Robert with some success to serve the queen and England as he had done himself, but it is doubtful whether the integrity or the judgment of the son equaled that of the father.

The best example of her wisdom in choosing, of course, is William Cecil, Lord Burghley; their working partnership is one of the most remarkable in English history. On the first day of public business after she was proclaimed queen, he was sworn in as a member of her Council and was also made principal secretary. "This judgment I have of you," she said, "that you will not be corrupted with any manner of gift, and that you will be faithful to the state, and that without respect of my private will, you will give me that counsel that you think best." Apparently she had taken his measure better than he had taken hers; about two years later, Cecil scolded the messenger of an ambassador for discussing a certain topic with the queen, "a matter of such weight being too much for a woman's knowledge." Cecil should have known better; he had been married some fourteen years to Mildred Cooke, a woman with a perceptive mind about political affairs. But Cecil learned. Later he said that the queen was "the wisest woman that ever was, for she understood the interests and dispositions of all the princes in her time, and was so perfect in the knowledge of her own realm that no councillor she had could tell her anything she did not know before."

Elizabeth was a successful queen because her ambition to be great as a ruler was the greatest urge in her life. That desire conquered her infatuation for Robert Dudley and any tendency toward a foreign marriage, for she certainly realized that a marriage inside or outside England would impose limitations. She had once said that she had a longing "to do some act that would make her fame spread abroad in her lifetime, and after, occasion memorial forever." She used well the qualities that have been mentioned here because her love of England had deep roots, with her aim centering on her people, not on herself. She wished to keep out of wars, especially wars of foreign conquest, and to give England peace and prosperity.

Mary Tudor placed her love of Spain and of her Catholic church above herself, but she lacked other qualities for ruling well; and she did not discover until too late that she loved England. Mary Queen of Scots, trained by a French mother for the French court, had no genuine love for either Scotland or England. She placed nothing, not even loyalty to her church, above herself and the gratification of her emotions. Elizabeth subordinated herself and her personal life to something greater than self: the welfare of England.

The success of Elizabeth as a queen has been sung by a large chorus, with a few sour notes usually rising from other emotional commitments. Puritans praised her as their Deborah, and both Puritans and Cavaliers throughout the seventeenth century celebrated her accession day. Camden, Speed, Stow, Francis Bacon, and even James I, at times, joined in the chorus. Conyers Read, in his article, "Good Queen Bess," summarized by saying that Pope Sixtus V and Henry of Navarre agreed about her, although they agreed about little else. Shortly after his election to the papacy in 1585, Pope Sixtus said: "She certainly is a great queen, and were she only a Catholic, she would be our dearly beloved. Just look how well she governs! She is only a woman, only mistress of half an island, and yet she makes herself feared by Spain, by France, by the Empire, by all."

# APPENDIX

# *Historical Background*

## *English and Scottish Rulers*

### *BEAUFORTS—Descendants of John of Gaunt, son of Edward III and his mistress, Catherine Swynford, later his third wife*

| | |
|---|---|
| John of Gaunt | 1340-1399 |
| John Beaufort, Earl of Somerset: son of John of Gaunt | 1373?-1410 |
| John Beaufort, Duke of Somerset: grandson of John of Gaunt | 1403-1444 |
| Margaret Beaufort: daughter and heir of Duke of Somerset; first husband, Edmund Tudor, son of Owen Tudor and Catherine of France, widow of Henry V | 1443-1509 |

## *STUART RULERS, SCOTLAND*

| | |
|---|---|
| James IV: m. Margaret Tudor, daughter of Henry VIII of England | 1488-1513 |
| Regency | 1513-1524 |
| James V: son of James IV and Margaret Tudor; m. Mary of Guise | 1524-1542 |
| Regency | 1542-1561 |
| Mary Queen of Scots | 1561-1567 |
| Regency | 1567-1578 |
| James VI: son of Mary Queen of Scots and Lord Darnley | 1578?-1625 |

## *SOME PRE-TUDOR RULERS, ENGLAND*

| | |
|---|---|
| Edward I | 1272-1307 |
| Edward II | 1307-1327 |
| Edward III: seven sons, oldest died before father, two others died young | 1327-1377 |
| Richard II: second son of Edward III | 1377-1399 |
| Henry IV: son of John of Gaunt by first wife, Blanche of Lancaster | 1399-1413 |
| Henry V: son of Henry IV | 1413-1422 |

Henry VI: son of Henry V and Catherine of France;
    two periods of rule                                        1429-1461
                                                              1470-1471

Edward IV: descendant of Edward III by younger son,
    Duke of York; two periods of rule                          1461-1470
                                                              1471-1483

Edward V: older son of Edward IV, nominal king April
    9 to June, 1483, but murdered in the Tower
Richard III: brother of Edward IV                              1483-1485

## TUDOR RULERS, ENGLAND—Henry VII, his son, and his three grandchildren

Henry VII: son of Edmund Tudor and Margaret Beaufort          1485-1509
Henry VIII: son of Henry VII and Elizabeth of York,
    daughter of Edward IV                                      1509-1547
Edward VI: son of Henry VIII by third wife, Jane Sey-
    mour                                                       1547-1553
Mary Tudor: daughter of Henry VIII by first wife, Cath-
    erine of Aragon                                            1553-1558
Elizabeth Tudor: daughter of Henry VIII by second wife,
    Anne Boleyn                                                1558-1603

## STUART RULERS, ENGLAND

James I: also James VI of Scotland, descendant of Mar-
    garet Tudor                                                1603-1625
Charles I: son of James I and Anne of Denmark                 1625-1649
    Protectorate. Oliver and Richard Cromwell                  1649-1660
Charles II: son of Charles I and Henrietta Maria             1660-1685
James II: son of Charles I and Henrietta Maria and
    brother of Charles II                                      1685-1688

The Tudor line ended in 1603 with the death of Queen Elizabeth, since no son or daughter of Henry VIII had any child. The right of Henry VII to the throne came from his mother, Margaret Beaufort. The right of James I to the English throne came from his ancestor, Margaret Tudor. If the Suffolk line had ever reached the throne, it also would have done so through female inheritance, by Mary Tudor, the younger daughter of Henry VII, who married Charles Brandon, Duke of Suffolk. Their only son died in 1533 as an adolescent. Their older daughter, Frances, married Henry Grey; the Greys had no surviving son; the oldest of their three daughters was Lady Jane Grey. But though Henry VIII apparently favored the Suffolk line and Edward VI definitely did so (perhaps because of their English birth and background) Queen Elizabeth did not.

## Elected Emperors — Called Roman Emperors and, earlier, Holy Roman Emperors

Maximilian I: son of Emperor Frederick III, the last emperor crowned in Rome

| | |
|---|---|
| Crowned emperor at Aix-la-Chapelle | 1486 |
| Died | 1519 |

Charles V: son of Philip of Burgundy and Joanna, sister of Catherine of Aragon; ruler of Netherlands and King of Spain

| | |
|---|---|
| Formally succeeded Maximilian I as emperor | 1519 |
| Crowned emperor at Aix-la-Chapelle | 1520 |
| Formally abdicated as emperor, having resigned earlier rule of Netherlands and Spain | 1558 |

Ferdinand I: grandson of Maximilian I and son of Philip and Joanna

| | |
|---|---|
| Crowned emperor at Frankfort | 1558 |
| Died | 1564 |

Maximilian II: oldest son of Ferdinand I

| | |
|---|---|
| Elected emperor | 1564 |
| Died | 1576 |

Rudolph II: son of Emperor Maximilian II

| | |
|---|---|
| Became emperor on father's death | 1576 |
| Died | 1612 |

## French Kings

| | |
|---|---|
| Louis XII | 1499?-1515 |
| Francis I | 1515-1547 |
| Henry II | 1547-1559 |
| Francis II (husband of Mary Queen of Scots) | July 1559-Dec. 1560 |
| Charles IX | 1560-1574 |
| Henry III | 1574-1589 |
| Henry IV | 1589-1610 |

# Notes and Sources

These abbreviations are used in the Notes and Sources:

| | |
|---|---|
| *AHR* | *American Historical Review* |
| BM | British Museum |
| *Cal. Pat. Rolls, Hen. VII* | *Calendar of Patent Rolls, Henry VII,* or *Edward VI,* or *Elizabeth* |
| *Cal. S. P. Dom. Ser.* | *Calendar State Papers, Domestic Series,* or *Foreign,* or *Spanish,* or *Venetian* |
| *DNB* | *Dictionary of National Biography* |
| EETS | Early English Text Society |
| *Econ. H.R.* | *Economic History Review* |
| *EHR* | *English Historical Review* |
| Hist. MS. Comm. | Historical Manuscripts Commission |
| *HLQ* | *Huntington Library Quarterly* |
| *JEGP* | *Journal of English and Germanic Philology* |
| *Letters and Papers* or *L. and P.* | *Letters and Papers, Foreign and Domestic of . . . Henry VIII* |
| PCC | Prerogative Court of Canterbury |
| PRO | Public Record Office |
| *STC* | *Short-Title Catalogue of Books . . . 1475-1649,* ed. A. W. Pollard and G. R. Redgrave |
| *Trans. R. H. Soc.* | *Transactions of the Royal Historical Society* |

CHAPTER ONE: *Mildred Cooke Cecil, Lady Burghley*

*Acts of the Privy Council,* ed. J. R. Dasent. London, 1890-1907. Volume for year and index.

Ascham, Roger. *The Whole Works,* ed. J. A. Giles. London, 1865. Ability to speak Greek, I, Pt. 1, lxx-lxxi.

Baker, Thomas. *A History of the College of St. John the Evangelist,* ed. J. E. B. Mayor. Cambridge, 1869. Queen and Lady Cecil, I, 157.

Ballard, George. *Memoirs of British Ladies.* London, 1775. Letter to Fitz-william, 128; Mildred Cooke, 130; Elizabeth Cooke, 136; Catherine Cooke, 142.

Beckingsale, B. W. *Burghley: Tudor Statesman, 1520-1598.* London, Melbourne, Toronto, New York, 1967. Plot of Northumberland, 43-51; estimate of Lady Burghley, 284.

Bennett, H. S. *Six Medieval Men and Women.* Cambridge, 1955. Fastolf's allowance to his wife, 32.

*Cal. S. P., Dom. Ser., 1547-1580.* London, 1856. Wish of Countess of Lennox to put son in Burghley's household, I, 428.

*Cal. S. P., Foreign, 1558-1559.* Vol. I, London, 1863. Vol. IV, London, 1866. Letters of important men to Cecil with greetings to his wife; in these and other volumes, see index.

*Cal. S. P. . . . Archives of Simancas, 1558-1567,* ed. M. S. Hume. London, 1892. Comments on Lady Cecil, I, 18, 382, 544, 620.

Cecil Papers. Hist. MSS Comm. *Cal. MSS, Hatfield House.* London, 1883-1971. Letters from Scots, I, 211, 215, 250, 252; her benevolences, IV, 334, 495, 526; the "staff of poor chaplains," 526; employment for a ranger of Enfield, 560; dates of Cecil family events, V, 69-71; XIII, 141-43; Frances Cecil's cure, IX, 383 (2); X, 335; appreciation by Whitgift and Fulke Greville, XI, 232.

Collins, A. J. *Jewels and Plate of Queen Elizabeth I: The Inventory of 1574.* London, 1955.

*Complete Peerage,* ed. Vicary Gibbs et al. London, 1910-1959.

*Dictionary of National Biography.* For John Gerard, Sir William Fitzwilliam, and wards of Burghley, under individual names.

Donaldson, Gordon. *Scotland: James V to James VII.* Edinburgh, London, 1965. General background.

Dunlop, Ian. *Palaces & Progresses of Elizabeth I.* London, 1962. Theobalds, Chap. 11.

Edwards, Richard. "The Praise of Eight Ladies of . . . Elizabeth's Court." See *Nugae antique,* ed. Harington and Park. London, 1804. The poem, II, 392.

Fulwell, Ulpian. *The First Parte of the Eyghth Liberall Science. . . .* 1576. STC 11471[a].

George, J. "William Cecil's Second Marriage." *Notes and Queries,* Vol. XXII, no. 7 [Vol. CCXX, continuous service], 294-95: "Nov. 21. Wm. Cecile & Mildred Cooke, of gentle birth, London diocese. Dispensation for marriage . . . without banns & within the prohibited time, 7 s. 2d." Item from Archbishop of Canterbury's Faculty Office, 1545. Advent, usually including four Sundays before Christmas, was a prohibited time.

Handover, P. M. *The Second Cecil.* London, 1959. The crippled daughter, 4, 244.

Haynes, Samuel. *A Collection of State Papers . . . 1542-1570.* London, 1740. Letters to Lady Cecil from Scots, with detail: Maitland, 293, 301, 359; Melville, 362; Earl of Arran, 363.

Howell, James. *Familiar Letters,* ed. Joseph Jacobs. London, 1892. Comment on Posthumous Hoby, I, 269.

Hurstfield, Joel. *The Queen's Wards.* London, New York, Toronto, 1958. Wards in the Cecil household, 247-50; Fermor wardship, 265.

Lodge, Edmund. *Illustrations of British History. . . .* London, 1791. Temporary coolness between Lady Burghley and the queen, II, 100.

Machyn, Henry. *Diary,* ed. J. G. Nichols. Camden Society, Vol. XLII, 1848. Festivities attended by Mildred Cecil, 288-89.

Miller. Amos C. *Sir Henry Killigrew.* . . . Leicester, 1963. Date of Catherine Cooke's marriage, 96.

Mulcaster, Richard. *Positions.* . . . 1581. *STC* 18253. Ability of women to speak the languages, Chap. 38. Donald S. Pady, Iowa State University Library, is compiling new material about Mulcaster's appreciation of woman's place in Elizabethan society; he taught male students about the benefits of a married woman's happiness through continual learning; some of his students later wrote, translated, and published fascinating methods by which the fashionable housewife educated herself.

Neale, J. E. *Queen Elizabeth.* London, Toronto, 1934. Money to the "Congregation" from the queen, 85-89.

———. *The Elizabethan Political Scene.* London, 1948. Gifts and fees to officials, entire article.

Nichols, John. *The Progresses* . . . *of Queen Elizabeth.* London, 1823. Places the queen visited, I, li; persons visited, liii; Burghley's gift of a basin, II, 427.

Peacham, Henry, The Younger. *The Compleat Gentleman.* 1634. Cecil's estimate of *De officiis,* by Cicero, 45. *STC* 19504.

Peck, Francis, *Desiderata curiosae.* London, 1779. Anonymous life, "The Compleat Statesman . . . Lord Burghley," 1-49. Household expenses, 22-23; order in the household, 24; young men in his service, 24; enlargement of Theobalds for queen, 25; precepts for son Robert and tribute to Robert's mother, 47.

Peller, Sigismund. "Births and Deaths among Europe's Ruling Families since 1500," 87-100, in *Population in History,* ed. D. V. Glass and D. E. C. Eversley. Chicago, 1965. Figures on infant deaths, 90, 92.

Read, Conyers. *Mr. Secretary Cecil and Queen Elizabeth.* London, 1955. Cecil's education, 23-30; first marriage and first son, 27-28; property assignment by Cecil's father, 34, 470, Note 22 [*L. and P.,* XX, Pt. 2, 455 cited]; in Parliament, 45; life at Wimbledon, 87-89; crisis at Northumberland's plot, 94-101; Cecil's letter to wife, 96; purchase of effects of Anne of Cleves, 113; Mildred's allowance, 114; her letters from leaders of Scots, 140, 169-70; Thomas Cecil, 212-17, 309; Guzman de Silva's talks with Mildred, 336.

———. *Lord Burghley and Queen Elizabeth.* London, 1960. Study schedule for Earl of Oxford, 125; Anne Cecil's marriage, 127-38; Lady Burghley's benevolences, 446-48; Read's estimate of Lady Burghley, 447.

———. Lord Burghley's Household Accounts." *Econ. H. R.,* 2nd ser., IX (1956), 343-48.

Royal Commission on Historical Monuments. *An Inventory* . . . *Essex.* London, 1921. Monument to Cooke Family, II, 203-4; picture opposite 203.

Rye, W. B. *England as Seen by Foreigners.* London, 1865. Rathgeb's account of Theobalds, 44-45.

*Short-Title Catalogue,* ed. A. W. Pollard and G. R. Redgrave. Dedications to Mildred, Lady Burghley: Thomas Drant (translation from Horace), 13805; Ockland and Sharrock, 18773, 18775[a], 18777.

Simpson, Alan. *The Wealth of the Gentry, 1540-1660.* East Anglian Studies, Cambridge, 1961. Gratuities to officeholders, 9-10; also index, under "Gratuities."

Stone, Lawrence. *The Crisis of the Aristocracy, 1558-1641.* Oxford, 1965.

Subversive books owned by Catherine, Duchess of Suffolk, 706; Puritan influences exerted by women, 734-39.

Summerson, Sir John. "The Building of Theobalds, 1564-1585." *Archaeologia,* XCVII (1959), 107-26; also plates.

Townshend Papers. Hist. MSS Comm. *Marquis of Townshend, 1572-1791.* London, 1887. Will of Sir Nicholas Bacon, 4-7.

Williams, Franklin B., Jr. *Index of Dedications . . . in English Books before 1641.* London, 1962.

Williams, Neville. *The Royal Residences of Great Britain.* London, 1960. Theobalds, Chap. 13.

## CHAPTER TWO: *Anne Cooke, Lady Bacon*

Bacon, Anne. *Certayne Sermons.* 1550 (?). *STC* 18766.

———. *Sermons Concernyng the Predestinacion and Election of God.* 1570 (?). *STC* 18768.

———. *An Apologie . . . in Defense of the Church of England.* 1562, 1564. *STC* 14590, 14591, and later editions.

Bacon, Francis. *Collected Works,* ed. James Spedding, R. L. Ellis, and D. D. Heath. London, 1867-1874. Apophthegms, VII, 144; Lady Bacon and her sons, VIII, Chaps. 5, 7; her plea for the Nonconformists, 40-42; her aversion to revels at Gray's Inn, 325-43.

Ballard, George. *Memoirs of British Ladies.* London, 1775. Anne Bacon, 132.

Birch, Thomas. *Memoirs of the Reign of Queen Elizabeth.* London, 1754. Advice to Anthony, I, 55-56, 227, 270-71; II, 61-65; Lady Bacon and Essex, II, 218-20.

Bowen, Catherine Drinker. *Francis Bacon: The Temper of a Man.* Boston, Toronto, 1963. Details of banquet house, Gorhambury, 27-28.

Clutterbuck, Robert. *The History and Antiquities of the Co. of Hertford.* London, 1815. Gorhambury, I, 88-92.

Collins, A. J. *Jewels and Plate of Queen Elizabeth I: The Inventory of 1574.* London, 1955.

Dunlop, Ian. *Palaces & Progresses of Elizabeth I.* London, 1962. Gorhambury, Chap. 12; water supply, 188.

Machyn, Henry. *Diary,* ed. J. G. Nichols. Camden Society, Vol. XLII, 1848. Wedding feast for James Bacon's daughter, 280; Mildred Cecil and Anne Bacon as godmothers, 288-89.

Nichols, John. *The Progresses . . . of Queen Elizabeth.* London, 1823. Queen's visit to Gorhambury, II, 55-60.

Puttenham, George. *The Arte of English Poesie,* ed. Willcock and Walker. Cambridge, 1936. Tribute to Sir Nicholas Bacon, 139.

*Short-Title Catalogue.* Dedications to Anne Bacon, 2005, 13805, 24995, 25620, 25627, 25695.

Spedding, James. *An Account of the Life and Times of Francis Bacon.* Boston, 1878. Anne Bacon's views on popery, religious observances, debts, theaters, revels, I, Bk. 1, Chap. 4, and other early chapters; plan to clear debts of Francis, I, 110; revels at Gray's Inn, 138-57; her illness and death, 623-24.

Williams, Franklin B., Jr. *Index of Dedications . . . in English Books before 1641.* London, 1962.

CHAPTER THREE: *Bess of Hardwick, Countess of Shrewsbury*

*Acts of the Privy Council,* ed. J. R. Dasent. London, 1890-1907. Statement of confidence in Shrewsbury, vol. for 1583-1585, index.

*Cal. S. P., Dom. Ser. . . . Eliz. 1581-1590.* London, 1865. Documents on conflict between Shrewsbury and wife, II, 450-55; queen's request that he receive a visit from his wife, 636; earl's fear of future family quarrels, 689. Complaints of Bess about earl's failure to honor agreements, III, 25. Addenda, queen's letter about punishment for Henry Jackson, VII, 39.

*Cal. of Pat. Rolls, Eliz.* London, 1939: Grant to William St. Loe, captain of guard, I, 258; grant as chief butler, 323. London, 1948: St. Loe's payment for Cavendish, II, 495.

Collins, Arthur. *Historical Collections of the Noble Families of Cavendish.* London, 1752. Family details, will of Bess, 9-20.

*Complete Peerage,* ed. Vicary Gibbs et al. London, 1910-1959.

Harman, Thomas. *A Caveat or Warening for Commen Cursetors.* 1567. STC 12787.

Hunter, Joseph. *Hallamshire.* London, 1869. Letter of Bess to Crompe, 107; letters to "My dear None," 111-12; other letters, 107-24.

Lees-Milne, James. *Tudor Renaissance.* London, New York, Toronto, Sydney, 1951. Hardwick Hall, 117-18; plates, nos. 98, 104, 126, 127.

Lodge, Edmund. *Illustrations of British History. . . .* London, 1838. Earl's expenses for Mary Queen of Scots, II, 179-81, 181-83; letter of Bishop Overton, 407.

Machyn, Henry. *Diary,* ed. J. G. Nichols. Camden Society, Vol. XLII, 1848. Funeral of Cavendish, 156; notes, 360.

Rawson, Maud S. *Bess of Hardwick and Her Circle.* London, 1910. General background.

Read, Conyers. *Mr. Secretary Cecil and Queen Elizabeth.* London, 1955. Rising of the North, Chap. 23.

―――. *Lord Burghley and Queen Elizabeth.* New York, 1960. Ridolfi plot, Chap. 3; Throckmorton's treason, 287; Babington conspiracy, 343-45.

Sitwell, Sacheverell. *British Architects and Craftsmen,* 3rd ed. London, 1947. Hardwick Hall, 26-29; quotation, 27.

Stallybrass, Basil. "Bess of Hardwick's Buildings and Building Accounts." *Archaeologia,* LXIV (1912-1913), 347-98, general background.

Stone, Lawerence. *The Crisis of the Aristocracy, 1558-1641.* Oxford, 1965. The 8,000 sheep Bess owned, 299; funeral costs, App. 25.

Williams, Ethel Carleton. *Bess of Hardwick.* London, 1959. Early life and first marriage, Chap. 1; Chatsworth, 18-19, 32-33, 38, 89-109, 171; poisoning episode, 43-44; Catherine Grey, 49-55; Eleanor Britton, 191-94, 197; Gideon tapestries, 204. (*The DNB* gives 1518 as her birth date; Williams cites Camden, *Britannia,* II, 308, for the statement that in 1607 she was 87.)

*Manuscript material from Folger Shakespeare Library*

Acct. Book of Sir William and Lady Cavendish, 1548-1550. MS. X. d. 486.
Bagot Letters. MSS. L. a. 1-1076. Bess and her employees. L. a. 843,844.
Edmund Whalley's Accompts (Steward, 1589-1592). MS. V. b. 308.

*PCC Wills, once at Somerset House, now at PRO*

1565. Saint Lo (Seintlowe), Sir William, knt. (Chatsworth, Darby). With sentence, 24 Morrison.
1590. Shrewsburie, Earle of, George (Sheffield, Yorks., Notts.). 86 Drury.
1608. Talbot, Elizabeth, Countess of Shrewsbury, lately wife of George, late Earl of S. [F. A. B. Hardwicke]. Derbys. 23 Windebanck; sentence 105 Fenner.


CHAPTER FOUR: *Catherine Willoughby, Duchess of Suffolk*

*Cal. S. P., Dom. Ser. . . . Eliz., 1547-1580.* London, 1856. Letter to queen on her accession, I, 120; letter to Cecil on queen's compromise, 123; return of Catherine's property, 135; letter to Cecil about Mary Grey, 297; to Cecil on exiles, 332; other letters, index.
*Cal. Pat. Rolls . . . Eliz., 1558-1560.* London, 1939. Denization of Peregrine Bertie, I, 25; summons of former bishops to consecrate Parker, 449; royal assent to another as Bishop of Exeter, 450.
Cecil Papers. Hist. MSS Comm. *Cal. MSS, Hatfield House, 1883-1971,* 22 vols. Other letters between Catherine and Cecil, index.
Coverdale, Miles. *Remains.* Parker Society. Cambridge, 1846, Vol. XIV. Biographical Notice, vii-xvi; his letter to Parker on finances, 529.
Ellis, Sir Henry. *Original Letters,* 2nd ser. London, 1827. Letter of Otwell Johnson on racking of Anne Askew, II, 172-78.
Erasmus. *The Seconde Tome . . . of the Paraphrase of Erasmus.* 1549. STC 2854.3. See prefaces by John Old. This number will be in the new edition of the *STC.*
Foxe, John. *Acts and Monuments.* 1563: No story of the Berties. STC 11222. 1570, 1576, 1583: Complete story of Bertie exile. STC 11223-11225.
————. *Acts and Monuments,* ed. Josiah Pratt. London, 1877. Complete story of exile, VIII, 569-76.
Garrett, C. H. *The Marian Exiles.* Cambridge, 1938. General background. Details about Catherine are probably erroneous.
Goff, Lady Cecilie. *A Woman of the Tudor Age.* London, 1930. General background.
Haydn, Joseph. *Book of Dignities.* London, 1894. List of bishops, 424-87.
Latimer, Hugh. *The Fyrste Sermon of Mayster Hughe Latimer . . . before the Kinges Majestie.* 1549. STC 15271.
————. *Seven Sermons Made upon the Lordes Prayer . . . in 1552.* 1572. STC 15284.
————. *Selected Sermons . . . ,* ed. A. G. Chester. Charlottesville, Va., 1968.
Leadam, I. S. "A Narrative of the Pursuit of English Refugees in Germany under Queen Mary." *Trans. R. H. Soc.,* new ser., XI(1897), 113-31. Efforts to deliver processes to Berties at Weinheim.
*Letters and Papers of . . . Henry VIII.* London, 1862-1910. Letters of Sir Christopher Willoughby, IV, nos. 3349, 3474, 4184, and index. Questions to Anne Askew on "my Lady of Suffolk," XXI, Pt. 1, no. 1181; letter of Chapuys about heretical influences, XXI, Pt. 2, no. 756.
Mattingly, Garrett. *Catherine of Aragon.* Boston, 1941. Return of Maria Willoughby to the dying queen, 429.

Mozley, John F. *John Foxe and His Book.* London, New York, 1940. Lodging of Foxe with the Duchess of Suffolk, 30, 48.

Read, Conyers. *Mr. Secretary Cecil and Queen Elizabeth.* New York, 1955. Comment on the duchess, 41.

Read, Evelyn. *Catherine, Duchess of Suffolk.* London, 1962. Early life of duchess, Chaps. 1, 2; final settlement with Sir Christopher Willoughby, 170; Bertie's answer to Knox, 170; accounts at Grimsthorpe, Chap. 9; Mr. Coverdale, not indexed, 149, 151, 157.

Stone, Lawrence. *The Crisis of the Aristocracy, 1558-1641.* Oxford, 1965. Subversive books owned by the duchess, 706.

Strype, John. *Ecclesiastical Memorials.* Oxford, 1822. Miles Coverdale in exile, V, 233.

Wilson, Thomas (ed.). *Vita et obitus duorum fratrum, Hen. et Car. Brandoni.* 1551. *STC* 25816.

———. *The Arte of Rhetorique,* ed. R. H. Bowers. Gainesville, Fla., 1962. Character of Brandon brothers, 27-30.

CHAPTER FIVE: *Mary Sidney Herbert, Countess of Pembroke*

Aubrey, John. *Brief Lives,* ed. O. L. Dick. London, 1949. Wilton House "like a college," 138-39.

Babington, Gervase, *The workes . . . STC 1077.*

Beza, Theodore. *The Psalmes of David,* transl. A. Gilby, 1580. Material available to the Sidneys. *STC* 2033.

Breton, Nicholas. *The Works.* Edinburgh, 1879. Chertsey Worthies' Library. "Wits Trenchmour," the house of a lady, II, 18-19. Breton's other titles, see *STC*.

Browne, William. *The Poems.* London, 1894. "An Elegy on the Countess Dowager of Pembroke," II, 248-55.

*Cal. Carew MSS, 1575-1588,* ed. John Brewer and George Bullen. London, 1868. Letter of Henry Sidney to Walsingham, no. 501, 334-60. (Source: PRO Dom. Eliz. clix, no. 1, fol. 38).

*Cal. Pat. Rolls, Edw. VI.* London, 1925, 1926. Grants to Henry Sidney, III, 174; V. 1, 7, 60, 201, 242.

*Cal. S. P., Dom. Ser., 1547-1580.* Lady Mary Sidney's plea against title, I, 442; queen's offer to take daughter Mary at court, 494. Henry Sidney's 1583 letter to Walsingham, II, 98-99.

*Cal. S. P., Spanish, 1558-1567.* Lady Mary Sidney as queen's intermediary, I, 95, 96, 98-100, 105, 107, 109, 112-13, 115-16. Mendoza's report on a loss of lodging at court, II, 682; meeting at Pembroke's house of those opposed to queen's marriage, 693.

Calvin, John. *The Psalmes of David . . . ,* with J. Calvin's commentaries, transl. A. Golding, 1571. Material available to the Sidneys. *STC* 4395.

Collins, Arthur. *Letters and Memorials of State.* London, 1746. Vol. I, *Memoirs of the Sidneys.* Gratitude of Duchess of Northumberland to Spanish, 33, 34; Henry Sidney's work in Ireland and Wales, 82-93; births, also marriage of Mary, 96-97; Leicester's payment on Mary's portion, 97; quarrel between Philip Sidney and Oxford, 101; Sir Philip's will, 109-13. Vol. I, *Letters and Memorials of State,* Henry Sidney's letter to a twelve-year-old son, 8; his letter to Burghley about his penury, 43; letter to Leicester about Mary's marriage, 88; Sir Philip Sidney's praise of his mother, 247; her letters to

Mollineux on lodgings at court, 271, 272; illnesses often attended by Dr. Goodrich, I, 363, 372; II, 120, 123, 124, 128.

*Complete Peerage,* ed. Vicary Gibbs et al. London, 1910-1959.

Daniel, Samuel. *The Complete Works.* London, Aylesbury, 1885-1896. For works mentioned here, dedications are reproduced. See also *STC.*

―――. *A Panegyrike . . . A Defence of Rhyme.* 1603. *STC* 6259.

Davies, John of Hereford. For titles and dates, see *STC.*

Dee, John. *The Private Diary,* Camden Society, Vol. XIX, 1842. Visits of Philip Sidney to Dee, 2, 20.

Fraunce, Abraham. *Amyntas, with Translation of the Lamentations,* ed. F. M. Dickey. Chicago, 1967. Dedication to countess, 8. For other titles by Fraunce, see *STC.*

*Gentleman's Magazine,* Vol. XXIV (1845). Three articles, "Lady Mary Sidney and her Writings," by H. T. R[oach], 129-36, 254-59, 364-70.

Goss, Charles W. F. *Crosby Hall.* London, 1908. Lease by countess, 89.

Halle, Edward. *Chronicle. The Union of the . . . Two Families. . . .* ed. Grafton. 1550. Additions by Sidneys, on blank pages between Edward IV and V, and Henry VII and VIII. Folger Shakespeare Library copy 2, *STC* 12721.

Harington, Sir John. *The Letters and Epigrams,* ed. N. E. McClure. Philadelphia, 1930. His letter praising Psalms of the countess, 87; epigram on women named Mary, 310.

Harvey, Gabriel. *Pierce's Supererogation.* London, 1815. His tribute, 89.

Herbert, Mary. *A Discourse of Life and Death* (by Mornay) and *Antonius,* transl. Countess of Pembroke. 1592. *STC* 18138.

Jayne, Sears. *Library Catalogues of the English Renaissance.* Berkeley, Los Angeles, 1956. Gift by William Herbert of Greek manuscripts to Bodleian, no. 1629.

Languet, Hubert. See Pears.

Luce, Alice. *The Countess of Pembroke's Antonie.* Weimar, 1897. General background.

Lysons, Daniel. *Magna Britannia. . . .* London, 1806. Mansion in Ampthill Park, I, 96.

Moffett, Thomas. *Nobilis,* ed. V. B. Heltzel and Hoyt Hudson. San Marino, Calif., 1940. Sidney's attitudes to astrology and chemistry, 75, 119; comment on Mary Herbert, 85.

Nichols, John. *The Progresses . . . of Queen Elizabeth.* London, 1823. Details on "Astrea," III, 529-31.

―――. *The Progresses . . . of King James the First.* London, 1828. I, 195, 327, 513; II, 99.

Osborn, James M. *Young Philip Sidney, 1572-1577.* New Haven, London, 1972. Contrast in Dudleys and Sidneys, 5-6; Philip Sidney's knowledge of Greek 89; meeting of anti-Alençon group at Baynard's Castle, 503; Sidney's rejection of astrology, App. 1.

Pears, S. A. *The Correspondence of Sir Philip Sidney and Hubert Languet.* London, 1845. Mood of Sidney in March 1578, 143-45.

Pembroke, Countess of. *A Discourse of Life and Death . . . Antonius, a Tragedie.* 1592. *STC* 18138.

Pembroke, William, Earl of, and Sir Benjamin Rudier. *Poems,* ed. John Donne the Younger. London, 1660. Rudier's poem on countess, 26.

Rathmell, J. C. A. *The Psalms of Sir Philip Sidney and the Countess of Pembroke.* Garden City, N.Y., 1963. Introduction, xi-xxxii; quotations, xvii, xx, xxi.

Sidney, Sir Philip. *Astrophel and Stella,* 1st ed. 1591. Film Acc. 366. 1, B. M. 22536. Used at Folger Shakespeare Library. For other works of Sidney, see *STC.*

Stillinger, Jack. "The Biographical Problem of *Astrophel and Stella.*" *JEGP,* LIX(1960), 617-39. First ed., 619.

Sweeper, Walter. *A Briefe Treatise.* . . . 1622. *STC* 23526. Original not available.

Taylor, John. *The Needle's Excellency,* 10th ed. 1634. *STC* 23776.

*Victoria History* . . . *Co. of Bedford.* London, 1912. Houghton House, Ampthill Park, III, 289-90.

Wallace, M. W. *The Life of Sir Philip Sidney.* Cambridge, 1915. Education and ability of Lady Mary Sidney, 17, 20; cause (about 1578-1580) of Philip Sidney's mood, 197-200, 226.

Williams, Franklin B., Jr. *Index of Dedications* . . . *in English Books before 1641.* London, 1962. Dedications to Mary Herbert, Countess of Pembroke.

Williamson, George C. *Lady Anne Clifford.* Kendall, 1922. Her view of Philip Herbert, 183.

Young, Frances B. *Mary Sidney, Countess of Pembroke.* London, 1912. Letters to Sussex about lodgings at court, 16-20; will of Henry Herbert (PCC 39 Woodhall, 1601) and his wife's dower, 77-82; death and burial of Mary Herbert, 117; reprint of her translation from Petrarch, 209-18.

CHAPTER SIX: *Margaret Beaufort, Countess of Richmond and Derby*

Armitage-Smith, Sydney. *John of Gaunt.* Westminster, 1904. Ancestry of Margaret Beaufort, 389, 390-92.

Axon, William E. A. "The Lady Margaret as a Lover of Literature," *Library,* new ser., VIII(1907), 34-41. "John Bokas" perhaps was Lydgate, 41.

Ballard, George. *Memoirs of British Ladies.* London, 1775. Her admission into the fraternity of five religious houses and her legacy of books, 6-19.

*Cal. of Letters* . . . *between England and Spain,* ed. G. A. Bergenroth. London, 1862. Foreign comments on influence of king's mother, I, 163, 178.

*Cal. Pat. Rolls, Henry VII, 1485-1509.* London, 1914, 1916. Grants to Margaret Beaufort, I, II, index.

Callis, Robert. *The Reading* . . . *upon the Statute* . . . *of Sewers.* London, 1647. Lecture "quarta," read in 1622, stating that Margaret was put in the commission, 199-201.

Cooper, Charles H. *Memoir of Margaret, Countess of Richmond and Derby.* Cambridge, 1874. King's letter to mother about bishopric for Fisher, 95; her renewal of the vow of chastity, 97; other details, 34, 45, 49, 52, 53, 56, 59, 66, 68, 74; first edition of *Mirror of Gold,* 108.

Dionysius, Carthusianus. *The Mirroure of Golde for the Synfull Soule,* trans. by the countess. 1522. *STC* 6895.

Ellis, Sir Henry. *Original Letters,* 1st ser. London, 1825. Letter of Henry VII approving his mother's transfer of funds to Cambridge, I, 43-46.

Fisher, John. *English Works,* ed. J. E. B. Mayor. EETS, ex. ser., Vol. XXVII, 1876 (repr., 1935). Estimate of the Lady Margaret, 289-310.

Fox, Richard. *Letters,* ed. F. S. Allen and H. M. Allen. Oxford, 1929. Fisher's assertion that Fox had been responsible for his success, 153.

Gairdner, James. *History of the Life and Reign of Richard the Third.* Cambridge, 1898 (repr., 1968). Chance meeting of Margaret and Buckingham, 116; other details of Henry's return to England, 137, 141, 158, 227, 242-44.

*Grove's Dictionary of Music and Musicians,* ed. H. C. Callas. New York, London, 1932. Hugh Aston, Vol. I.

Halsted, Caroline A. *Life of Margaret Beaufort.* London, 1839 [repr., 1945]. General background.

Ingrim, John K. (ed.) *The Earliest English Translation of . . . De imitatione Christi.* EETS, ex. ser. Vol. LXIII, 1893 (repr., 1908). Lady Margaret's translation of fourth book, 259-83; Atkinson's version of first three, done at her special command, 153.

Jayne, Sears (ed.). *Library Catalogues of the English Renaissance.* Berkeley, Los Angeles, 1956. Lists of MSS she gave Christ's College, Cambridge, 94.

Knowles, Dom David. *The Religious Orders in England.* Cambridge, 1959. Houses noted for integrity of life, III, Chaps. 17-19.

Lees-Milne, James. *Tudor Renaissance.* London, New York, Toronto, Sydney, 1951. The Lady's tomb, 28-29; portraits, 61; plates 8, 16.

*Letters and Papers of . . . Henry VIII.* Darcy's note on position held by "king's grandam," Vol. XII, Pt. 2, no. 186 (38).

Mattingly, Garrett. *Catherine of Aragon.* Boston, 1941. Margaret's hostility to Catherine, 115.

More, Thomas. *The History of Richard III,* ed. R. S. Sylvester. New Haven, London, 1963. General background.

Mullinger, James Bass. *The University of Cambridge from the Earliest Times . . . to . . . 1535.* Cambridge, 1873. King's College Chapel, 451-52; colleges founded with help of Lady Margaret, 446-70.

Nicholas, N. H. *Testamenta vetusta.* London, 1826. Will of Lady Margaret, 316-24; will of Anne Stafford, 356-57.

Plomer, Henry R. *Wynkyn de Worde & his Contemporaries.* London, 1925. *Brevarium . . . Hereford,* 30; *Scala perfectionis* and *The Fifteen Oes,* 51.

Pollard, A. F. *The Reign of Henry VII.* London, New York, Bombay, Calcutta, 1913. Signature of Lady Margaret, I, 217-20.

Putnam, Bertha H. *Early Treatises on the Practice of the Justices of the Peace in the Fifteenth and Sixteenth Centuries.* Oxford Studies in Social and Legal History. Vol. 7. Oxford, 1924. Women on commissions, 194-97.

Reid, Rachel R. *The King's Council in the North.* London, New York, Bombay, Calcutta, Madras, 1921. General background, Chaps. 1-3; Lord Darcy's comment, 87; Noye's comment on her arbitraments, 87-88; her fitness for the position, 88-89; also App. 2, 487.

Reynolds, E. E. "St. John Fisher and the Lady Margaret Beaufort," *Moreana,* Vol. VI, no. 23, 1969. Signature of Lady Margaret, 32.

*Rotuli Parliamentorum, 1278-1504.* London, 1767. Statutes about property of the Lady Margaret, VI, 250, 284, 387.

Routh, Enid M. G. *Lady Margaret: A Memoir.* London, 1924. Plans to put Henry on throne, 42-48, 54-56; rewards he gave later, 60; his mother's later place in family affairs, 90-95.

Thomas à Kempis. *A Full . . . Treatyse of the Imytacion . . . of . . . Criste.* 1503. *STC* 23955.

*Victoria History . . . Co. of Dorset.* London, 1908. Chantry at Wimborne Minster, II, 111.

Williams, Franklin B., Jr. *Index of Dedications . . . in English Books before 1641.* London, 1962. Dedications to Lady Margaret Beaufort.


CHAPTER SEVEN: *Catherine of Aragon*

Armitage-Smith, Sydney. *John of Gaunt.* Westminster, 1904. Catherine's English ancestry, 300; also Chap. 13.

*Cal. S. P., Venetian.* London, 1867. Chieragato's account of pardon of apprentices, II, no. 887, 385.

Chambers, R. W. *Thomas More.* London, 1935. More's part in Evil May Day, 147-51; his comment after his condemnation, 341.

Fisher, H. A. L. *The History of England from the Accession of Henry VII to the death of Henry VIII.* London, New York, Bombay, Calcutta, 1910. Treaty with Aragon and 1512 campaign, 171, 174-77; the 1513 invasion of France, 179-84; Catherine's regency, 185; Flodden, 185-89.

Mattingly, Garrett. *Catherine of Aragon.* Boston, 1941. Isabella's influence, 3-11; expulsion of her niece, 5; Catherine's education, 8-11; Isabella's expulsion of the Jews, 11-12; Catherine's early connection with England and journey there, 14, 19-22, 29-30; her appearance, 36-38; difficulties as Arthur's widow, 50-103; coronation, 125-26; ambassador and political advisor, 137-41, 149-52; 163-65, 170-71, 173-74; work as regent, 155, 157-61; her children, 141, 142-43, 174-75; later years as queen, 175-79; her charities, 177-80; Evil May Day, 180-81; her encouragement of scholars, 181-86; plans for her daughter's education, 183, 186-89; Henry's first talk with her about the guilt of their union, 249-52; her appeal at the legatine court, 285-88; Henry's departure from her, 334; her refusal of trial at Cambrai, 329-32; her surrender of the jewels, 350; refusal of title, "Princess Dowager," 364-66; refusal of certain residences, 377-80; refusal to assent to Act of Succession, 389-90; ripeness of England for revolt, 394-406; Mary's illness, 412-15; Catherine's death, 424-30; also index.

Prescott, H. F. M. *Mary Tudor.* New York, 1952. Quotation on education of Princess Mary, 26.

Rogers, Elizabeth F. (ed.). *St. Thomas More: Selected Letters.* New Haven, London, 1961. More's early praise of Catherine, 2-3.

Scarisbrick, J. J. *Henry VIII.* Berkeley, Los Angeles, 1968. The nature of Henry's illnesses, 426, 484-87, note on 485.

Vocht, Henry de. *Monumenta humanistica Lovaniensia: Texts and Studies about Louvain Humanists.* Louvain, London, 1934. Bibliography of works by Vives.

Watson, Foster. *Vives and the Renascence Education of Women.* London, 1912. English version of Vives' dedication to Catherine, 32-38.


CHAPTER EIGHT: *Catherine Parr*

*Acts of the Privy Council,* ed. J. R. Dasent. London, 1890. Vol. I, 1542-1547. Individuals accused of heresy, index.

Ascham, Roger. *The Whole Works,* ed. J. A. Giles. London, 1865. Vol. I, Pt. 1. His Latin letters to Mary Parr, nos. XLI, XLII.

Ballard, George. *Memoirs of British Ladies.* London, 1775. Catherine's letter on secret visits of Seymour, 67-68.

Burnet, Gilbert. *The History of the Reformation of the Church of England.* London, 1830. Catherine Parr, I, 523-25; also III, index.

*Cal. of Letters . . . England and Spain,* ed. M. S. Hume. London, 1904. Talks of Chapuys with Catherine and Mary, VIII, 2, 104-5.

*Complete Peerage,* ed. Vicary Gibbs et al. London, 1910-1929. Edward Burgh, not the husband of Catherine Parr, II, 422. Edward Burgh, who married Catherine Parr and died while his father was living (d. v. p.) and without issue (s. p.), II, 423.

Cooper, Charles. H. *Annals of Cambridge.* Cambridge, 1842. Appeal to Catherine, her reply, the king's action, I, 429-31.

Cope, Sir Anthony. *A Godly Meditacion upon XX Select Psalmes of David.* 1547. *STC* 5717.

Devereux, E. J. "The Publication of the English Paraphrases of Erasmus," *Bulletin, John Rylands Library,* LI (Spring, 1969), 348-67. Influence of the English *Paraphrase,* 367.

Edward VI. *Literary Remains,* ed. J. G. Nichols. London, 1857. Catherine's Italian Petrarch, I, cccxxvi; Edward's teachers, II, 209-10.

Elizabeth, Princess. *The Mirror of the Sinful Soul,* ed. Percy W. Ames. London, 1897. Preface, 3-45.

Ellis, Sir Henry. *Original Letters.* 2nd ser, London, 1827. Otwell Johnson's report on racking of Anne Askew, II, 177-78.

Elton, G. R. *England under the Tudors.* London, 1955. Comment on Catherine Parr, 195.

Erasmus. *The First Tome . . . of the Paraphrase of Erasmus upon the New Testament.* 1548. *STC* 2854.

————. *The Seconde Tome . . . of the Paraphrase of Erasmus.* 1549. *STC* 2854.3. The volume with this number is not listed in the present edition of the *STC* but will be in the new edition. Both the number and the use of the volume are available at the Folger Shakespeare Library.

Fisher, H. A. L. *The History of England from the Accession of Henry VII to the Death of Henry VIII.* London, New York, Bombay, 1906. Estimate of Catherine Parr, 453.

Foxe, John. *Acts and Monuments,* ed. Josiah Pratt. London, 1877. Mention of queen's servant at trial of John London, V, 494; trial and execution of Anne Askew, her refusal to implicate ladies of the court, 537-50; Gardiner's action against Catherine Parr, 553-61; flight and exile of Catherine Bertie, VIII, 569-76.

Halliwell, James O. (ed.). *Letters of the Kings of England.* London, 1846. Edward's letters translated into English, II, 8, 15, 22, 25.

Haugaard, William P. "Katherine Parr: The Religious Convictions of a Renaissance Queen." *Ren. Quart.,* XXII (1969), 346-59. Influence of the *Paraphrase,* 348-49; household of Lord Latimer, 349-50; Catherine Parr's funeral, 352.

Haynes, Samuel. *A Collection of State Papers . . . 1542-1572.* London, 1740. Catherine's letters to Seymour, 61, 62.

Hoffman, G. Fenno, Jr. "Catherine Parr as a Woman of Letters," *HLQ,* XXIII (August 1960), 349-67.

Hughes, Paul L., and James F. Larkin. *Tudor Royal Proclamations.* New Haven, London, 1964. Injunctions, I, 287, 395. Also *STC* 10088.

*Letters and Papers of . . . Henry VIII.* London, 1862-1910. Letters of royal children to Catherine, and hers as regent, XVIII, XIX, XX, XXI, index; Cranmer's license for king's marriage, XVIII, Pt. 1, no. 854; account of the marriage, 873; commission of regency for Catherine, XIX, Pt. 1, no. 1035 (78); "Life Grants" of property to Catherine, XIX, Pt. 1, 644; Catherine's letter to Cambridge University, XXI, Pt. 1, no. 279; Chapuys to Mary of Hungary, Pt. 2, no. 756.

McConica, J. K. *English Humanists and Reformation Politics under Henry VIII and Edward VI.* Oxford, 1965. Mary's circle for study, 157; Catherine's influence, 201, 234, and Chap. 7; royal school, 213-18; Catherine's discussions of scripture at court, 224; the queen and Anne Askew, 224-27; Henry's concern over Catherine's independence of mind, 226; the Royal Injunctions, 240.

Madden, Frederic. "Narrative of the Visit of the Duke of Nàjera. . . ." *Archaeologia,* XXIII(1831), 344-57. His talk with the queen and the Princess Mary, 352-53.

Martienssen, Anthony. *Queen Katherine Parr.* New York, St. Louis. San Francisco, Dusseldorf, Mexico, 1973. Account of royal school for Princess Mary with Catherine Parr as a pupil, 21; first husband of Catherine Parr, follows the old tradition of the elderly widower, 36; reports that each of the two Parr daughters was assigned £ 800, but the will provides that sum "betwixt them," 37; gives a complete account of Catherine's interview with the king, to secure release of Throckmorton, save his property, and incriminate Cromwell, but without adequate evidence, 115-18.

Muller, James A. *Stephen Gardiner and the Tudor Reaction.* New York, 1926. Attempt to arrest Catherine, 138-39.

Mullinger, James Bass. *The University of Cambridge from . . . 1535 to the Accession of Charles I.* Cambridge, 1884. Founding of Trinity College, 76-86.

Nicholas, N. H. *Testamenta vetusta.* London, 1826. Will of Sir Thomas Parr, knt., "I will that my daughters, Katherine and Anne, have DCCC 1. betwixt them, except they prove to be my heirs or my son's heirs. . . . ," 548. The complete will is reproduced, 548-49.

Noye, William. *A Tretise of the Principall Grounds and Maximes of the Lawes of this Kingdome.* London, 1641. Nuncupative wills, Chap. 65, 112-13. Cf. Holdsworth, *A History of English Law.* London, 1942 (repr., 1966). III, 537-39.

Parr, Catherine. *Prayers . . . Medytacions. . . .* 1545, STC 4818-26.

———. *The Queene's Praiers. . . .* STC 3009-13.

———. *The Lamentacions of a Sinner.* 1547. STC 4827-29.

Pollard, A. F. *Henry VIII.* London, 1970. Substance of the Six Articles and discussion, 313.

Read, Conyers. *Mr. Secretary Cecil and Queen Elizabeth.* New York, London, 1955. His comment on Catherine, 39.

Ridley, Jasper. *Thomas Cranmer.* Oxford, 1962. Men who exposed the plot by John London, 242.

Ryan, Lawrence V. *Roger Ascham.* Stanford, London, 1963. Tutors for royal children, 102-8.

Scarisbrick, J. J. *Henry VIII.* Berkeley, Los Angeles, 1968. Nature of Henry's illness, 484-86, with note, 485; estimate of Catherine, 433, 456-57.

*Statutes of the Realm,* ed. A. Luders, T. E. Tomlins, J. Raithby et al. London,

1810-1828. Transfer of colleges to the will of the king, III, 37 Henry VIII, c. 4; right of Mary Parr to inherit, IV, Edward IV (1549-1550), c. 14.

Strickland, Agnes. *Lives of the Queens of England.* . . . London, 1860. Sir F. Madden's translation from Latin of Catherine's request that Princess Mary publish her work, using her name, III, 229.

———. *Lives of the Queens.* . . . London, 1890. Her plea before the king for Throckmorton property, II, 402; some reasons for lack of records about Catherine, 464-65.

*Victoria History of Wiltshire,* London, 1962. Disastrous fire at Wilton House, VI, 6.

Wriothesley, Charles. *A Chronicle of England.* Camden Society, Vol. XI, 1875. Racking of Anne Askew after her sentence to death, 167.


CHAPTER NINE: *Queen Elizabeth* (1533-1603)


*Acts of the Privy Council,* ed. J. R. Dasent. London, 1890-1907. See index of volume for the year named.

Ascham, Roger. *The Scholemaster,* ed. Edward Arber. London, 1870. Diligence of Elizabeth as a student, 67; her method of learning, 95-96.

———. *The Whole Works,* ed. J. A. Giles. London, 1865. Comments to Sturm on Elizabeth's scholarship, I, Pt. 1, lxii-lxiv.

Bacon, Francis. *Works,* ed. J. Spedding, R. L. Ellis, and D. D. Heath. London, 1878. Bacon's view of queen's morality, VI, 317. (Winfreid Schleiner, University of California, Davis, called my attention to the passage.)

Bradner, Leicester (ed.). *The Poems of Queen Elizabeth I.* Providence, R.I., 1964. Introduction, xiv, xv; original poems, 3-10; verse translations, 13-68.

Camden, William. *The History of* . . . *Princess Elizabeth, Late Queen of England,* ed. Wallace T. MacCaffrey. Chicago, London, 1970. Reform of coinage, 57-58.

Cross, Claire. *The Puritan Earl* . . . *Henry Hastings* . . . *Huntingdon.* London, Melbourne, Toronto, New York, 1966. Queen's consolation of his countess, 271-73.

Dunlop, Ian. *Palaces & Progresses of Elizabeth I.* London, 1962. Reasons for and methods of progresses, Chap. 7.

Elton, G. R. *England under the Tudors.* London, 1956. Necessity of Mary's execution, 370.

Harrison, William. *The Description of England,* ed. Georges Edelen. Ithaca, 1968. Order at court, 227-33; queen's visits to noblemen's houses, 227.

Neale, J. E. *Queen Elizabeth.* New York, 1934. Seymour episode, 18-28; the Mass, 33; other problems under Mary, 35-51; coronation procession, 58-63; ability to control emotions, 82; letter to Lord Hunsdon, 187; visits to Coventry, Warwick, Norwich, Sandwich, 205; visits to universities, 206; hasty action about Stubbs, 239-40; comment on execution of Mary, 280; handling of finances, 282-85; corruption in recruiting and military pay, 288-91; oration at Tilbury, 296; visit to Hatton, 318; congratulations to Peregrine Bertie, 319; reply to Polish ambassador, 344; "Golden Speech," 383-85; letters to Mountjoy, 386; also index.

Nichols, John. *The Progresses* . . . *of Queen Elizabeth.* London, 1823. Lists of places visited, I, li; of persons, I, liii, also index, III; coronation procession, I, 38-60; queen's visits to universities, I, 149-50, 206-17; III, 144-60.

Osborne, James M. (ed.). *The Quenes Maiesties Passage through the Citie of London . . . the Day before her Coronacion.* New Haven, 1960.

Parker, Matthew. *Correspondence.* Parker Society, Cambridge, 1853. Queen's gift of a stag, XXXIII, 190.

Pollard, A. F. *England under Protector Somerset.* London, 1900 (repr., 1966). Finances of Tudor rulers, 45-52.

―――. *The History of England from the Accession of Edward VI to the Death of Elizabeth.* London, New York, Bombay, Calcutta, 1910. Financial situation at Mary's death, 186-87; Elizabeth's early financing, 221-22.

Read, Conyers. "Good Queen Bess," *AHR,* XXXI (July 1926), 647-61.

―――. *Mr. Secretary Cecil and Queen Elizabeth.* New York, 1955. "The Rising of the North," Chap. 23.

―――. *Lord Burghley and Queen Elizabeth.* New York, 1960. Ridolfi plot, 38-44; Throckmorton "Enterprise," 287-88; Babington conspiracy, 343-47.

Rice, George P., Jr. *The Public Speaking of Queen Elizabeth.* New York, 1951 (repr., 1966). Brief remarks to officials of London, 63; speeches at universities, 71, 74, 98; speech to Parliament, 81.

Ryan, Lawrence V. *Roger Ascham.* Stanford, London, 1963. Grindal as tutor, 42, 102-3; Ascham as tutor, 102, 112, 216-17, 223-24.

*Statutes of the Realm,* ed. A. Luders, T. E. Tomlins, J. Raithby et al. London, 1810-1828. Volume for year named and index for topic.

Williams, Neville. *The Royal Residences of Great Britain.* London, 1960. General background.

―――. *Elizabeth, Queen of England,* London, 1967. Attendants in coronation procession, 56-57.

# Index